Critical Disability Studies Disabled Child

This book examines the relationship between contemporary cultural representations of disabled children on the one hand, and disability as a personal experience of internalised oppression on the other. In focalising this debate through an exploration of the politically and emotionally charged figure of the disabled child, Harriet Cooper raises questions both about what it means to 'speak for' the other and about what resistance means when one is unknowingly invested in one's own abjection.

Drawing on both the author's personal experience of growing up with a physical impairment and on a range of critical theories and cultural objects – from Frances Hodgson Burnett's novel *The Secret Garden* to Judith Butler's work on injurious speech – the book theorises the making of disabled and 'rehabilitated' subjectivities. With a conceptual framework informed by both psychoanalysis and critical disability studies, it investigates the ways in which cultural anxieties about disability come to be embodied and lived by the disabled child.

Posing new questions for disability studies and for identity politics about the relationships between lived experiences, cultural representations and dominant discourses – and demonstrating a new approach to the concept of 'internalised oppression' – this book will be of interest to scholars and students of disability studies, medical humanities, sociology and psychosocial studies, as well as to those with an interest in identity politics more generally.

Harriet Cooper is currently Senior Research Associate in Health and Medical Humanities at the University of East Anglia, UK. Having worked across both critical disability studies and health sociology, she is interested in how (inter)disciplinarity imagines itself and polices its operations, as well as in the ways in which concepts of inclusivity, involvement and democracy animate and shape academic agendas. The themes of disability and emancipation connect all of Harriet's work to date, yet as a methodologist she continues to be irked by the question of how best to combine academia and activism.

Interdisciplinary Disability Studies

Series editor: Mark Sherry, The University of Toledo, USA

Disability studies has made great strides in exploring power and the body. This series extends the interdisciplinary dialogue between disability studies and other fields by asking how disability studies can influence a particular field. It will show how a deep engagement with disability studies changes our understanding of the following fields: sociology, literary studies, gender studies, bioethics, social work, law, education, or history. This ground-breaking series identifies both the practical and theoretical implications of such an interdisciplinary dialogue and challenges people in disability studies as well as other disciplinary fields to critically reflect on their professional praxis in terms of theory, practice and methods.

Identity (Re)constructions after Brain Injury
Personal and Family Identity
Chalotte Glintborg

Global Perspectives on Disability Activism and Advocacy
Our Way
Edited by Karen Soldatic and Kelley Johnson

Disability Hate Speech
Social, Cultural and Political Contexts
Edited by Mark Sherry, Terje Olsen, Janikke Solstad Vedeler and John Eriksen

Sexual Citizenship and Disability
Understanding Sexual Support in Policy, Practice and Theory
Julia Bahner

Critical Disability Studies and the Disabled Child
Unsettling Distinctions
Harriet Cooper

Critical Disability Studies and the Disabled Child

Unsettling Distinctions

Harriet Cooper

Routledge
Taylor & Francis Group

LONDON AND NEW YORK

First published 2020 by Routledge

2 Park Square, Milton Park, Abingdon, Oxon OX14 4RN

605 Third Avenue, New York, NY 10017

*Routledge is an imprint of the Taylor & Francis Group,
an informa business*

First issued in paperback 2022

Publisher's Note

The publisher has gone to great lengths to ensure the quality of this
reprint but points out that some imperfections in the original copies
may be apparent.

British Library Cataloguing-in-Publication Data
A catalogue record for this book is available from the British Library

Library of Congress Cataloging-in-Publication Data
Names: Cooper, Harriet (Senior research associate), author.
Title: Critical disability studies and the disabled child : unsettling
distinctions / Harriet Cooper.
Description: Abingdon, Oxon ; New York, NY : Routledge, 2020. |
Series: Interdisciplinary disability studies | Includes bibliographical
references and index.
Identifiers: LCCN 2019050373 (print) | LCCN 2019050374 (ebook) |
ISBN 9780367183066 (hbk) | ISBN 9780429060694 (ebk)
Subjects: LCSH: Children with disabilities. | Disability studies.
Classification: LCC HV888 .C656 2020 (print) | LCC HV888 (ebook) |
DDC 362.4083–dc23
LC record available at https://lccn.loc.gov/2019050373
LC ebook record available at https://lccn.loc.gov/2019050374

ISBN: 978-0-367-18306-6 (hbk)
ISBN: 978-1-03-233668-8 (pbk)
DOI: 10.4324/9780429060694

Typeset in Times New Roman
by Integra Software Services Pvt. Ltd.

'Lefty', a painting by Em Cooper, 2019.

Contents

Acknowledgements

Though only one person is named as the author of this book, many people have enabled it to come about.

Firstly, I'd like to express my heartfelt thanks to Mark Sherry, the series editor for Routledge Interdisciplinary Disability Studies, for responding to my book proposal with such animation. Mark is a gem of an academic: our field needs more people like him in it! I'm also extremely grateful to my editor at Routledge, Claire Jarvis, for her thoughtful guidance and support throughout the book production process, to Georgia Priestley, for her helpful responses to my queries and to the anonymous reviewers for their encouraging and constructive feedback.

I am grateful to the Arts and Humanities Research Council for funding the PhD project that became this book. It is an incredible privilege – in this day and age especially – to be paid to think.

Deepest thanks to Joanne Winning, my PhD supervisor, for nurturing me through the process of finding my voice. Thank you, Jo: you trusted me, and knew how to bring out the best in me. I am also extremely lucky to have had the opportunity to work with the brilliant Lisa Baraitser. Lisa has been a very kind and generous mentor to me over the years. Thank you, Lisa, your support has meant so much! Huge thanks also to the two wonderful academics who examined the PhD on which this book is based: Gayle Letherby and Dan Goodley. Your optimism, warmth and enthusiastic endorsement of my project has been invaluable.

I was really lucky to be based in the School of Arts at Birkbeck, University of London for my PhD. This book is very much a product of that vibrant environment, which taught me so much about how to think and how to live. Special thanks to my dear friends Sophie Jones and Fiona Johnstone, for the many stimulating conversations we shared as PhD students, and for your thoughtful and motivating responses to an early version of my manuscript. Thank you also to Kathy Boxall, Ally Davies, Eve Lacey and Rachel Robertson for your feedback on conference papers or chapter drafts. I've really appreciated your input.

Massive thanks too, to the many thinkers and activists I've got to know through the 'Theorizing Normalcy and the Mundane' conference and the disability studies community in Sheffield/Manchester. I want to mention in particular Tillie Curran, Rebecca Mallett, Katherine Runswick-Cole, Jenny Slater and

Donna Reeve, who've become firm friends over the years, and have, in their different ways, each played a significant role in supporting the intellectual and emotional labour that resulted in this book.

I'd also like to thank Tom Shakespeare and Fiona Poland for their dedicated mentorship over the last few years. It's a privilege to work with you both. Our conversations have provoked me to think harder about methods and evidence across the humanities and social sciences, and what I'm learning has sharpened my thinking immeasurably.

How can I begin to thank my family (Coopers, Eyres, Whitehouses), for being there for me throughout this process? To my parents, Jane and Phil: thank you from the bottom of my heart. This book may not be an easy read for a parent, but you've encouraged me throughout the writing of it with generosity and love. To Em and Ol: where would I be without you guys?

Em: thank you for the stunning painting of Lefty. It is such a special gift!

I couldn't have finished this book without childcare help: the un-glamourous but necessary labour that doesn't accrue either social status or a wage. Mum and Nick deserve a special mention here. Gratitude doesn't feel like it's enough, but I want to express it anyway. Thank you both!

The shape that the book has taken is in many ways a result of the incredible process of psychoanalytic psychotherapy. I owe a huge debt of gratitude to my psychotherapist, whose work with me has made it possible for me to explore the difficult terrain that I wanted to broach in my work. Her interpretations have enabled me to think in new and unique ways about my oppression.

I really don't know how or where to begin to thank Nick Hocking, for being such an extraordinary interlocutor. Nick, you have enabled this project in more ways than I can count and I'm not sure it would have come to fruition without you. Our challenging and inspiring conversations about theory, culture and politics have formed the backdrop to this work, and have enriched my thinking – and my feeling – no end.

Abbreviations

A few acronyms are used in this book to refer to literary texts for the duration of an extended close reading. Where the text is mentioned in passing elsewhere, I revert to an author-date system. Full bibliographic information is provided in the reference list.

Acronym	Title	Author(s)	Date of edition
DDJE	A Day in the Death of Joe Egg	Peter Nichols	1967
FC	The Fifth Child	Doris Lessing	2007
SG	The Secret Garden	Frances Hodgson Burnett	1987
TWQ	Two Weeks with the Queen	Morris Gleitzman	1989
WLF	Ways to Live Forever	Sally Nicholls	2008

Introduction

At a book launch for *Disabled Children's Childhood Studies: Critical Approaches in a Global Context* that took place in 2014, editors Tillie Curran and Katherine Runswick-Cole explained that, in the field of enquiry inaugurated by the book, the disabled child is seen through a new lens.[1] Runswick-Cole and Curran pointed out that most (sociological) studies of disabled children evaluate whether service provision meets children's needs, or consider how specific impairments pose particular challenges in children's lives. Such studies are designed with an adult agenda in mind. They answer the questions that adults ask about disabled children. The field of 'disabled children's childhood studies' reframes the debate, posing a different sort of question altogether. What do disabled children want to tell us about their lives?

This book is motivated by a similar interest in the voices of disabled children, and by a desire to bring about change in the lives of disabled children. It is, more specifically, interested in these voices and lives as ones that have been 'made' in a particular way by cultural, ideological and psychosocial forces. I argue in the book that before we can begin to *resist* disabling discourses, gazes and practices, we first need to understand how they have *made* us, and what they have done to our voices. In my quest to explore the 'making' of the 'disabled child' (a contested term whose parameters I shall consider shortly), I defamiliarise some of the tropes that populate and structure adult discussions of childhood disability in contemporary Euro-American culture, such as the 'normal child' and the 'developing child'. Drawing on my personal experience of growing up with a physical impairment, I also reflect on the significance of certain scenes in the 'making' of the disabled child, including in particular the 'diagnostic scene' and the 'rehabilitative scene'. The constitutive nature of the relational encounter is also examined in a discussion of the pre-verbal infant's experience of the gaze.

Drawing on Sara Ahmed's (2006, p. 1) deployment of the concept of 'orientation' as something we may not even notice until we experience its opposite, my project asks what it means to be orientated within contemporary Euro-American medical culture and other dominant cultural practices, by foregrounding the literal *disorientation* that these same practices produce in the life of the (pre-verbal) disabled child. Although notions such as the 'normal child' and the 'developing child' make sense in the context of medical discourse, we forget that reason and language are the tools we require in order to *make* them make sense. In viewing these discursive objects[2] – as reason-able adults – through the lens that medical discourse supplies, we are already orientated.

My goal, throughout the process of working on this book, has been to make a contribution to the political and social emancipation of disabled children and adults, especially those whose lives have been touched by internalised oppression.[3] I draw on psychoanalysis, as well as on the critique of ideology, and on the notion of the '*discursive formation*' (Foucault, 2002, p. 41, emphasis in original), to explore what burdens us in the versions of ourselves that we carry with us knowingly and unknowingly. The contribution I make is awkward to define. It is about grappling with ideas and processes as much, if not more than, about reaching any conclusions; it is interested in the spaces between the known and the unknown – that is, the speculative, the half-remembered and, drawing on a psychoanalytic register, the ever-to-be-repeated.

I open this introduction by asking: can we define 'the disabled child'? This discussion provides a way into a review of the theoretical and disciplinary terrain in which the book intervenes. I map key developments in disability studies here. I consider what we mean by 'the child', although I do not seek to present an outline of the whole field of childhood studies here, which is vast and disparate: where I engage with this field, notably in Chapter 2, I discuss the relevant theories in the context of that chapter. The introduction then moves on to ask questions about my focus: am I interested in the figurative child, or in 'real' children? If the answer is 'both' – and it is – what are the disciplinary implications of this focus? This leads me on to a discussion of interdisciplinarity and methodology, before I turn to the question of my personal experience, its impact on the book and my use of personal writing as an exploratory technique. I briefly discuss the ethics of writing about personal experience, before a short section reflecting on the limitations of this project. At the end of the introduction, I provide an outline of the chapters.

Who is the 'disabled child' of this book?

Writing in 1984, Jacqueline Rose observed that: 'Childhood [...] serves as a term of universal social reference which conceals all the historical divisions and difficulties of which children, no less than ourselves, form a part' (p. 10). Has this tendency to essentialise the child, and to regard childhood as a monolithic category, changed since these words were written thirty-five years ago? A more recent observation suggests that Rose's claim still holds in the contemporary moment:

> Currently, multiple and contrasting ideas of childhood coexist with an apparently hegemonic idea of 'the' child. To put it more colloquially, it is still culturally accepted (and not only in everyday language) to refer in passing to what children are and what we should expect them to do, while – fortunately – more than one eyebrow would be raised if we were to state confidently what women are or what they ought to do.
>
> (Caselli, 2010, p. 243)

This is an intriguing state of affairs. Whereas in recent years, identity politics has grappled with the problem of essentialism in relation to a wide range of subject positions, the figure of the child remains curiously untouched by such debates – or at least within the humanities, as Karín Lesnik-Oberstein (2011) points out. Noting that the concept of the child as 'constructed' has been more widely accepted in the social sciences, Lesnik-Oberstein views the humanities' attachment to an essential child as arising out of a 'liberal humanist investment [...] in particular ideas of the family and emotion, where the child is the guarantee for a transcendent human emotion' (p. 3). As I go on to argue, the figure of the disabled child troubles a naturalised connection between the child and emotion, and we might speculate that it is precisely this figure's disruption of the 'guarantee' that triggers such strong emotional responses when it comes to discussing disability and the child.

The notion of the unknowability of the child is an important starting point. Jacqueline Rose's (1984, p. 9) compelling observation that '[c]hildren's fiction emerges [...] out of a conception of both the child and the world as knowable in a direct and unmediated way' has been taken up and developed by Lesnik-Oberstein (2011, p. 6), who argues that Rose's (1984) monograph is an indispensable contribution to 'all work on childhood' and not just to the study of children's literature. It is difficult, I find, to stay with this unknowability; indeed Lesnik-Oberstein remarks that in spite of the fact that '(de)constructivist approaches to the child in the humanities have been widely discussed, written about, and even much advocated' in recent years, it is often the case that 'childhood [...] continues after all to be retrieved as "real" in the end' (p. 4). Even those texts that claim to be interested in the discursive child posit the existence of a 'real' child that is beyond and outside of the reach of discourse (Lesnik-Oberstein, 2011). The critical 'mastery' of the child by the adult seems to be part of what is at stake in such situations (J. Rose, 1984, p. 10; see also Lesnik-Oberstein, 2011). Rose (1984, p. 13) suggests that we want to see childhood as situated firmly in the past, as 'something separate which can be scrutinised and assessed'; we are uncomfortable with Sigmund Freud's notion of childhood as 'something in which we continue to be implicated' (J. Rose, 1984, p. 12).

Perhaps all research projects are, by their very nature, caught up in a desire to know. This book is no different, in that, in a certain sense, it does aspire to 'find' the child.[4] Yet, in addition to aspiring to an 'idea of mastery', which may, in part, be connected with 'securing the child's rationality' (J. Rose, 1984, p. 10), this book is interested in questioning the ground on which adult rationality is built. It is interested in the experiences of an adult (me) whose childhood continues to make itself known to her. It is interested in using psychoanalysis to think about what a disabled childhood might have felt like, yet in using psychoanalysis it recognises that this childhood (especially the pre-verbal part) is knowable only in the way that it 'persists' in the present (J. Rose, 1984, p. 12). This focus has some implications for the status of knowledge in this book, which I discuss later in this introduction, as well as throughout the book.

There are times in this book when I invoke a concept of 'the disabled child' as though this were a defined and knowable category. It should be noted that I sometimes use this term rhetorically with my childhood self in mind (and this is why this child almost invariably becomes a 'she'); the term becomes a site of my rage and loss on behalf of a child who was unable to speak angrily herself. Gayatri Spivak's concept of 'strategic essentialism' is helpful here (1987, p. 205).[5] Although Spivak has latterly sought to distance herself from the term on the grounds that it has been overused and misused, I feel that we need a way to defend the value of distinct identity categories when they are used in the service of obtaining political recognition. Yet, when thinking in terms of identity, it is important to consider who is included and who is excluded from such recognition (Puar, 2017a, 2017b, 2015, 2009).[6] Not only are experiences of disability diverse, but the discourse of disability is structured to keep certain bodies outside of it (Puar, 2017a, 2015). We are all at risk of becoming disabled,[7] but we are not equally exposed to this risk (Puar, 2009). Can we define 'disability' at all, and is it politically desirable to do so?

At this point it is necessary, I think, to discuss the chequered recent history of the term 'disability'. During the course of the twentieth century, disability was increasingly seen through the prism of medical discourse (Cooper, 2013a; Davis, 1995). As a result, it was often perceived as a 'tragedy, rather than [...] a phenomenon which may be explained in a number of ways' (Oliver, 1983, p. 19). In order to counter this 'individual model of disability' (Oliver, 1983, p. 15) – also known as the medical model – disability was reconceptualised by activists in the 1970s according to a 'social model' (p. 23). In this period, the following definitions were proposed to distinguish between 'impairment' on the one hand, and 'disability' on the other:

> [...] we define impairment as lacking part of or all of a limb, or having a defective limb, organ or mechanism of the body; and disability as the disadvantage or restriction of activity caused by a contemporary social organisation which takes no or little account of people who have physical impairments and thus excludes them from participation in the mainstream of social activities.
> (Union of the Physically Impaired Against Segregation (UPIAS) and The Disability Alliance, 1976, p. 14)

These definitions focus on physical impairment at the expense of cognitive impairment. This may reflect the particular standpoint of the activists who formulated the concepts. Subsequently this imbalance has been highlighted (Chappell, 1998). The very deployment of a physical/cognitive binary, or indeed of any kind of impairment label at all, is, as some have argued, a reinstatement of a medical model of disability, and, therefore, a depoliticising act.[8] I admire those who seek to withhold impairment labels in the face of a cultural 'urge to know' impairment (Mallett and Runswick-Cole, 2016). Yet this position is, as Mallett and Runswick-Cole (2016) acknowledge, an ambivalent space to occupy. Moreover, it is complicated by that of the disabled subject who mostly passes as non-disabled, for whom laying claim, publicly, to a particular impairment label may be felt (at least partly) as an emancipatory 'coming out'. This tends to be my own experience. I return to these unresolved questions later, but for now I would like to echo the sentiments of Alison Kafer (2013), who, whilst critiquing aspects of the medical model of disability, argues that to reject it entirely is to condemn those who seek more comfortable lives via an engagement with medicine.

Since the 1970s, scholarship in disability studies has critiqued the social model from a variety of angles, developing and reworking it. In her excellent review of the debate, Donna Reeve notes that the social model 'has been criticised for focussing on structural disabling barriers' at the expense of 'experiential and cultural aspects of disability' (2008, p. 28). As Reeve (p. 30) also observes, a 'naturalised concept of impairment' has troubled theorists including Dan Goodley (2001, 2000), who draws attention to it as a social construction. This point has also been made by Shelley Tremain, who has argued in the context of reproductive politics that 'descriptions of certain phenomena *as* foetal impairment have caused "prenatal impairment" to emerge as an object of discourse and social existence' (2006, p. 37; see also Hughes, 1999). An impairment can only be understood as such within a particular social and discursive context. Meanwhile, other models of disability have come to the fore both alongside the social model and since its advent: Goodley (2011) identifies a North American 'minority model' (p. 12), a North American 'cultural model' (p. 14) and a Nordic 'relational model' (p. 15). I draw on a range of theories and models of disability in this book, but am particularly influenced by the theories of those working within a 'cultural model', such as Lennard Davis (1995). Davis' (1995) work repositions the focus of our gaze on normalcy rather than on disability, which strikes me as an emancipatory shift. By altering our perspective in this way, Davis argues, we obtain a better understanding of how, historically speaking, disability has come to be seen as problematic.

Another development in the discipline, which has influenced my work, is the advent of critical disability studies. Goodley (2011) stresses that this sub-discipline emphasises intersectionality and the connections between disability studies and other related, politicised fields, for example queer theory, which has also influenced my own thinking greatly. I see my own work as contributing to a project of critical disability studies in the sense that not only does it draw out connections between disabled subjectivity and other oppressed or marginalised subjectivities (of which the child is arguably one),[9] but it also asks critical questions of disability studies by bringing psychoanalysis to bear on it, as well as seeking to ask critical questions of psychoanalysis with the help of disability studies. I am not the first to bring together these two fields: Goodley, for example, sees a role for 'social psychoanalysis' (2011, p. 94), whilst sounding a note of caution about the tendency of some branches of psychoanalysis to frame disability as tragedy. As we shall see, there are good reasons to be wary of psychoanalysis, given that some psychoanalytic authors have uncritically essentialised and pathologised disabled people (Watermeyer, 2013). Yet it seems that the politics of engagement with psychoanalysis are an animating factor for critical disability studies, as though such engagement might contaminate or taint the ideological purity of the field. Brian Watermeyer's important book

Towards a Contextual Psychology of Disablism (2013) maps the interstices between the fields with a critical honesty and clarity that is sometimes absent elsewhere.

Turning then to the question of what terminology to use in this book, my outline of the contours of contemporary disability studies will have made it clear that there are no uncontested terms. We have a real difficulty on our hands: to invoke disability is to draw a distinction – to make a troubled and troubling exclusion, even (Puar, 2017a, 2015). Given this difficulty, I am keen to draw the reader's attention to the specificity of what my project is doing (and therefore what it is not doing) as I turn to the subject of language. The book is about my own struggle to find a critical vocabulary for disability that would describe what it is like to embody a cultural anxiety without knowing it; in this sense, it is wholly bound up with questions of language and naming, and these are not issues to be discussed in the introduction and then dispensed with, but rather ongoing tussles.

Given the ongoing prevalence in disability studies of the social model, it is hard not to at least *begin with* a distinction between 'impairment' as a category of bodily experience and 'disability' as signifying the social and structural exclusion occasioned by that impairment. But I have necessarily sought to complicate and move beyond this model, which problematically reifies impairment as though it were something we could access in an unmediated way. Following the aforementioned shift in the field towards the denaturalisation of dominant or normative identities (Davis, 1995), I have generally sought to focus attention on notions such as the 'normal child', the 'developing child', 'the child as gift' and 'the child as futurity', as well as on formative 'scenes' including the diagnostic scene and the rehabilitative scene. Such an approach brings our attention to what it is that makes disability appear. It also sits more comfortably with choosing to use the term 'non-disabled people': it is this term, rather than 'able-bodied', that I tend to use, and I follow contemporary UK disability theorists including Goodley and Lawthom (2013) in so doing. Although this term does not evade a binary opposition, at least it decentres the able-bodied world.[10]

The trajectory of the book takes me towards the idea of disability as a political identity, as one that may have to be claimed or recovered by the subject.[11] I am speaking here of a notion of disability pride. Yet if this is the kind of definition I am ultimately working with, it leaves me with a question about whether the term 'the disabled child' is oxymoronic, or even 'impossible', in Jacqueline Rose's terms (1984, p. 9). By this I mean that there is a contradiction between the use of the term 'disabled child' by an adult who ascribes this identity to a child, and the idea of being disabled as an identity that is self-chosen and claimed. In my case, the latter could only come after I had begun to emancipate myself from the structures that sought to label me as 'handicapped' as a child (a term that has pejorative associations in contemporary British culture, but which seems to have been widely used, and regarded as neutral, in the 1980s). These issues bring me on to the question of the agency of the child, because the contradiction I describe only operates if we conceive of the child as a passive subject, and as a non-subject, as far as political will is concerned.

Agency is a major theme in the book, as it is in the new social studies of childhood, which has sought to challenge the conceptualisation of the child as passive, and as a victim of circumstance (James et al., 1998; see also Hockey and James, 1993). However, it is only in the late stages of my book that the potential agency of the child comes to the fore, and even here my focus is not so much on the child as actor, but on the agency of the adult who has a childhood that 'persists' (J. Rose, 1984, p. 12). If the disabled child emerges as a passive figure initially, this is, I think, because I was that passive child, and I have wanted to understand, through the process of writing, what it was that made me that way and precisely why resistance was so difficult for me for so very long. The agency that I have recovered through psychoanalysis was a long time in the (un)making (a term I discuss further in due course).[12] I suspect that I try to perform a similar kind of unmaking on behalf of the disabled child, peeling back the layers of 'making' which have oppressed her. Such a metaphor, I am aware, implies that I might reach a kernel of truth, a 'real', pre-made child within: I am back to fantasies of knowing. It is to these that I turn now.

Real and figurative children

For a long time during my work on this project, I was troubled by my bifurcated interest in both the 'figure' of the disabled child and the 'real' disabled child, as well as by (what I perceived as) my inability to decide which of these categories was my subject. My discovery of the debate around 'realness' and 'knowing' (Lesnik-Oberstein, 2011, 2008; Caselli, 2010; J. Rose, 1984) suggested to me that what I had regarded as a problem might in fact be a symptom of a broader cultural and disciplinary issue, relating to the ways in which attempts to 'know' can sometimes inadvertently be about prising apart the discursive and the experiential, even as they gesture towards the process of bringing the two together.[13] This book can be read as an attempt to follow, get lost in, get stuck with and hopefully ultimately to *think with* this paradox.

As someone with a background in cultural and critical theory (and prior to that, English literature), I have always known that I was interested in representations. In the early stages of my work on this project, my one-sentence dinner-party summary of my doctoral thesis referred to 'cultural constructions of the disabled child'. Yet as I went deeper, I began to wonder whether the object of my research was not in fact, at least partly, myself. Although I had known at the outset that personal experience drove my interest in my research topic, I had not imagined that the process of writing would become so intertwined with my own recovery, nor that my thesis – and this book – would bear the mark of the personal in quite the way that it has. The place of personal material in the book is explored in more detail shortly, however I refer to it here to note that my neat one-sentence summary collapsed when I realised that the project in which I was becoming immersed was as much about the formation of a particular kind of subjectivity as it was about representations of that subject. It was about both the figurative disabled child and disabled children living in the world (or at least, about an adult with an experience of having been a 'handicapped' child). Above all, it was about the relationship between these two categories.

It seemed to me initially that wanting to explore this relationship entailed a kind of disciplinary blasphemy. Even though interdisciplinarity is a key term in the contemporary academy, the question of what it actually involves is rarely discussed (Callard and Fitzgerald, 2015). It remains the case that, broadly speaking, the realm of the discursive is understood as proper to the humanities whilst the realm of experience is seen as the domain of the social sciences (Lesnik-Oberstein, 2011). The *intersection* of cultural representation and lived experience is still under-theorised. The *mechanics* of how the 'outside' gets in and the 'inside' gets out is a subject that straddles the disciplines, in such a way as to mobilise interdisciplinary questions which, it seems to me, challenge disciplinary norms and conventions. This, for me, is what makes these questions interesting, but I have also felt at times as though I lacked a critical vocabulary for talking about representation and experience together. I hope that this book has taken some steps towards the development of such a language. Even the relatively recent discipline of cultural studies, which brings together methods from literary studies and methods from sociology in a bid to render 'everyday' and 'low' cultural objects worthy of academic attention, did not seem to me to have all the answers here, although I have been inspired by this discipline and am much indebted, in my development as an academic, to the pioneers of the British school of cultural studies, especially Raymond Williams (see, for example, Williams, 1977). For all the emphasis on interdisciplinarity in contemporary UK academia, my own experience of pursuing questions that cross disciplinary boundaries is that such work carries certain risks – risks associated with the perceived contravention of methodological principles (see Callard and Fitzgerald, 2015). I will illustrate what I mean here with reference to my use of literary texts in the book, where the issue of my dual interest in the 'figural' and the 'real' child starts to seem problematic.

Although I discuss literary texts in the book, what I do with them is not always literary analysis, or at least not always in the sense in which this procedure is usually understood now, in this (post-)theoretical moment. I deploy Frances Hodgson Burnett's (1987) children's book *The Secret Garden* as a resource for thinking through, and developing, relational theories of the formation of disabled subjectivity. The text, controversial as it has been for disability studies, turns out to be a kind of focal gathering point, where the philosophy of Jean-Paul Sartre (2003) meets with the psychoanalytic theories of Sándor Ferenczi (1999) and Kenneth Wright (1991) to produce new ways of thinking about how the disabled child gets 'made', both on the page and in the world. In another unconventional treatment of a novel, Jane Messer (2013, p. 12) speaks of 'work[ing] with the text as a (fictional) auto-ethnography': my approach to *The Secret Garden* is perhaps similar. What I mean by this is that I am interested in the figure of Colin as exemplifying a particular kind of disabled subjectivity that we might also encounter in the 'real world'.

The way I read *The Secret Garden* in Chapter 1 will seem, at some points, naïvely caught up in the 'realness' of the characters-as-people, almost as though I am mimicking the credulity of the child-reader who identifies with the protagonists as though they were her friends. It is not insignificant that I am drawn into such a mode of reading in relation to *The Secret Garden* in particular – a text that enthralled me as a child and which still has the power to cast a certain spell over me. It beguiles a part of my being that precedes the development of the critical faculties instilled in me by a training in English literature, just as Dickon entrances the creatures on the moor with his flute.

In my reading, it is almost as if Colin is a fleshly body, and I am making the assumption that I can access him as a fleshly body via my experience of the text. And yet I am a literary studies academic, schooled in the idea that there is no 'outside-text', to take Jacques Derrida (1997, p. 158) at his word. What is going on here? I ask the reader to bear with me in Chapter 1; this way of 'reading' (or should I say experiencing?) *The Secret Garden* is a stage in a process that unfolds over the course of the book – a process of thinking about how we come to live and embody particular cultural representations, and how they live through us. If my mode of reading seems regressive or unschooled, I would draw attention to the way in which my research project seemed to demand of me – at that point in time – that I regress. The archive that I came upon seemed to help me to meet that demand, because of the way it resonated with Harriet-the-Adult-Reader remembering Harriet-the-Child-Reader. *The Secret Garden* spoke to me of an embodied experience that I knew; it helped me to become an embodied reader and writer, (re)connecting with something in myself that I was, at that time, struggling to embody. This book tries to take on the question of what it means to regress and to progress in the context of both literary criticism and disabled subjectivity. But it does not necessarily want to align literary-theoretical reading practices (or the analysis of discursive formations) with 'progress': indeed, in the final chapter, I return to something of this 'embodied' mode of reading in my discussion of Pedro Almodóvar's film *The Skin I Live In* (2011).

If, as David Mitchell and Sharon Snyder (2000, p. 6) observe, disability is used in literary texts as a 'narrative prosthesis' – as a vehicle that 'inaugurates the act of interpretation' and that causes a particular, predictable story to develop – mightn't we, in our critical gestures, want to resist being interpellated into this kind of hermeneutic approach, or at least to examine how it operates?[14] For Mitchell and Snyder (p. 50), 'the artifice of disability binds disabled characters to a programmatic (even deterministic) identity'. This observation raises questions about the relationship between disability as a textual phenomenon and as a lived experience – as Mitchell and Snyder are themselves only too aware.[15] In order to avoid reproducing 'programmatic' identities, we might need an approach that questions the received 'programme' of literary analysis.

Disciplinary status anxiety: What are my methods?

My book draws on a range of theoretical frameworks, often using critical vocabularies from more than one paradigm at once. I am drawn to working at the intersections of different approaches, enjoying the challenge of attempting to put together things that do not ordinarily fit. Indeed, I would argue that it is fitting for a book in disability studies to value mis-fitting at the level of theory as well as in interpersonal encounters (see Garland-Thomson, 2011).[16] If we only value 'fitting' and 'fitting in' as aspirational qualities in academic endeavours in the humanities, we may reproduce normative and oppressive modes of thinking. This seems particularly pertinent in the neoliberal academy, where the experience of material precarity can intensify the difficulty of speaking honestly and critically for a junior academic. I include critical disability studies here as a disciplinary and institutional structure that has its own blind spots and its potential to coerce: it too may exclude under the sign of 'inclusion'. It is partly with this in mind that I argue for a re-evaluation of psychoanalysis in this book.

In this introduction, and across the book as a whole, I advocate for reflexivity around method (Cook, 2013; Wiegman, 2012; Baraitser, 2008; Law, 2004). It is sometimes assumed that 'research methods' is a term that does not apply in the humanities at all, as noted by Gabriele Griffin (2013, p. 1). We need to explore how invocations of methodological rigour and of political commitment function across the humanities and social sciences (Wiegman, 2012; Baraitser, 2008; Law, 2004), as well as thinking about what happens when there is no appeal to such concepts, and when authorial desire remains a subtext. The aims voiced by John Law (2004) in the introduction to *After Method* provide the means for thinking critically about the way method *itself* (as opposed to 'methods' plural) has operated as a kind of legitimising device. To this end, Law argues that he 'would like to divest concern with method of its inheritance of hygiene' (p. 9). He elaborates:

> I want to move from the moralist idea that if only you do your methods properly you will lead a healthy research life – the idea that you will discover specific truths about which all reasonable people can at least temporarily agree.
>
> (Law, 2004, p. 9)

For me, as a scholar of disability studies, method becomes much less appealing once its 'inheritance of hygiene' is foregrounded: my immediate associations to this phrase are thoughts of the eugenics movement. If leading a 'healthy research life' entails rooting out and eliminating that which is complicated or messy, then I would much rather be leading an unhealthy one. Moreover, I have been very struck – given that notions of 'making', 'unmaking' and 'remaking' are central to my own project of exploring the construction of disabled subjectivity – that Law should use these very terms to conceptualise his work on method: '[m]y aim is thus to broaden method, to subvert it, but also to remake it' (p. 9). Soon afterwards, exploring the implications of this project, Law notes that 'we will need to unmake many of our methodological habits' (p. 9). In the book, I explore how the disabled subject is 'made' (or, as I later come to understand it, 'unmade') by disabling cultural practices. What if method itself were one of those cultural practices that, in its un-deconstructed form, is disabling?

Explaining her decision to interweave the theoretical with the anecdotal in *Maternal Encounters*, Lisa Baraitser (2008, p. 12) draws on Law's work as she argues for 'a refusal or desisting of a hierarchy of method'. It is all too easy, especially in a research culture that privileges 'evidence-based' work, to start to feel insecure about one's own methods when their relationship with evidence is complex. This book is about what it means to have a complex and plural relationship with one's evidence, and about what happens when one to tries to probe that relationship, without any guarantees about the outcome. My book works with different kinds of 'evidence': literary and film texts; (canonical) works of critical theory; anthropological essays; childcare manuals; psychoanalytic theories (as texts and – problematically, perhaps – as evidence of the psyche's operations); personal writing that reconstructs scenes from my childhood; a notion of 'my lived experience' and of a *speculative* lived experience – that is, one that I cannot directly remember. Following Robyn Wiegman (2012), I might ask: what did I *want* from my 'evidence'? I think the most honest way of answering that is to say that what I wanted evolved in the process of working on this subject and with these materials. In this sense, the notion of following a 'method' feels like giving this process order and regularity post-hoc. As Jon Cook writes in relation to the question of how creative writing can function as a research method in English Studies:

> To have a method implies that you know what you are about, that your work will not be undermined by accident, digression or irrelevance. To possess a method assumes a kind of reassurance about the future, even an insurance against it. Method promises results and it promises them in good time.
>
> (Cook, 2013, p. 207)

This definition of method, as Cook points out, seems fundamentally at odds with the idea of writing-as-discovery, for which he is making a case, mainly to serve creative and practice-based PhDs. Method provides a structure and a system; writing, on the other hand, has the potential to disrupt this because we do not know what might emerge in and from it (Cook, 2013). Method 'implies an economy' (Cook, 2013, p. 201), it reassures that something will emerge within a given timeframe; writing seems to offer no such guarantees. Cook identifies a binary in the way that method and writing are set up in the discourse of research methods: writing is viewed as the mode of presenting an argument, 'the identity of which has been determined apart from the act of writing itself' (p. 203). I have continuously sought to remain open to what happens in the act of writing itself. The distinction between 'writing' and 'writing up' is destabilised by this kind of approach, as is the shrouding of research practices. Law (2004) argues that if the inscription devices used in the construction of knowledge were more routinely *seen* rather than being swept away and kept out of the write-up, the idea of knowledge as 'constructed' would no longer seem so alien.

In the course of the creation of the first version of this manuscript, I became interested in the traffic between my conscious and unconscious versions of myself; I started to see these as inseparable from my practice as an academic –

an approach that might be commonplace in creative writing (Cook, 2013), but not in academic writing (but see Taylor, 2014; Hollway and Jefferson, 2013).[17] Academic writing is usually governed by the need for a rational argument. In certain ways my book privileges 'unreason' and 'unsoundness' over 'reasonableness' and 'soundness'. Reason is one of the chief strategies through which we are interpellated to 'face' in a particular direction, and to take a particular 'path' without realising it (Ahmed, 2006, pp. 29, 16). This is, of course, not to say that I could have extricated myself from the tentacular clutches of reason, given its dominance in academic discourse, and its embeddedness within the linguistic structures of argumentation. I too wanted to build a rational argument, a case about how the disabled child is 'made' by culture, ideology and psychosocial factors. But I was interested in the question of how my rational argument came to be, on what grounds it stood, whether its rationality was in some sense 'my' rationality. In a wonderful letter to 'Mr Reasonable' at the start of their book, disability theorist Jenny Slater writes:

> What you are not, Mr Reasonable, is the *overtly* nasty person that it's easy to be angry with. In fact, you could be that person I occasionally find myself describing as 'alright really'.
>
> (Slater, 2016, p. 1)

Here, rather than allowing reason to interpellate them fully, Slater personifies reason precisely so as to interpellate *it* (or indeed, him). By explicitly hailing reason in this way, Slater demands that reason accounts for its role in orienting us towards particular objects and not others (Ahmed, 2006). According to reason, the disabled child (as a disabled person) would be luckier, happier, better off, without a disability. According to reason, the disabled child (as a child) does not know what is best for her: she must rely on reasonable adults to make reasonable decisions for her. These decisions are apparently in her best interests. But what kinds of 'new understandings' can we generate by de-naturalising these 'common sense' propositions?

It could be argued that this approach is some form of deconstruction (Derrida, 1997): deconstruction has already done this work, showing how a reasoned argument can unravel; psychoanalysis too has played its role. Yes, this is true; what I am doing is nothing new – I am simply drawing on the tools of 'methods' that are now canonical in literary studies. But sometimes (though not always), these approaches for analysing texts are used in quite a clinical or de-personalised way; there is no sense of how the author's *own* unconscious, or her emotional life, might be unravelling the intentions of her argument, even as, at a conscious level, she seeks to bolster and underpin it. If this book makes a contribution to questions of how knowledge is made, it is, I hope, in its attention to the some of the points of desire and tension in its own argument, where, for example, my desire to create a unified and unifying theory of internalised oppression clashes with my need to problematise the possibility (and desirability) of such a thing. If this approach troubles the overall coherence of my argument then this is partly to pose questions about the grounds upon which coherence rests in academic arguments.

In case this preamble should be seen as an attempt to deflect attention from an actual account of my methods – which it may be, given my insecurity about the validity of what I 'did' – I shall now briefly recount what I 'did' to produce this manuscript. I began with the figure of the disabled child, and I shifted early on, with input from my PhD supervisor Joanne Winning, from the idea of doing a 'pure' cultural history to something more critical-theoretical and concept-driven. At this point, I began to realise that I was interested in viewing the figure of the disabled child through more than one critical lens, and that I was intrigued by the compatibilities, clashes and contradictions between approaches that place emphasis on psychic life, approaches that think in terms of discursive formations, and approaches that foreground the critique of ideology. By this stage of my work, I had also gone into psychoanalysis. My critical-theoretical voyage of discovery was happening in tandem with the labour of suffering, the labour of living with intensifying anxiety. Sometimes I wrote with/about/against my anxiety as a way of helping myself to keep on going, and sometimes the writing process or the analytic process suddenly and dramatically shone a light on something I was trying to understand. It was difficult to disentangle myself-as-discoverer-of-theory from myself-as-self-discoverer and myself-as-sufferer. I came to realise that what I was writing about, fundamentally, was internalised oppression – I was interested in the question of how the outside gets inside, in ways that make it all but invisible. But what is the nature of this invisibility? How can it be studied? How is it inscribed within discourse, within the psyche, in what ways is it hegemonic, and can its hegemony be shifted?[18] Gradually, then, my project began to constellate around a key concept: 'making'. How is the (figure of the) disabled child 'made', in culture, in body, in psyche? What is the role of internalised oppression – often so difficult to detect – in these processes of making?

As this account shows, the quest to determine my topic and my research questions was, itself, iterative, and in constant dialogue with my materials – my cultural objects – and my methods. Broadly speaking, I focus on the disabled child in contemporary Euro-American culture, and I look at British culture in particular. But the objects I have written about have not been chosen according to a strict delineation of a time-and-space-bound field of study, and are instead present in the book more because of the way they speak to me, and enable me to elucidate something of my own experience of having been 'made' as a disabled child. While I was working on the thesis that was to become this book, I hated the questions 'what is your thesis about?' and 'what texts are you looking at?' because they seemed to expose the fraudulence of this bizarre project, which at some points seemed to be spiralling further and further away from being *about* something, and becoming more and more myopic. I had, and I continue to have, insecurities about the epistemological validity of the gear shifts I make: there is an ongoing fear that each shift takes me into disciplinary territory in which I lack expertise and will be 'found out'. By what right do I juxtapose close textual analysis on the one hand, and claims about a lived experience of internalised oppression on the other? What kind of knowledge am I generating when I analyse, say, diagnosis as a speech act and then follow this with a claim about how it gets embodied and lived on the basis of *how I feel* or *how I theorise I must have felt in the past*? When I use personal experience as a legitimising device, can I claim that my conclusions are relevant to anyone other than me? And when I am speculating about an experience of which I have no conscious memory, I am not even operating in relation to 'evidence', am I?

Where I answer these kinds of questions by invoking a psychoanalytic or deconstructionist epistemology, I frame things in terms of speculation and fantasies of knowing (Lesnik-Oberstein, 2011, 2008; J. Rose, 1984). I do have recourse to this approach, but arguably one criticism of my book could be that it does not take the insights of such epistemologies to their proper conclusions because it moves back into a more ontological mode: my desire – perhaps over-reaching myself, or at least betraying my own ambition – to make a contribution to disability theory. In pointing out this very tension, perhaps I will be read as an over-defensive early career academic, wanting to insulate her work from all possible unanticipated angles of critique. This point recalls the insightful connection that Eve Sedgwick (2003) draws between the paranoid reader and the insecurely attached infant, both of whom maintain a 'terrible alertness' (p. 128) as they seek to defend themselves against '*bad surprises*' (p. 130, emphasis in original). But, even though it is indisputable that I would like to prevent such surprises when it comes to the reception of my work, I hope there is also another way of reading this aspect of my work, to which I have been gesturing. This way of reading has to do with entertaining a playful desire to explore what theory can do, and a desire to hold differences, and difficulties, in tension. Baraitser (2008) provides a helpful template here as she charts the tensions inherent in her approach to the maternal, which she sees as having pulled her in two directions at once. On the one hand, she recognises that she has been drawn towards producing a new account of maternal subjectivity, yet at the same time she notes that she continuously seeks to 'undercut [her] own grandiose aims' by pulling herself back from this project, to focus instead on the 'mundane' aspects of the maternal, via a phenomenological methodology (p. 152). Yet nor is a disinterested phenomenological account entirely satisfactory, Baraitser (2008) comments. There is a need to reconnect with the political, and so she is again drawn back towards theorising subjectivity. What I cherish in Baraitser's (2008) account is the honesty and clarity with which she details this zigzagging, ambivalent state of being pulled in two directions by her subject matter and the difficulties it presents. This is not to mention the humbling way she brings her own fears and ambitions into view: this remains a relatively rare act in the recent academic work I have read, in spite of the rise of self-disclosure culture, on which I will touch in the next section.

What is the place of 'the personal' in an academic book?

The arc of this book is also the arc of a personal, psychoanalytic journey into the darker territories of my own childhood: I explore the place of my impairment in my early life. I have hemiplegia, a mild form of cerebral palsy, which was caused by a birth injury, and diagnosed when I was eleven months old. It has been painful, but also cathartic, to think and to write about how the diagnosis of my impairment, and my subsequent 'rehabilitation' through physiotherapy, has affected and shaped my life. As explained, while I was working on this project, I realised that I wanted to incorporate personal, 'creative' writing into the body of my book alongside conventional academic prose, as a way of working with un-metabolised early experience; my hope was that such writing would not only help me, but that it might also help others who have had similar (or different) childhood experiences, and that along the way it might generate new ways of thinking about disabled subjectivity.

During the course of my work on this project alone, there has been a rapid rise of a culture of self-disclosure in the public sphere (Han, 2017). Although facilitated by the recent evolution of online social media ecologies and their conventions, this inflection can also be seen in terms of a longer-term rise of the genre of memoir and of a confessional mode in literary culture, which has been seen as contemporaneous with the advancement of individualism (Couser, 2012; Segal, 2009; Gill, 2006; Miller, 2002). My own project no doubt participates, in some way, in this cultural moment; it is beyond the scope of this book to examine the question of 'how' in detail, although I hope to explore cultures of self-disclosure further in future work. Of course, the idea of drawing on a personal register in political and academic writing is by no means new. In 1969 the feminist thinker Carol Hanisch famously wrote that 'The Personal Is Political' and feminism in this period inaugurated new ways of thinking about the relationship between the public and the private spheres, for example in relation to the conceptualisation of housework (Oakley, 2018; Federici, 2012).[19] Today there exists a large body of feminist academic work on the relationship between researchers' selves and their objects of study.[20] Within some parts of sociology, it has become almost *de rigueur* for academics to give an account of how they see their relationship to the subject of their research, as a stage in a process of reflexivity whose function is to augment the rigour and trustworthiness of the research by bringing possible biases into view. As previously noted, there is less of an established tradition of doing personal writing in humanities academia, although this too is changing, especially in the cluster of fields that Wiegman (2012, p. 1) terms 'identity knowledges' (see, for example, Wiegman, 2014; Cvetkovich, 2012; Baraitser, 2008; Stacey, 1997). There is also a growing number of so-called 'cross-over' books by academics or para-academics, where personal memoir is interwoven with academic discussion (see, for example, Nelson, 2016; Jacques, 2015; Taylor, 2014; Preciado, 2013). As I argued in the previous section, my own justification for exploring personal material in an academic book is that it brings unconscious motivations more overtly into the subject of the study and allows me to acknowledge the ways in which their (non)resolution shapes the trajectory and findings of my project. Personal experience was shaping my work whether I liked it or not, so I decided to entertain it, and see where it led.[21]

Do we value academic writing whose objects are personal memories and internal worlds? Baraitser (2008) cites the influence of Jane Gallop's (2002) work on anecdotal theory as she presents her sections of italicised personal writing, which facilitate exploration of 'key moments in which we are [...] dislodged by motherhood, but perhaps in very minor, transitory, mundane, silly or occasional ways' (2008, p. 11). Anecdotes interrupt Baraitser's theoretical prose and represent 'something of the indigestibility of maternal experience' (p. 13). Although my personal writing is not anecdotal in quite the same way, in that it is more often a reconstruction of an *un*remembered past than a reconstruction of a remembered moment, I use imaginative writing alongside analytical writing, to tell of a pain that seemed (at first) to refuse to be assimilated into theory. Doing the personal writing seemed to enact the undoing of oppression that I was simultaneously seeking to explore in theory; it was, then, in itself a way of 'doing theory'. Lesnik-Oberstein (2008, p. 180) deconstructs a conceptualisation of emotion as 'resistant to analysis', troubling the notion that analysis is 'an invasive and "cold-hearted" instrument of dissection and anatomization that does not understand emotion, but negates or restrains and disciplines it'. Drawing on this idea, and on the attempts by Gallop (2002) and Baraitser (2008) to get theory to take itself less seriously, I would seek to defend a more generous and inclusive notion of theory, which attends to the ways in which affective or 'undisciplined' modes of operating come to be split off from it. These are also ambitions shared by proponents of the 'reparative turn' in literary studies who, drawing on Sedgwick's (2003) work, have sought to query the dominance of hermeneutic modes of reading and their obsession with 'exposing' something in the object of study. Although, following Wiegman (2014, 2012), I would want to query what motivates the turn to reparation, as well as the possibility and desirability of rejecting interpretation, I believe that the Sedgwick essay makes a vital point about the need for reflexivity around reading practices, and for the place of feeling in these.

It is not possible to ascribe a single function to my 'personal writing' in the book (and nor should 'the personal' be considered to start and stop with the italicised sections of text). I have chosen to retain these sections of italicised reflective writing because, as interludes, they provide an opportunity for thinking differently about the ideas I am seeking to theorise. In one sense, these passages are 'data' with a similar status to the literary texts and other cultural objects I examine, and I do subject my personal writing to analysis just as I interpret the other texts I explore. Yet these interludes have also been about allowing a different mode of processing 'disability experience' – perhaps we might say, in a Winnicottian 'space free from [the] intrusions' of academic expectation (Wright, 1991, p. 35), to draw on an image that is very meaningful for me in this book. However, it might be more accurate to say that these sections of text (and the commentaries they produce) dramatise intrusion. This is a book that is very much in dialogue with its interlocutors, by which I mean both the imagined supportive community of scholars I conjure as I write and the more hostile (internalised) voices which are sometimes even being apostrophised with a disparaging 'you' in the personal sections of the book (the 'you' of the physiotherapist that I wanted to hail in my childhood, perhaps – of which more later). Since writing the PhD thesis that was to become this book, I have reflected a lot on the different voices preserved in the manuscript: whom do they address, and what is their motivation? Like Baraitser (2008) I am interested in what happens when one interrupts oneself with writing that deploys a different register. Although normative academic conventions about genre do not always make it easy to work in this way, the fact that my personal writing persistently evades classification as either 'illustrative' or 'theoretical' – but instead helps me to develop my argument by doing something I struggle to classify – is helpful and enriching in a project that aims to unsettle what we think we know about the making of the disabled child.

My past – the past of others? The ethics of drawing on personal material

As the paragraph above makes clear, the personal elements in this monograph tell *my* story,[22] *my* version of the past and of the childhood that 'persists' into the present (J. Rose, 1984, p. 12). In Barbara Taylor's terms, 'this is my version of my history, and nobody else's' (2014, p. xvii). This is important for two reasons: firstly, because the book is about my struggle to develop a version of my history that *is* distinct from the narratives of it that I have inherited, which have sometimes (although not always) been oppressive. Secondly, this book can only claim to be speaking about my past *as I experienced it* – or as I am able to understand it via a process of repeating and working through (Freud, 1958a) – and cannot speak about how certain experiences *may have been intended to feel*. I know that my parents made their decisions about my care and treatment out of love for me. Sometimes the decisions they had to make were extremely difficult ones. They did the best that they could for me, in circumstances that were not always easy to navigate or negotiate. I would even say the same about individual medical practitioners.

My book is not interested in individual decision-making, but in a culture that individualises decision-making. As Nikolas Rose has argued, post-war discourses of child-rearing create a double-bind for parents when it comes to decisions:

> The family is simultaneously allotted its responsibilities, assured of its natural capacities, and educated in the fact that it needs to be educated by experts in order to have confidence in its own capacities. Parents are bound into the language and evaluations of expertise at the very moment they are assured of their freedom and autonomy.
>
> (N. Rose, 1999, p. 208)

Rose identifies this trait as particularly dominant in the work of the psychoanalyst Donald Winnicott who, writing during in the post-war period, simultaneously affirmed the natural maternal capacities of the 'Ordinary Devoted Mother' whilst also constructing both mother and child in terms of norms and the need for monitoring (N. Rose, 1999; Winnicott, 1957, p. 1). For Rose (1999), this state of affairs is part of a broader contradiction in the changing conceptualisation of the family in the twentieth century as at once private and responsible for its own affairs, and yet peculiarly public and subject to state surveillance and intervention. I hope that the intensity of the personal sections of this book can be read with a sense of this frame in mind.

At many times in the process of writing, I have been concerned about doing writing that implicates my parents in a history that has made me angry. Yet, not to have done such writing would be to thwart the voice, the academic creativity and the conviction that psychoanalysis has helped me to find, and which my parents have encouraged me to foster in myself, both in the present and when I was a child. Indeed, I am deeply grateful to both of my parents for their generous and supportive responses to this work. Although it is a cliché, my suffering has been the making of me as a person with something distinct to say, and it seems important to take up the challenge of trying to say it, even though, or perhaps *because* it differentiates me from those from whom I spring. Elsewhere I have written that disability potentially presents us with the opportunity for 'an identity politics that does not run in the family' given that impairment can, in many cases, signify a break with the parental embodiment (Jones et al., 2014, n. p.). In my case, claiming disability as an identity has entailed a process of psychic separation, through which I have begun to be able to move away from the automatic concealment of my impairment and towards a place of choosing to display it. In allowing my voice to come through in this book, I am enacting a similar process of bringing something out into the open, and of choosing to query the norms I have inherited. This is not to reject my inheritance, but rather to occupy a place in which I am able to think about it, so that I can take from it that which nurtures me, and understand why other parts of it have been problematic for me.

I am therefore arguing for an ethics of different voices that sit alongside one another. To the extent that my parents do figure in this narrative, I have sought not to individualise their role and the decisions they made, but to see these as part of a much broader tapestry of dominant cultural positions associated with disability. Where there is anger, there is also an acknowledgement that whatever was done was done with the best of intentions.

Limitations of my work

In the course of my work on this book, I have become increasingly aware of the ways in which I am invested in an identity-based model of disability, in which disability is seen as exception (Puar, 2017a, 2015). As Jasbir Puar (2017a, 2015) notes, the body that is recognisable as 'disabled' is one that has already been retrieved for rights, empowerment and rehabilitation. Puar's term 'debility' – which highlights how, at the level of population, certain bodies are marked out for life whilst others are designated for death or for maiming – is not an identity, but it is that which allows disability to be produced as an 'empowered status' (2017a, p. xvii). Drawing on Puar's work in *Terrorist Assemblages* (2017b), which was first published in 2007, Robert McRuer (2010) draws attention to 'disability nationalism',[23] which affords certain privileges to some disabled subjects (often on the basis of nationality and/or skin colour), at the expense of others whose identity as 'disabled', and whose right to be protected as such, remains problematically invisible, and is, furthermore, *made* invisible by the structuring of these issues in terms of disability.

In what ways does the notion of debility change how we interrogate the 'making' of the disabled child, and how would it change the parameters of this project? It would require that I acknowledge that all of the ways in which I theorise 'making' are in relation to a subject that has *always already* been retrieved for life, which might initially appear paradoxical, given that this subject is in receipt of the kinds of attention that are supposed to be retrieving it for life (diagnosis, rehabilitation). Under pressure from 'debility', 'disability' is shown to rely for its coherence on practices of retrieval that must necessarily leave some bodies behind, unrecognised, not-fitting. In this context, it feels important to remind ourselves of the overwhelming whiteness of disability studies as a discipline (Bell, 2017), and of its ongoing reproduction of cultural imperialisms (Grech and Soldatic, 2015), which persist even as it articulates the need to problematise its tendency to centre the Global North (Watermeyer et al., 2019).

It makes me deeply uncomfortable to think that my acts of 'retrieval' in this book may be predicated on the non-visibility of debilitated bodies, and on complicity with discourses of 'disability nationalism' (McRuer, 2010). There is no doubt that there is a preponderance of white, middle-class disabled children in this book, and this is a limitation of the work – one that emerges in large part from the inseparability of my archive from my personal disability history (I was a privileged, white, middle-class disabled child), but which cannot be disentangled from the hegemony of disability-as-exception in Anglo-American disability studies, which Puar (2017a, 2015) so acutely diagnoses. Insofar as my approach in this book is animated by the category 'making', it too is interested in the question of what constitutes a recognisable disabled body and (more problematically) a disabled subjectivity. Whilst I would, like Puar, seek to critically interrogate the exclusions of liberal discourses of recognition, I nevertheless want to retain and develop a critical vocabulary – drawn from psychosocial studies and medical humanities – to unpack the inter- and intra-subjective character of internalised oppression. This means moving between an analysis of the operations of biopolitical strategies and discourses on the one hand (for which debility is, I would argue, *the* most useful and disruptive concept to have emerged in disability studies this decade), and, on the other hand, a more phenomenological, ontological, microscopic mode, for which an alternative lexicon is required. That is a project which this book takes on.

Outline of chapters

The book is divided into four chapters, each of which explores a particular question or issue relating to the 'making of the disabled child'. The progression of the chapters is associated with the unfolding of new ways of understanding my self and my struggle to resist internalised oppression, and the development of my thought and feeling can be observed in the book. It would, I feel, be a betrayal of myself to attempt to disguise or conceal this development, especially since my process of psychic 'working-through' has helped me to feel strong enough not to mask the person that I am or the disabled body that I have (Freud, 1958a, p. 155). It is important to me that the body of work presented here is imperfect (or perhaps I should say, disabled), in the sense that it does not wholly conceal the development of a subject (its author) over time. This is not to say that I have *not* made revisions in the process of finalising the work, but it is to say that the book bears the imprint of a political consciousness in the making, of a journey towards resistance.

In Chapter 1, 'The look that made me: The early gazing relationship and the construction of disabled subjectivity', I explore the place of intersubjectivity, and specifically the formative qualities of the look, in two novels that feature ambiguously 'different' children: Doris Lessing's (2007 [1988]) *The Fifth Child* and Frances Hodgson Burnett's (1987 [1911]) *The Secret Garden*. The chapter uses a conceptual framework informed by object relations psychoanalysis – in particular Winnicott's (1971a) essay on the mirroring function of the mother's face, and Kenneth Wright's (1991) work *Vision and Separation*, which draws on that work to theorise the role of the look in parent–infant relationships. I also draw on Teresa Brennan's (2004) book *The Transmission of Affect* to reflect on the interpersonal and intergenerational mobility of states of feeling and sensation associated with disability. This analytical framework necessitates a discussion about the epistemological status of my acts of reading in the chapter and the kinds of claims to knowledge that I am making, questions that are revisited in later chapters as I approach the issue of 'making the disabled child' from other theoretical angles. In Chapter 1, I introduce the metaphor of the 'over-looking/overlooking' gaze to theorise my own early experience of being looked at, and explore the relevance of this concept for critical disability studies and for reading practices more generally.

Chapter 2, 'Making her better? Denaturalising the notion of the "developing child"' takes an altogether different approach to the question of 'making', one in which the key concept – development – is analysed as a discursive entity. The chapter reflects on the role played by discourses of development in the life of the disabled child, highlighting and working with my ambivalent attachment to 'development'. I draw on the work of critical psychologist Erica Burman (2008a, 2008b), who has emphasised the relationship between development as a culturally imperialist geopolitical and economic notion, and development as a property of the child's 'natural' progress in the discipline of developmental psychology. I also deploy Mikhail Bakhtin's (1981) notion of the chronotope – which underscores the interconnectedness of space and time in literary expression – to interrogate the discursive construction of developmentalism. Using fictional and non-fictional examples, I argue that a hegemonic developmental logic structures the decisions that are made about disabled children's lives even when the opposite might appear to be the case. Once again, I use personal writing to reflect on my own relationship with developmental time, and I begin to consider the role of the 'pathological' symptom in resisting the developmental unfolding of existence – a theme to which I return subsequently.

In Chapter 3, '(Un)making the child, making the future: On gifts, commodities and diagnostic speech acts', I argue that the arrival of the disabled child disrupts the potential of the child of liberal individualism to figure as a signifier of futurity and promise (Mollow, 2012; Ahmed, 2010; Edelman, 2004). Drawing on Marxist theories of commodification (Marx, 1976; Lukács, 1971), on Derrida's deconstruction of the gift (1992), and on recent and contemporary scholarship in feminist theory, queer theory and disability studies, I dwell on the role of the disabled child in drawing attention to the commodification of childhood, the child and the process of child-rearing itself. I focus in particular on the effects of the rhetoric of the child-as-gift. Having set this scene, I then turn to the cultural practice of diagnosis. I am interested in the performative properties of the 'diagnostic speech act'. What does the diagnostic speech act, pronounced by the consultant, mean for the family of the disabled child: how does it change how the child and her future (and her value as an investment for the future) are understood? And what of the pre-verbal child's experience of this diagnostic scene: where does it lodge in her body? I consider these questions with reference to Judith Butler's (1997a) work on injurious speech acts, Frantz Fanon's discussion of the 'bodily schema' (1986, p. 110) and Sándor Ferenczi's (1999, p. 299) concept of 'introjection of the aggressor'; I also draw on my own experiential knowledge. The injurious speech act – including the concept of being able to 'counter the offensive call' (Butler, 1997a, p. 2) – then goes on to take centre stage in the final chapter as I theorise resistance.

Chapter 4, 'Making, unmaking, remaking? Finding a position from which to resist', is the most personal of the chapters. By drawing a parallel between physiotherapy as a practice that 'unmade' me and psychoanalysis as a practice that has necessarily had to repeat the original wound, I investigate the issue of how we can really undo the knot of internalised oppression. In order to examine the speculative question of what rehabilitation might feel like from the point of view of a young child, I juxtapose discussion of my personal experience with analysis of a disturbing and disorienting film about forced 'remaking' – Pedro Almodóvar's *The Skin I Live In* (2011). I take up a question I posed towards the end of Chapter 3, in which I queried Butler's insistence that the injurious power of speech is also the making of us as subjects that are capable of 'counter[ing] the offensive call' (1997a, p. 2). Reflecting on the paradox of speech as that which masks as well as that which can unveil, I examine the place of language as a '"second skin"' (Bick, 1968, p. 484) in my own belated experience of coming to inhabit a self that can take up a position of resistance.

Chapter 4 is followed by a short 'Conclusion', in which I explore the ground covered in the chapters through a discussion of agency; I analyse why the disabled child has predominantly been read in the book as the object of practices of making, rather than as an actor in her own right. I reflect on the movement towards agency in the trajectory of the book, which parallels my personal shift towards a capacity to resist. I also draw some conclusions about my disciplinary position in relation to critical disability studies and psychoanalysis, the antagonism of which has been a major feature of my work. I conclude by advocating a 'disagreeable' politics of disability,[24] which would help us to think again about how disabled childhoods are 'made'.

Notes

1 The book launch for *Disabled Children's Childhood Studies* took place at Birkbeck, University of London on 31 January 2014. The perspectival shift that Curran and Runswick-Cole discussed then is also in evidence in their Preface to the (2013) edited collection. They note, for example: '[d]isabled children's childhood studies are very different from studies of child development or children's impairments' (p. x).

2 In my use of the term 'discursive', I am drawing on Foucault's (2002) notion of discourse.

3 I first encountered the term 'internalised oppression' in Mason (1992, p. 27), and I believe this to be an early usage of the term. However, it is widely used in disability studies and I do not think the term can be attributed to an individual author, so I avoid putting it inside quotation marks. David and Derthick (2014) locate the origins of the concept in Fanon's work on colonial oppression (they cite Fanon, F. (1965) *The Wretched of the Earth*, New York, Grove). Within disability studies, Kumari Campbell (2008, p. 151) has drawn on critical race theory to flesh out the concept of 'internalized ableism', which could be seen as synonymous with internalised oppression. For my purposes in this book, I have a slight preference for the latter term, because of the way it hints at an oppressing self, and because it connotes a mode of self-oppression that extends beyond disability.

4 In relation to the idea of '[f]inding the [c]hild', see Steedman (1995, p. viii).

5 Here Spivak refers to 'a *strategic* use of positivist essentialism in a scrupulously visible political interest' (1987, p. 205, emphasis in original). This comes to be known as 'strategic essentialism' later in Spivak's work.

6 A politics of recognition and rights is arguably grounded in a liberal individualist model of subjectivity, which I would want to contest. See the 'Limitations' section of my introduction.

7 Marks (1999, p. 18) notes that the term 'temporarily able-bodied' was deployed by activists in the late 1980s 'to challenge the security of the "able-bodied" position'.

8 For a discussion of the way in which the social model potentially reinscribes impairment as natural or biological, see Goodley (2001). For a discussion of the social role of impairment labels, see Mallett and Runswick-Cole (2016).

9 In relation to the idea that both disability and childhood function as signifiers of 'dependence that is so often desired though repressed', see Goodley and Lawthom (2013, p. 170).

10 Goodley and Lawthom (2013) argue that this term enables them to 'emphasize the cultural, relational and psychological processes involved in distancing the non-disabled self from the disabled other' (p. 165). They suggest that '[t]he term also acknowledges the tensions and defence mechanisms – in the broadest socio-cultural senses – to be found in a dominant culture that struggles with the precarious nature of trying to be what it often is not' (p. 165). The company EQuality Training (n.d., p. 5) also advocates use of the term 'non-disabled' in their online training materials.

11 In relation to the political dimension of the term disability, see Mallett and Runswick-Cole (2016).

12 'Making' and 'unmaking' are also terms used by Scarry (1985). I draw on Scarry's definitions in Chapter 4.

13 This is a point that reverberates throughout Lesnik-Oberstein's (2008) book, *On Having an Own Child*.

14 I use the term 'interpellation' in a broadly Althusserian sense: see Althusser (1971).

15 The authors observe that '[n]arrative prosthesis [...] is our way of situating a discussion about disability within a literary domain while keeping watch on its social context' (2000, p. 9).

16 Rosemarie Garland-Thomson argues for the term '*misfit*' as 'a new critical keyword' for disability studies, stating that it 'emphasizes context over essence, relation over isolation, mediation over origination' (2011, pp. 592, 593, emphasis in original).

17 Hollway and Jefferson (2013) draw on ideas from psychoanalysis to argue that social researchers need to take account of the *effects* of their own subjectivity and the transference in the research encounter. They examine how these factors impact on data collection. Arguably, then, the personal is already the stuff of academic writing, whether or not we choose to make it so, since we are drawn to particular research questions by our unconscious conflicts as well as by our conscious interests and desires (Taylor, 2014). Taylor writes that '[t]he book that emerged from my PhD thesis, *Eve and the New Jerusalem*, was a historical defence of the values underpinning "The Family of Man" exhibition' (pp. 17–18). This was an exhibition at the Museum of Modern Art in New York, the catalogue for which was an important document in Taylor's childhood, and a visual representation of her parents' left-wing politics, which Taylor came to idealise. Taylor notes that she did not see her PhD research in this light at the time of undertaking it, but states that 'it is obvious to me now' (p. 18): this discussion highlights the role of the unconscious in the selection of subject matter.

18 I draw on the work of Antonio Gramsci (1971) in my use of the term 'hegemonic'.

19 It should also be noted that within a context of feminist disability studies, Carol Thomas (1999, p. 73) has challenged the 'private/public dualism' that she finds in Michael Oliver's work on the social model of disability.

20 For an excellent discussion of the researchers' relationships with their subjects see Letherby et al. (2013).

21 By this point it will be clear to the reader that my psychoanalysis has impacted on both the content of the book and its form. In my movement towards recovery, there have been times when I have seemingly become more ill and closer to madness than prior to psychoanalysis. A non-psychoanalytic theoretical approach would struggle to deal with this strange route to health and its implications for my method, which I work through in Chapter 4. Taylor's (2014) memoir has been an important touchstone as I have sought to validate my approach. Her observations about her 'craziness' being her 'salvation' (p. xiii) have been inspiring for me – she writes: 'the person I am, I became through my madness: not by "recovering" from it, which implies a return to a previously healthy state, but by entering into it and travelling to its roots' (pp. xviii–xix). I feel similarly that the suffering associated with the so-called 'pathological' parts of myself is something from which I am paradoxically being released by learning to inhabit, and this is a shift I trace in the book.

22 As my book progresses, the unity of this 'my' may be up for discussion.

23 This term is used in the title of McRuer's essay.

24 Here I am drawing on Ahmed's (2010) politicisation of 'disagreement'. Ahmed (2010) observes that '[t]o suffer can mean to feel your disagreement with what has been judged as good' (p. 210), pointing out that '[a]cts of revolution' are '*protests against the costs of agreement*' (p. 213; emphasis in original).

1 The look that made me

The early gazing relationship and the construction of disabled subjectivity

What do you see when you see me? You doctors, binding my legs in plaster, putting me in plaster boots. They're supposed to make me walk correctly. I am lying on the stretcher. You are smearing the wet, cold plaster along my legs. I'm up here. You are down there, talking amongst yourselves, talking about my legs, wrapping them, weighing them down so they can no longer move.

Solidified legs.

Great blocks of rock on my feet. You don't look at me, up here in my head: you stay with the legs. They are easy to manage, they are just legs. Not a person.

Where am I?

***

The chapter considers the role of the look in the formation of disabled subjectivity. It is a chapter that calls into question the relationship between subjectivity and objectivity, between the 'I' and the 'you', the inside and the outside, the past and the present. In the brief personal account that opens this chapter, the childhood experience of being regarded as an object while being imprisoned inside plaster boots is endured as an intrusion that co-opts the body for someone else. The present-day narrator of this retaliatory piece apostrophises those doctors of the past (who are somehow simultaneously looking and unlooking) in a speech act that deprives the 'you' (plural) of agency, making the (now voiceless) doctors both the subject and object of *my* sentence ('you don't really see me'). Even as the doctors are portrayed as agents, the narrator's language wrests control of how we read the scene. According to Johnson (1986, pp. 29–30), the rhetorical device of apostrophe – 'the direct address of an absent, dead or inanimate being by a first-person speaker' – 'manipulates the I/Thou structure of *direct* address' by animating and by ventriloquising the absent 'you' (p. 30, emphasis in original). Drawing on this analysis, then, we could say that in my account it is the child narrator figure (voiceless at one time) who is given voice, and the doctors whose position is manipulated via my apostrophe. My narrator's address attempts to reverse the original structuring of the I/Thou relation, such that it is almost as if the doctors are being forced to embody the alienation of the – my – objectified body: 'you stay with the legs', 'they are just legs'. It is my child narrator's apostrophe that linguistically forces the doctors into the position of 'the oppressors', thereby creating a parallel with the physically restrictive position that I had to inhabit whilst wearing the plaster boots. Yet the narrator's oppression (a term whose ambiguous transitivity I am deliberately engaging here) is incomplete: the doctors might just be placing their attention elsewhere ('talking amongst yourselves'), or threatening to move on to the next patient, rather than actively being the oppressors that my narrator would have them be. The final, plaintive, 'Where am I?' conjures an ambiguity around deprivation-of-self versus agentic escape. As this writing suggests, what interest me in this chapter – and indeed throughout the book – is the instability of the categories 'I' and 'you' in the formation of disabled subjectivity. What is the role of the exchange of gazes in this process?

If this chapter makes a contribution to the literature in disability studies that probes the connection between seeing and knowing (oneself), it does so by asking what it means for an experience of oneself to be transmitted via the gaze, and what kind of knowledge about disability is created via the exchange of gazes. It could be said that in choosing to focus on the eye, my work reproduces the tendency in the European, masculinist philosophical tradition to privilege the gaze as our primary means of knowing the world,[1] and that this chapter may re-inscribe ocularcentrism. Yet I choose to focus on sight partly *because* of its hegemony (Vidali, 2010). By attending to the linguistic imbrication of seeing and knowing, Amy Vidali (2010) draws attention to the naturalisation of this connection. She points to the work of Rod Michalko, who has highlighted the numerous ways in which metaphors of sight are used to invoke perception and enlightenment: 'seeing the point'; 'not being blind to the facts'; 'looking at things objectively' (Michalko, 2003, p. 76). Meanwhile – as Vidali (2010) notes – Georgina Kleege reminds us that people who are 'clear-sighted' are 'probably also level-headed and open-minded' (1999, p. 111). Following Davis' (1995) recommendation that disability theorists examine and de-centre the dominant terms, I hope that whilst I *am* positing the dominant role of sight in the founding of disabled subjectivity, I am *also* – like Vidali (2010) – probing what it means to know ourselves – or not to know ourselves – via the gaze.

The performative character of the look has long fascinated philosophers and social theorists. Jean-Paul Sartre's (2003) canonical essay on 'The Look', written in the 1940s, drew attention to the profoundly disabling quality of the experience of being looked at. The essay's narrator explains: 'in the shock which seizes me when I apprehend the Other's look, [...] suddenly I experience a subtle alienation of all my possibilities, which are now associated with objects of the world, far from me in the midst of the world' (p. 288). Sartre emphasises the arresting quality of the scrutinising look – its power to thwart the expansion of a sense of self, and to turn self-perception into an experience of objecthood. In 1963, Erving Goffman (1990) famously figured the relational experience of stigma in terms of exposure and intrusion. Within disability studies, Bill Hughes (1999, pp. 156, 157) has described the gaze as both 'constituted' by cultural formations and 'constitutive' in the sense that it produces experience. Donna Reeve draws on Hughes' (1999, p. 168) notion of the gaze as 'disfiguring' in her work on psycho-emotional disablism, arguing that this gaze can lead disabled people to 'restrict their life choices' (Reeve, 2008, p. 41). Rosemarie Garland-Thomson (2009) considers staring as a biological and a cultural phenomenon, while Susan Lingsom (2008), among others, has worked on the notion of passing, exploring how the ability to 'pass' as non-disabled is both enabling and disabling.

In this chapter, I seek to build on this scholarship to argue that we need to analyse the experience of being 'looked at' not only as a culturally and historically situated phenomenon, but also as a process with a temporality – a temporal thickness. Scholarship in disability studies tends to focus on the look as a synchronic phenomenon, as does Sartre (2003). My interest here, however, is in the look as both a synchronic experience and a diachronic one – as something that resonates in the present because of the ways in which it re-enlivens something from the past. The look is lived over time, and our biographies and past experiences affect how we respond to it (Reeve, 2008). I shall consider not only how the looks we receive give form to our later responses to the gazes of the Other, but also how our *own* uses of the gaze – upon ourselves, upon the Other and upon the texts we read through the prism of this gaze – shape the world even as they are also shaped by it.

Because the work I am doing in this chapter reflects on the ways in which disability is brought into being via acts of perception and interaction, most of the texts I discuss feature characters whose status as disabled is ambiguous – where disability is not a known entity. I am working with, and building on, a 'relational model of disability', which sees people with disabilities as *'disabled through dynamic relationships of body/mind and the environment'* (Goodley, 2011, p. 17; emphasis in original). All of the texts discussed exemplify aspects of a model of 'looking' which I am proposing here, and which – I hope – has implications both for disability studies and more widely for disciplines that are interested in subject formation. The look can have an effect even in the absence of visible impairment, or in the absence of a clear diagnosis. It is not that I want to prioritise the productivity of the look and downplay embodiment, or vice versa, but that I am interested in highlighting complexity in this context.

The chapter begins by introducing the key ideas that have informed my theoretical framework in the chapter, including a section on object relations psychoanalysis and one on Brennan's (2004, p. 1) notion of the 'transmission of affect'. Within these sections, I raise questions about the status of psychoanalytic and experiential knowledge, which come under discussion at various stages of the chapter. Next, I turn to Lessing's (2007 [1988]) novel *The Fifth Child* (*FC*).[2] In my analysis of the novel, I argue that we can read the characters as seeking to disavow the 'transmission of affect' and the relationality of difference, and that the narrative structure invites the reader to critique this position. Subsequently, in my consideration of Hodgson Burnett's (1987 [1911]) *The Secret Garden* (*SG*), which follows in the next section,[3] I home in on the gaze as a transmitter of affect, grounding my discussion in Sartre's (2003) theory of 'The Look' and in the work of Winnicottian psychoanalyst Kenneth Wright. Then, looking more closely at Wright's (1991) work on the gaze, I draw on my own experience of growing up with an impairment to theorise the specificity of the disabled infant's experience of the look. I develop the concept of the 'overlooking/over-looking' gaze, as one whose double meaning is both specific to my experience and – I hope – relevant to others who have grown up with an impairment. I explain what this concept has to offer the field of critical disability studies, including a discussion of the experience of passing as non-disabled. Lastly, I propose that the doubting, diagnostic gaze – which I enact upon myself and the world – can be understood as a mode of reading and of (insecure) knowing, whose the dialogic properties have been in play in the course of the chapter.

Why object relations psychoanalysis?

Like the relational model of disability described above, object relations psychoanalysis sees the infant as formed in relationship with primary caregivers. It destabilises clear-cut distinctions between the 'I' and the 'you'. It foregrounds the primacy of 'intra-psychic and (close) interpersonal explanations for personality development' (Watermeyer, 2013, p. 53). The gaze has been a subject of interest within this branch of psychoanalysis (see Wright, 1991; Winnicott, 1971a). While the thought associated with object relations psychoanalysis is by no means homogenous (and some may contest my framing of this school and its proponents), there are nevertheless a number of common themes in the work of the analysts generally regarded as working within this tradition. Before attending to these themes, I will briefly explore in a little more detail why psychoanalysis has been seen as a controversial set of ideas within disability studies and more widely in the academy, and why I nevertheless find it compelling.

It is reasonable to ask how a psychoanalytic approach can be used in the service of a politics of resistance. Psychoanalysis and radical disability politics make uneasy bedfellows: as Watermeyer (2013) points out in his review of the intersections between the two fields, historically, where psychoanalysis has paid attention to disability, it has tended to conceptualise it in terms of pathology and to theorise psychological difficulties as a response to impairment rather than to the psychosocial experience of exclusion. He gives the example of Niederland's (1965)[4] paper, in which disabled people are regarded as 'carrying *inherent psychological difference* emanating from organic factors' (Watermeyer, 2013, p. 60, emphasis in original). Nor is Niederland's work an isolated example – Watermeyer (p. 59) explains that this author is able to cite Freud in support of his argument, since 'Freud's own utterances on disability are quite ambiguous'. Although, as Watermeyer goes on to explain, we do also find more nuanced, multifactorial accounts of disability in the psychoanalytic literature, it is not especially surprising that disability studies has been, and remains, suspicious of psychoanalysis, given this history of problematic accounts.

Relatedly, one might object that there is a risk in this chapter, focussing as it does on the exchange of gazes between mother and baby that the mother is simply placed back in the 'object-position as container, mirror, receptacle for intolerable feelings' (Baraitser, 2008, p. 5). As Baraitser observes (p. 161, note 4), although much work has been done at the intersection between feminism and psychoanalysis to retrieve the mother from being viewed solely through this 'functional' lens, the persistence of a focus on 'development' in psychoanalytic theory means that 'child-centred accounts' continue to dominate. In the next chapter, I take up and problematise the concept of 'development' (including in relation to psychoanalysis), but, as far as this chapter is concerned, my perspective is certainly informed and coloured by a developmental and child-centred paradigm, even as I seek to remain aware of the limitations of such an approach. Doing critical disability studies means taking on questions that make us afraid, because they take us into difficult places – places where a radical politics comes up against major challenges, where it perhaps even starts to come undone. The 'critical' in critical disability studies ought, in my opinion, to mean confronting ideas that confound our political compass. And in my opinion we cannot afford to ignore the formative role of the gaze in early childhood: if the way I am seen now, in the present, restricts me, how much more am I restricting *myself*, on the basis of gazes that are perhaps no longer physically present, but which I internalised in a time before memory began?

Amongst the various schools of psychoanalytic thought, object relations has a particular attachment to the developmental paradigm (Mitchell, 1988). This means that in terms of disciplinary orientation, the theory of object relations sometimes reads as though it is making scientific claims, in contrast with Lacan's thought, for example, which is more easily read (and indeed has been read) as a canonical contribution to literary theory.[5] There are, therefore, interesting tensions in object relations psychoanalysis (which are mirrored in my interests in this chapter and across my book), between what is knowable and what is unknowable, between what is empirically verifiable and what is speculative. The central claim of psychoanalysis, about the existence of an unconscious that can never be fully known, *undoes* epistemological certainty (Roustang, 1984) and thus it seems to work against sweeping claims to theory, either in relation to development, or in relation to how we 'explain' disability. As we shall see, object relations seeks to offer a more-or-less coherent theory of development, which is sometimes, but not always, attuned to its own ambivalence about the idea of being a developmental theory, as well as to the difficulties associated with having the status of a theory whilst positing the existence of the unconscious. To some extent, this contradiction is at work across psychoanalytic theory, but it is, I think, especially marked in object relations. These are meta-theoretical questions to which I return; for the time being, I want to highlight some of the theories that help us to explore the early gazing relationship and its role in subject formation.

Object relations psychoanalysis places emphasis on the (relational) body as the locus of early infantile experience – experiences must be understood in sensory terms as there is no way of symbolising them. According to Wilfred Bion's (1963) model of infantile development, the infant needs the primary caregiver to 'contain' overwhelming bodily sensations, to metabolise them and then to return them to the infant in a form that can be managed. This model proposes that the Kleinian processes of projection and introjection operate from the start of life

(Klein, 1997a), as the infant's crying allows her to hurl 'the pain sensation out and away, over and over again' (Stern, 1991, p. 34). The object relations psychoanalytic tradition usually conceptualises early life as a phase in which there is a lack of differentiation between self and Other. For Winnicott (1990a, p. 45), the psyche is regarded as 'indwelling in the soma' – a representation of the mind/body relationship that challenges the dominance of the Cartesian split. In *Diary of a Baby*, Daniel Stern (1991) uses the metaphor of the weather to describe the baby's moods. Stern suggests that it is not always clear to the baby what comes from within the body, and what comes from without, so that when the baby starts to cry, voice and crying are not perceived as one, as if 'the wind and its sounds have separated' (p. 33). Continuing with this theme of (non) differentiation, we can turn to Winnicott's influential account of the maternal mirroring function, in which the role of sight is crucial to the perception of difference:

> What does the baby see when he or she looks at the mother's face? I am suggesting that, ordinarily, what the baby sees is himself or herself. In other words the mother is looking at the baby and *what she looks like is related to what she sees there.*
>
> (Winnicott, 1971a, p. 112; emphasis in original)

For Winnicott, it is through looking into the mother's face that the baby begins to obtain a sense of him/herself. Ordinary mirroring is the source of creativity in that it is 'the beginning of a significant exchange with the world, a two-way process in which self-enrichment alternates with the discovery of meaning in the world of seen things' (p. 113). If for some reason this mirroring function does not take place satisfactorily, this process of exchange is replaced by an imperative for perception. Studying the mother's face 'to predict [her] mood' becomes the baby's main preoccupation (p. 113). For Winnicott, this baby 'will organize withdrawal, or will not look except to perceive, as a defence' (p. 113).[6]

These theories of the becoming-self are necessarily speculative. How does the psychoanalyst 'know'? As discussed, psychoanalysis has struggled since its inception with the question of how to authorise what it claims to see (Roustang, 1984). Winnicott's discussion of seeing, becoming and knowing mirrors this epistemological tension. We might note the perspectival hall of mirrors implied by the phrase '*what she looks like is related to what she sees there*'. Condensed in this short phrase is the idea of the undifferentiated baby's face as the mirror that determines how the mother looks: i.e., how she sees herself and *also* how she is seen by the baby, whose impression is itself impacting on the mother's self-image and *also* reflecting something back to the baby about who or what s/he is. So many reflections! Where do they begin and end? This rather confusing compression, where pronouns seem to remove the (always male) baby's role, underscores the difficulty of tracing what belongs to whom in this space of ever-receding images bouncing back and forth. Yet Winnicott (1971a) proposes that while the exchange of gazes remains playful and engaged, it is possible to tolerate a notion of identity as relational, co-constructed and in flux (the image without origin). It is, these passages suggest, when the flow of gazes is impaired or interrupted that there is a need for 'knowing', for fixity. Winnicott's ontology could be understood as an analogue for the epistemological tussle in which both the psychoanalyst and the interdisciplinary humanities scholar (me) are engaged. Where does perception end and speculation begin? How do I ground my knowledge in this chapter, if I am moving between the subject of experience on the one hand (requiring inward perception that is impossible for the Other to verify, as well as speculation, free association and intuition) and the subject of representation on the other (requiring empirical perception and close textual analysis)? And yet, if speculation relates to the *specular*, to that which is mirrored, then isn't this space at the intersection none other than the desired space of mother–infant co-creation, indeed of making representations, that Winnicott advocates?

Object relations psychoanalysis, then, is in a certain sense a theory of the transitive grammar of sensation and emotion; a mode of thinking about the affects which refuses to take them for granted as fixed attributes of a person, but which rather seeks to investigate their mobility and their relationality. What if the question *'what do you see when you see me?'* is also a question about how I am 'made' as a disabled subject by the affects that move via the gaze? To develop this line of thought, I now want to consider, in more detail, what the notion of the 'transmission of affect' (Brennan, 2004, p. 1) can contribute to an analysis of how we come to know ourselves through the early gazing relationship.

The transmission of affect

The notion of the 'transmission of affect' (Brennan, 2004, p. 1) enables us to probe the space of perceptual uncertainty, this space in which the ownership of feelings and sensations cannot always be clarified. Brennan's key insight is that the perception of the subject as self-contained is in itself a cultural production. The transmission of affect is a potentially powerful concept, which breaks down distinctions between subject and object and between the biological and the social. Even though it may be a social process at one level, the transmission of affect can also be 'deeply physical in its effects' (Brennan, 2004, p. 23). Thus, although projective identification is a social and affective phenomenon, it may engender a physical change in the body. Projective identification is just one of the mechanisms of transmission that Brennan analyses in her book, even as she maintains a degree of critical distance from (Freudian) psychoanalysis, which she characterises as maintaining the illusion of self-containment via its investment in the individual psyche as 'the origin of the drives and affects' (p. 12). Brennan is also critical of the 'foundational fantasy', through which the mother is figured (in psychoanalysis, and in culture more widely) as 'the natural origin of rather than the repository for unwanted affects' (p. 12). This point introduces the possibility of a maternal-feminist critique of the positioning of the mother in much psychoanalytic literature. Furthermore, and significantly for my work in this chapter, Brennan's critical reading of psychoanalysis excludes 'the post-Kleinians', R. D. Laing and Daniel Stern (p. 14), whom she aligns more closely with her own theory, which, in her words, 'postulates an origin for affects that is independent of the individual experiencing them' (p. 13). Distancing herself from Gilles Deleuze, whose approach she seems to find too generalising (p. 14), Brennan is interested in understanding how transmission happens, what it does to the distinction between subject and object and also, why it is so commonly disavowed in some cultures. Brennan emphasises the cultural prioritisation of sight, arguing that although there is widespread scepticism of the notion that affect moves between individuals, when theorists do attend to this idea, 'sight is the preferred mechanism in explaining any form of transmission' (p. 10). She comments:

> [W]hat is interesting about the question [of transmission via sight] is the resistance it reveals to the idea that a foreign body – something from without – can enter into one's own. If entrainment is effected by sight, then on the face of it, our boundaries stay intact.
>
> (Brennan, 2004, p. 10)

Thus, the perceived distancing effect of sight, and its role in creating individuals who regard themselves as bounded, cannot be ignored. Sight is bound up with the question of what is inside and what is outside, and with the interplay between surface and depth.

How can we examine subject formation, except with recourse to a language of subjects and objects? Arguably one of the limitations of Brennan's work is an optimism about the potential to reshape language in the image of a mode of understanding that is not organised along the lines of a subject/object boundary. Nevertheless, her concepts allow us to defamiliarise the relationship between the subject and the object. Discourse is, in itself, productive of subjectivity, yet this is a highly abstract idea: how does this happen, in practice? Judith Butler (1997b) poses the question in terms of a space inside the body – asking, with reference to the conceptualisation of the body in Foucault's work: 'Is this a space of pure malleability, one which is, as it were, ready to conform to the demands of socialization?' (p. 89). Whereas discourse seems to act on bodies that cannot resist or move outside of it, except in pre-determined ways, a notion of the 'transmission of affect' (following Brennan, 2004) implies a breakdown of the very certainties around what constitutes a subject, an object, a body and a psyche. Although this notion problematises the very idea of 'the subject', in so doing it focuses in on the *processes* and *mechanics* of subject formation, which, for Butler, remain rather opaque in Foucault's work, as implied by her enquiry about precisely *how* norms are internalised (1997b). She writes: 'Is the norm first "outside," and does it then enter into a pre-given psychic space, understood as an interior theater of some kind?' (p. 19). If my aim in this chapter is to explore the movement, or the embedding, of such norms in the intimate space of the family, and in the psychesoma of the disabled child, the concept of the 'transformation of affect' opens up a potential space in which characteristics that might ordinarily seem to be attached to one individual or another can be understood as mobile. How does this mobility (or, as is more often the case, perceived fixity) come to be expressed in narratives in which disability is an 'issue' or a 'problem'? How is it figured, grammatically and syntactically? Does a discussion of its construction (or disintegration) in narrative bring us any closer to responding to Butler's question in *The Psychic Life of Power* (1997b) about how the outside gets inside?

Once again, I seem to be back with the question of what it means to be inside experience, what it means to be inside discourse, and why, time and again – as Lesnik-Oberstein (2008) notes – these two categories are made distinct and separate. What is it about language that keeps pulling the two apart? This question must wait until later in the book for a response; even then, I approach it with difficulty and do not find ready answers. For the time being, I turn to a case study that foregrounds the disruptiveness of the concept of the transmission of affect.

The optics of difference: Seeing, knowing and relating in *The Fifth Child*

As discussed, Brennan (2004) argues that the human is seen as affectively self-contained in contemporary European culture. In this section, I will read Lessing's (2007 [1988]) novel *The Fifth Child* (*FC*) with the concept of the transmission of affect in mind, suggesting that Lessing's novel presents an approach to the 'different' child that highlights particular features of British culture in the 1980s in which the idea of the self-contained individual comes to the fore. In the novel, characters disavow the movement of affect and the relational construction of difference, yet the narrative nevertheless pursues the idea that belonging is achieved via the connection made by gazing relationships. The look, however, is also expected to provide certain knowledge about the perceived difference of a child, and to establish the biomedical nature of this difference.

The Fifth Child explores the disintegration of a family following the birth of the fifth child, Ben, who is perceived as different from his siblings and as problematic. His arrival threatens to rupture the domestic idyll that his parents, Harriet and David Lovatt, have created. As a foetus, Ben is described as 'the enemy' (*FC*, p. 54), with the narrator clearly ventriloquising Harriet's thoughts at this point (a point to which I shall return). Harriet experiences the foetus as 'trying to tear its way out of her stomach' (p. 49). For the Lovatt family, 'the abnormal' is located in Ben, but there is a struggle to find a satisfactory description or label for this abnormality. Ben is described as being large for his age and his appearance is unlike that of the others in the family. Harriet perceives him as being 'like a troll, or a goblin or something' (p. 61) and describes him as 'Neanderthal baby' (p. 65). Members of the family comment on his appetite as a baby, noticing how painful Harriet finds the process of breastfeeding Ben as he drinks so much. Ben is seen as prone to violence, so that bars have to be installed on the windows of his bedroom. Later, the family decides that Ben must be sent to an institution, although there has been no medical diagnosis of his perceived difference. Throughout the novel, Harriet yearns for such a diagnosis, and recognises her plight in the following instance of free indirect discourse, which occurs in the closing stages of the novel, while she is waiting to consult a specialist:

> What am I hoping for, this time? What she wanted, she decided, was that *at last* someone would use the right words, share the burden. [...] She wanted to be acknowledged, her predicament given its value.
>
> (p. 124, emphasis in original)

Here, naming – in and of itself – is desired as an act that will bring relief. During the consultation, Harriet poses a question about Ben's humanity, but the doctor fails to respond convincingly one way or the other, noting that Harriet thinks Ben is a 'throwback' but refusing to affirm this suggestion (p. 127). Diagnosis thus eludes Harriet constantly: at the end of the novel, the third person narrator, implicitly speaking Harriet's thoughts, declares that '[n]o schoolteacher, or doctor, or specialist had been able to say, "That is what he is"' (p. 158). The closure associated with knowing is continually deferred.

What is the role of sight in these attempts to 'know'? Fascinated by the descriptions of Ben as the enemy *in utero*, I felt that my forward momentum as a reader was driven by the question of whether the opportunity for Harriet to exchange gazes with her son would alter her perception of him as her nemesis. Might there be an acknowledgement of the relational construction of difference? Harriet too fantasises about the moment 'when they actually set eyes on each other, after this long blind struggle' (p. 59); she wonders what she will see, as though seeing would bring knowledge and closure. There is thus a privileging of the gaze as the primary means through which subjectivity is revealed; however, when Harriet finally does 'exchange looks with the creature who, she had been sure, had been trying to hurt her', we are told that 'there was no recognition there' (p. 60). Although the phrase 'there was no recognition there' is implicitly a description of Ben's eyes, the use of the passive voice here allows for ambiguity. Is it actually Harriet who is unable to recognise her son, whose face remains unmoved when she sees him? The ambiguity is heightened by the fact that the pair are described as 'exchanging looks' in this sentence – the possibility of a mutual lack of recognition remains open. In Harriet's first encounter with Ben, his eyes are described as being 'like lumps of soapstone' (p. 60): by drawing a comparison with stone, the text highlights the hardness and solidity of these eyes, suggesting that rather than being a window through which a Winnicottian creative exchange might happen, these eyes let nothing either in or out. Yet the use of the term soapstone – with its reputation as a soft rock – implies a tantalising possibility that the stone might dissolve. Perhaps it will dissolve upon finding 'recognition' in the eyes of the mother? Instead, Harriet's focus moves swiftly onto drawing an unfavourable contrast between Ben's eyes and the eyes and face of Ben's older brother Paul, musing about the latter that she 'loved the look of him, the comical soft little face, with soft blue eyes – like bluebells, she thought' (p. 62). The repetition of the adjective 'soft' to describe Paul's face attempts to disavow any similarity with Ben, and the 'bluebells' connote new life, in contrast with the inanimate soapstone. For Harriet, Paul is a 'real baby' (p. 62), and Ben's siblings are distinguished from him throughout the text by the term 'real children'.

At the level of the characters, the possibility of the relational construction of normalcy (or its obverse) is not entertained. Ben's difference from his siblings is located in his body by his parents and relatives. But what of Ben's experience? Why is Ben's version of events excluded from the narrative? Why does the narrative begin to focus exclusively on Harriet's internal monologue after Ben's conception and birth, when prior to these events there is a greater sense of a shared reality in the novel? What are the politics of these narrative choices? In order to probe these questions further, I turn first to a paper that discusses the novel in terms of Derridean notions of hospitality and Otherness. I then connect this reading of the novel with my own discussion of it as a critique of dominant cultural approaches to the 'different' child. I explore how the notion of the 'transmission of affect' might come to the assistance of the novel's internal critique of its characters' rigid views about difference.

For Richard Brock, the novel offers an example of Derrida's opposition between the 'foreign other' and the 'absolute other' (2009, p. 10). The foreign Other is 'one who is prepared to acquiesce to the values pertaining within the host's realm, and whose otherness is therefore both knowable and capable of regulation' (Brock, 2009, p. 10). The guests who come to stay with the Lovatts for days and sometimes weeks during the holidays fall into this category. For Brock, Ben represents Derrida's 'absolute other', since his Otherness is not knowable (p. 11). Indeed, Harriet becomes obsessed, as the novel progresses, with seeking to know 'what he is', although her desire is not met (*FC*, p. 158). Ben brings into the domestic space precisely those 'elements of "society"' that Harriet and David have sought to exclude (Brock, 2009, p. 12). According to Brock, Harriet and David's

> domestic practices [...] encompass a variety of Thatcherite ideals, including the insistence on the primacy of the family over 'society,' the paranoid defence of space against the ideological 'other,' and the enthusiastic embracing of the 1980s capitalist dream of home ownership.
>
> (p. 10)

Yet this defence is not viable when 'the other' intrudes, as Brock observes, 'from within', as Ben does in the novel (p. 11). Ben becomes the kind of social misfit that Harriet and David would always have viewed as being someone else's child, not their own.

Brock concludes by proposing that the novel problematises Thatcher's (1987, n. p.) statement that 'there is no such thing as society' by demonstrating what happens if we seek to deny or exclude 'society' (2009, p. 12). As Brock notes, '[s]ociety, Lessing's novel tells us, is inherently both inside and outside: to deny its free passage over the domestic threshold, to deny even its very existence – to refuse it, in every sense, *admission* – is to undermine the very fabric which supports the individual, the family, and the home' (pp. 12–13, emphasis in original). The idea that society is being denied 'free passage over the domestic threshold' is reminiscent of Brennan's contention that Western culture sees the individual as an 'energetically self-contained or bound entity, whose affects are his or hers alone' (2004, p. 24). Indeed, Brennan notes (p. 2) that '[n]otions of the transmission of affect are suspect as non-white and colonial cultures are usually suspect'. This idea chimes with the Lovatts' sense, early in the novel, that it is by 'guarding that stubborn individuality of theirs' that they have succeeded in maintaining 'this fortunate place, their family', since beyond this 'place' lie 'the storms of the world' (*FC*, p. 29). The Lovatts' domestic happiness is contrasted with Harriet's sister's conjugal misery; indeed, this unhappy marriage is blamed for the emergence of a child with Down's syndrome. The foreshadowing irony here underscores the brittleness of the protagonists' apparent happiness and its reliance on the expulsion of the image of the disabled Other. The characters' world ultimately unravels as a result of their intransigent identification with a fragile ideal of domestic bliss. This early moment of narratorial insight into the couple's views on their relatives' disabled daughter foreshadows the marital divisions between David and Harriet: he dismisses her theory of how the 'mongol' child came to be born to her sister as 'silly hysterical thinking' (p. 29). Yet it also shows how a character's willingness to think in terms of the power of affect (that is, Harriet's explanation of events) is regarded as illogical and comes to be associated with her femininity. Here, perhaps influenced by the characters' need to exclude it, the transmission of affect has taken on a kind of supernatural form in Harriet's imagination, as it is later to do with greater force, with the arrival of Ben.

The very fabric of the novel – the narrative – enacts the characters' belief that 'there is no such thing as society' and in this way demonstrates that this position is untenable. The effects of this belief are played out through a gradual reduction of the narrator's access to different subjectivities, so that as the novel reaches its conclusion, the narrator has access only to Harriet's thoughts. Initially the narrator appears to have equal access to the subjectivities of both Harriet and David. The couple's shared reality – conservative values and the dream of a large family, with '[s]ix children at least' – permits the narrator insights into both of their internal worlds (*FC*, p. 14). Indeed, for the first third of the novel, the third-person narrator appears relatively impartial and any sense of its constructive role is minimised; it reports on Harriet and David's burgeoning relationship in a tender, if somewhat distant, tone, referring to them as 'these two eccentrics' (p. 10), and giving equal weight to its consideration of their family backgrounds – whilst always signalling that social class, and (non)identification with a notion of Englishness, will be crucial to the dynamics of the story. It is only once Harriet becomes pregnant with Ben that the narrative begins to report more on Harriet's subjectivity than on that of any other character. Thus, in the very early stages of the pregnancy, when Harriet is upset, we learn that '[David] felt [...] that she was breaking the rules of some contract between them' (p. 45), but from this point onwards we rarely have access to David's feelings. Harriet is portrayed as increasingly isolated with her thoughts and feelings, in the sense that, whereas the rest of the family is willing to simply exclude Ben, it is she who undertakes the hard work of maintaining ambivalence about Ben, oscillating between a tendency to locate abnormality firmly in the child – 'of a different substance, so it seemed to Harriet' (p. 62) – and a desire to reclaim him as a 'little child' and even '*our child*' (p. 90, emphasis in original). As the novel progresses and Ben's difference becomes its main theme, the narrow focus of the narrative induces a sense that there really is 'no such thing as society', only Harriet's internal world and her attempts to relate to Ben. With no one else to mediate our understanding of Ben, the reader may grow suspicious of Harriet's reliability, especially in light of her tendency to interpret Ben's difference in supernatural terms. In one sense, then, the text invites readers to view the characters through an individualising lens.

This enclosed, dyadic narrative focus increasingly supplants the spatially expansive narrative view that dominates the first third of the novel, with its preoccupation with the enormous family house and the wilderness of a garden, which appear to substitute for the lack of any sense of genuine social connection – hinted at by the speed with which time passes in the early part of the novel and the accumulation of family gatherings made up of unnamed 'people' who 'came and went' (*FC*, p. 27). As the novel progresses, the reader is offered less and less insight into David's subjectivity, and more and more free indirect discourse ventriloquising the painful duality of Harriet's observations about Ben. For example:

> Altogether, he was easier. Harriet thought: Well, any ordinary child is at its most difficult for about a year after it gets to its feet. No sense of self-preservation, no sense of danger: they hurl themselves off beds and chairs [...] And they are also, she added, at their most charming, delightful, heart-breakingly sweet and funny.
>
> (*FC*, p. 84)

Here her thoughts move between a yearning to be convinced that her sense of Ben's difference is imagined, and her hopelessness as she acknowledges that it is not. These sections of text give voice to a specimen of maternal ambivalence (Parker, 1997) – albeit a strain of this experience that appears particularly unbearable. Indeed, it is Harriet who is in agony over the decision – taken by the extended family – to institutionalise Ben, and who ultimately rescues him from the horrific place to which he has been consigned, telling her reproachful husband, 'I couldn't stand it' (*FC*, p. 105). When her husband deliberately (mis)interprets this phrase as descriptive of her experience of living with Ben at home, Harriet notes that David 'didn't see' the institution, to which he tellingly replies, 'I was careful *not* to see' (p. 105, emphasis in original). The refusal to *know* ambivalence is thus shown to be bound up with a refusal to *see*, or rather with an obscene attention to the avoidance of seeing. As this example reveals, if the narrative structure initially casts doubt on Harriet's sanity, encouraging collusion with an individualising reading of the text by arousing suspicion of Harriet's invocation of the register of science fiction with epithets such as 'Neanderthal baby' (p. 65), it ultimately undoes this very reading by drawing attention to the pain of Harriet's repeated, failed attempts to really connect with and know her son:

> Did he feel her eyes on him, as a human would? He sometimes looked at her while she looked at him – not often, but it did happen that his eyes met hers. She would put into her gaze these speculations, these queries, her need, her *passion* to know more about him – whom, after all, she had given birth to, had carried for eight months, though it had nearly killed her – but he did not feel the questions she was asking. Indifferently, casually, he looked away again, and his eyes went to the faces of his mates, his followers.
>
> (*FC*, pp. 156–157, emphasis in original)

This excerpt suggests an almost parodic reversal of the Winnicottian maternal mirroring function; here it is the mother expecting the child's face to act as a mirror, to reflect back to her something she can recognise of her world, peopled by 'human[s]' (a grouping from which she excludes Ben). The blank, indifferent face in this exchange is not that of the mother, but that of the son, whose face – or at least in his mother's reading of it – offers only a refusal to be penetrated. Although, as this excerpt suggests, Harriet is not wholly redeemed for taking a stance which always demands that her son become 'one of hers', the narrator's narrowed vision towards the end of the novel at least allows for an intensity of focus on the figure of the mother grappling with the difficult question of how to see – and therefore how to know – her son; she is engaged with questions of knowing (and doubting), collectivity and belonging. This stands in contrast both to the attitude of some of the other characters and to the expansive but superficial gaze of the narrator in the early part of the novel, which is unable to maintain intensity on any object for any length of time, operating in a mode that mirrors the preoccupation with exteriority and the appearance of the family tableau.

The question of whether Ben is innately physically, socially and emotionally different, or whether he carries a range of familial projections of Otherness, is never answered satisfactorily in the novel. Arguably it is this ongoing doubt that both tears apart the fabric of the family (unstably built on maintaining an illusion of sameness and of self-contained individuals) and leads to a shift in the narrator's gaze, away from its early panoramic perspective and towards Harriet's agonised internal world, where her own desire for answers is matched by the failure of *her* gaze to provide them. The use of free indirect discourse seems at once to offer access to Harriet's thoughts and yet to withhold something of her subjectivity, as if mirroring Harriet's own struggle to know her son, in which moments of apparent insight are matched by moments of doubt and ongoing, painful opacity.

If, as Mitchell and Snyder (2000, p. 6) have noted, disability 'inaugurates the act of interpretation' in narrative, then this is a novel about what is inaugurated by the ongoing inability to interpret. Interpretation, and the need to be able to know-what-it-is-one-sees, has taken up the space in the narrative where community, and connection, might have otherwise been situated. As we have seen, this can be read as a commentary on the encroachment of individualism in this period, and on how, in such a cultural context, a family's struggle with the perceived difference of a child leads to atomisation rather than collectivity. In my reading of *The Fifth Child*, I have sought to stay with the unresolved doubt inaugurated by Ben's arrival: for reasons that emerge later in the chapter, relating to my own experience of embodying a doubting gaze, I am interested in the question of what it means for epistemologies of disability not to be able to say, with certainty, 'That is what [Ben] is' (*FC*, p. 158). I have struggled with my own anxious need to 'know-what-it-is-I-see', and my own experience of visual undecidability, which I shall be exploring as a function of disabling diagnostic gazes. We should also note, finally, that Ben's view of 'what he is' is unknown: Ben is an aporia at the heart of the novel, a character whose perspective is structurally absent, and who is always constructed through the Other's words. He is the figure of the unknowable child (Lesnik-Oberstein, 2011, 2008; Caselli, 2010; Rose, 1984). There is a resonance here between Lessing's doubting-Harriet and my own personal writing at the start of the chapter, in which the disabled child on the stretcher seems to disappear from the doctors' view; it is also a subject to which I return later in the chapter in the context of my discussion of gazes that enact 'overlooking'/'over-looking'.

The Secret Garden: Producing disabled subjectivity through the look

My focus in this chapter now shifts back in time, from 1988 to 1911: in this next section I consider the significance of the look in Frances Hodgson Burnett's novel *The Secret Garden (SG)*, drawing on Sartre's phenomenology of the gaze, and Kenneth Wright's psychoanalytic discussion of Sartre's work. Although this novel could certainly not be called 'contemporary', I want to suggest that we might read the tropes in *The Secret Garden* as – to use Raymond Williams' (1977, p. 121) terms – an '[e]mergent' version of that which later becomes '[d]ominant'. Elsewhere, I have argued that *The Secret Garden* is one of the texts that inaugurates a new cultural construction of the disabled child (see Cooper, 2015): in the Edwardian period the figure of the frail/weak child begins to be perceived in binary opposition to a notional 'normal child', the latter being an emergent category at the time. Furthermore, the fact that *The Secret Garden* was made into a film for cinema in 1993, with another version anticipated in 2020,[7] suggests that it remains, in some sense, a culturally dominant representation of the disabled child. Indeed, as Lois Keith has written, 'today it is the most enduring and popular of [Hodgson Burnett's] titles, reproduced on television and in film many times over and published in hundreds of different editions' (2001, p. 119). Even if it is regarded and consumed as a 'historical' portrayal of disability, allowing the (adult) reader or viewer perhaps to feel confident in their critical distance from its values, the broad cultural reach of *The Secret Garden* is hard to deny.

In the reading that follows, I invite my reader to knowingly participate in a naïve credulity; I play with the question of what it might mean to re-engage the Child Reader's sense of connection with the characters – Mary Lennox and Colin Craven – as people, as animated subjectivities. Let me be frank. When I first wrote this chapter, I think that at some level I wanted to reject my literary training and to re-engage a 'damaged' part of myself – a part that childhood reading experiences had (in my view) helped me to preserve and protect. I argue that my 'naïve' readings enact an aspect of the *struggle* for a way of thinking about disability experience (or perhaps I should say a way of experiencing disability) that weaves in and out of the subject's experience of herself and her interaction with a cultural object. My reading of the characters arguably reinstates a dualism between experience and its representation (Lesnik-Oberstein, 2011, 2008), yet this is symptomatic of the very struggle that my book takes on: not to resolve, but to play and think with both the figural child and the 'real' child. If the dominant mode of writing was of 'struggling' for something to come to light, the reason for retaining these sections is partly to honour that struggle, but it is also much more than that – it is also about honouring the idea of *playing* as a mode of engagement that can be valued as much as *being trained*. Here, of course, I am also alluding to the role of the physiotherapist in the life of a disabled child. I shall return to these tropes later in the book.

The Secret Garden tells the story of Mary Lennox, the 'sickly, fretful' only child of a father who 'had held a position under the English Government' (as a colonial administrator in India) and a mother who 'had been a great beauty who cared only to go to parties' (*SG*, p. 1). Mary, who is orphaned at the start of the novel by a cholera outbreak, travels to Yorkshire to live with her uncle, a seemingly remote and uncaring aristocrat. Mary befriends Colin, her cousin, who is kept hidden from view in the manor house, and is expected to turn out as a 'hunchback' like his father (p. 128). The novel depicts India (and colonial life) as unhealthy and degenerative whilst romanticising the English countryside, the English fresh air and the rural working classes in England. The working-class characters in the novel are represented as earthy and connected with nature.

The Secret Garden represents disability as undesirable, and as necessarily requiring a cure, which may be troubling for the contemporary reader, as Lois Keith has noted (2001). Yet the fact that such a text has become and remains canonical in British culture is potentially revealing in terms of what it suggests about the ongoing status of disability as abjection, and also about the persistence of a troublingly seductive, nationalistic fantasy of the restorative properties of the English 'earth' and 'air' (*SG*, pp. 45, 121). What is it about this toxic admixture that has such lasting appeal? How does the novel key into something in the white

English psyche, mobilising and reproducing a particular racialised, classed, gendered and abled notion of national identity ready for consumption by another generation of white, middle-class children (mainly little girls)?[8]

I was one of those little girls, enthralled by the magic of the 'garden' and uncritically/unconsciously absorbing ideas about disability, race, gender and class as I read. Although it would be legitimate to ask whether anything other than outright critique of *The Secret Garden* can be justified, and although I agree with Keith (2001) that aspects of this text are repugnant in terms of the representation of disability (and of other identity categories) – not least its insistence on figuring physical impairment as hysterical symptom – my re-reading of this formative text from my childhood is not, first and foremost, a 'paranoid' one, but bears some features of 'reparative' reading (Sedgwick, 2003, p. 123).[8] I do not unambivalently want to redeem or rehabilitate *The Secret Garden* for disability studies, but it seems important to dwell on my ongoing enchantment with it, including my discomfort about that, and to ponder why I am drawn to this novel as an object for study. In finding the courage to proceed in this way, I have received succour and nourishment from Wiegman's (2012) unflinching analysis of the political desires (for social change) that academics invest in their objects. I wonder, then, whether – with a relatively unconscious part of myself – I seek to play the role of the physiotherapist in relation to *The Secret Garden*, in spite of my ambivalence about the concept and practice of rehabilitation.

It would not be surprising if I were to be caught enacting a 'rehabilitative gaze' upon this text, trying to retrieve it for literary studies as an object of intrigue and value, given my own intense experience of having been the subject of a gaze of this kind. I am, in part, drawn to *The Secret Garden* because it depicts an experience of subject formation that is familiar to me from my own past: Colin Craven, one of the novel's protagonists, is significantly disabled by the look of the Other. Although I have had a physical impairment from birth, in my infancy my impairment was barely visible, yet I was the subject of many scrutinising gazes as the early signs of my impairment began to show themselves on my body. As I reveal in the personal writing later in the chapter, these gazes have been very disabling for me – more disabling, I argue, than the impairment itself. *The Secret Garden* is an object lesson in the mechanics of the disabling gaze, and it is in this sense that I contend that it has something important to offer critical disability studies.

The son of Mary's aristocratic uncle, Colin is well-known as the 'disabled' boy in the story, secreted away in the manor house, who gradually regains his strength and learns to walk via his curative encounters with the secret garden. There are frequent references in the text to Colin's persecutory experience of Others' gazes. During his first encounter with Mary, he remarks: '[s]ometimes I have been taken to places at the seaside, but I won't stay because people stare at me' (*SG*, p. 129). He explains to Mary that the reason she was unaware of his existence is that, 'I won't let people see me and talk me over' (p. 128). In both utterances, the agency of the subjective 'I' at the start of the sentence has become diminished into a self-objectifying 'me' by the end of the sentence, gesturing to the difficulty of controlling the transformative capacity of the Other's gaze. These utterances are reminiscent of Sartre's phenomenology of 'The Look' (2003), in which subjectivity is diminished, by the look, into objectivity. Sartre uses the example of the individual standing in a corridor looking through the keyhole of a closed door at other people inside a room. Initially, the watching individual perceives himself to be alone, but then he hears a sound in the corridor and realises that he himself may be the object of another's gaze. This perceived change of circumstances in the external world precipitates a shift in terms of how the individual experiences himself at an internal level (Friesen et al., 2009). The first internal state can be characterised in terms of the disappearance of the lived body, and the second internal state in terms of 'acute awareness' of the body (Friesen et al., 2009, p. 86). The subject now sees himself from the outside; he becomes an object to himself. As Sartre puts it: 'I have my foundation outside myself' (2003, p. 284). Our ability to perceive ourselves objectively is predicated on the existence of the Other, for Sartre, since the Other is 'the being *through whom* I gain my objectness' (p. 294, emphasis in original). He goes on: '[i]f I am to be able to conceive of even one of my properties in the objective mode, then the Other is already given' (p. 294).

Colin is depicted as a subject who virtually always has his foundations outside of himself. When Mary questions Colin about his conviction that he will not live into adulthood, he is described as answering her 'indifferently', as though he were speaking objectively about a matter of no emotional import, rather than about his own future (*SG*, p. 132). He states:

> I don't suppose I shall [live]. [...] Ever since I remember anything I have heard people say I shan't. At first they thought I was too little to understand and now they think I don't hear. But I do. My doctor is my father's cousin. He is quite poor and if I die he will have all Misselthwaite when my father is dead. I should think he wouldn't want me to live.
>
> (*SG*, pp. 132–133)

Colin's own death is treated as an event which has been conceived of by the Other, as though the Other's conviction about it and assumed desire for it is what makes it certain, rather than any lived experience of frailty and suffering. The verb 'suppose' suggests that this is an issue that can be discussed with detached rationalism.

Although at first glance, the role of sight in existential questions appears to relate primarily to Colin, in fact, one of the key themes in the novel is the relationship between what is seen and what is cared for. The book opens with the line: 'When Mary Lennox was sent to Misselthwaite Manor to live with her uncle everybody said she was the most disagreeable-looking child ever seen' (*SG*, p. 1). Here, Mary's connection to 'disagreeableness' is simultaneously affirmed and rendered unstable by its status as a property of the look and the relational realm. A few lines later we learn that Mary's mother:

> [...] had not wanted a little girl at all, and when Mary was born she
> handed her over to the care of an Ayah, who was made to understand that
> [...] she must keep the child out of sight as much as possible.
>
> (*SG*, p. 1)

When everyone around Mary dies of cholera, she is entirely forgotten, mainly
because those outside of the household have never seen her and barely know
of her existence, as utterances such as this one illustrate: 'I heard there was
a child, though no one ever saw her' (p. 6). There is a parallel, then, with
Colin, who is also a subject of shame and secrecy and is kept out of public
sight. A minor character comments revealingly of Mary's mother: 'I believe
she scarcely ever looked at [Mary]' (p. 11), alluding to a relationship between
the deprivation of the look and Mary's lack of 'pretty ways' (p. 11). Again,
there is a symmetry here between the cousins: as we later learn, Colin's father
is unable to look upon his son because of the feelings stirred up in this
encounter, which I shall discuss shortly. Yet, in the housekeeper's account,
Colin's father himself directly rejects human contact: 'He cares about nobody.
He won't see people' (p. 16). The syntax seems to render the relationship
between choosing to 'see' people and 'caring' deliberately ambiguous, but in
the context of the novel's continuous drawing together of seeing/caring, it is
possible to read this speech act as implying that the sight of the Other
somehow triggers a painful form of caring for that Other, which is experienced
as an unmanageable burden. According to this logic, opportunities to see must
be minimised, in order to minimise the unbearable feelings that seeing might
unleash. Thus, the secret garden is locked up after the death of Mrs Craven,
out of sight.

As the examples above suggest, *The Secret Garden* shows a fascination with
the diachronic experience of the look, and its role in subject formation.[9] Colin's
account of his relationship with his father suggests an almost too-knowing
perceptivity about the origin of his own difficulties with the look. He explains
to Mary, of his father: '[h]e doesn't want to see me' and 'My mother died
when I was born and it makes him wretched to look at me' (p. 129). Martha
provides a comparable version of events:

> Mr. Craven went off his head like when he was born. [...] It was because
> Mrs. Craven died like I told you. He wouldn't set eyes on th' baby. He just
> raved and said it'd be another hunchback like him and it'd better die.
>
> (*SG*, p. 142)

Here, the act of looking is again represented as evoking something unmanageable
for the one who looks; it animates an intersubjective and intergenerational
connection (between father, dead mother and son), which, in this account, the
looker would rather leave to 'die'.

To probe these ideas further, I turn to the psychoanalyst Wright's (1991) account
of the gaze, which looks to the work of Winnicott to develop a version of Sartre's

synchronic model of the look that engages with questions of time and memory. Wright characterises Sartre's model as exhibiting a 'paranoid relation to the Other' (p. 33), asking why objectivity – 'the Other's view' – has to 'annihilate the subject' (p. 33). The account which follows contrasts the Sartrean experience with a less persecutory phenomenology:

> Why and when does the look of the Other bring about a collapse of the subjective self into the objective image that the look provides? I suggest that this occurs when there has been insufficient good early experience with the mother of a confirmatory kind; when the self is not founded on the rock of "good enough mothering" it cannot stand firm. [...] [I]f we think for a moment, with Winnicott, of the mother watching over the child's play, preserving for it a space free from intrusions, we again have a counterpoint to the kind of mother represented by Sartre's Other, who *looks at* but does not *look after.*
>
> (Wright, 1991, pp. 34–35, emphasis in original)

By introducing Winnicott into the equation, Wright contends that the diachronic dimension is important in terms of how the Other is experienced. The effect of the Other's gaze upon the body in the present moment depends on how the Other's gaze has been experienced in the past. Has it been a harsh, critical gaze that assesses and evaluates (a gaze that 'looks at' in Wright's terms) or a gaze that nurtures and allows the self to 'be' (a gaze that 'looks after')? This account – whose pathologisation of the Sartrean look, and focus on maternal responsibility I would certainly want to call into question[10] – nonetheless seems to intersect fruitfully with *The Secret Garden*'s own aetiology of 'disability', which emphasises the grief-stricken or neglectful look's formative properties. For Colin, the gaze has always been associated with judgements about his embodiment. Colin's father only comes to see him while he is sleeping because he cannot bear to look at his son. Colin is also subjected to another oppressive gaze, that of the 'grand doctor' who once 'came from London to see [him]' and said that the brace on his back was 'stupid' (*SG*, p. 129). The novel suggests that Colin's subjectivity has been formed by a pathologising gaze, for which seeing has become synonymous with scrutinising and assessing.

How exactly does Sartre's individual come to identify so closely with the Other's view of him? Wright argues that the infant who experiences the parental gaze as cold, or critical, or unresponsive, may associate this gaze with the sense of wrongdoing. The infant may unconsciously conclude that 'a behavior that so seriously jeopardizes the relationship with the mother must come to be avoided at all costs' and identifies a 'survival value' in 'seeing what the mother sees' (Wright, 1991, p. 45). The child in this situation 'joins forces with this mother who looks, disowns the self which the mother could not contain and which caused the rupture, and thenceforward regards this threatening self as an Other' (p. 46). The detachment displayed by Colin with regard to the value of his own life can thus be theorised in terms of a displacement of the self. To wish for life in a context in which animation provokes the parental desire for the child's non-existence is dangerous. Thus the rather surprising indifference that Colin exhibits in relation to Mary's questions – '[d]o you think you won't live?', '[d]o you want to live?' (*SG*, p. 132, p. 133) – can be read as Colin's adoption of his father's view of him as his own. The psychoanalyst Sándor Ferenczi describes this arrangement of functioning as arising from a '[c]onfusion of [t]ongues between [a]dults and the [c]hild' (1999, p. 293). For Ferenczi – who is theorising the psychic organisation of survivors of childhood sexual abuse – the child *'reacts to sudden unpleasure not by defence, but by anxiety-ridden identification and by introjection of the menacing person or aggressor'* (p. 299, emphasis in original). Colin, having introjected a view of himself as Other, effectively speaks from his father's subject position. In Chapters 3 and 4, I return to Ferenczi's concept of identification with the aggressor to explore the question of resistance in the context of disabled subjectivity. For now, I now turn to my own experience of the scrutinising gaze, and, using personal writing to explore how this feels, I seek to develop a theory of what I shall call 'overlooking/over-looking'.

Looking after, looking at and overlooking/over-looking

As I move out of the house, into the world, I look, I look, I look. I drink in what is mundane with my eyes but still it does not go inside. The sight does not penetrate. I cannot take it in. I have to look again. I cannot seem to satisfy my doubt. And the more I look, the more I seem to doubt. The less I am able to see, to really see. Looking and doubting. Looking and doubting.

Where does it come from, this daily straining of the eyes and the daily struggle to take in what I see AS IT REALLY IS? The door is locked, the gas is off. The window is shut. I look and look and yet I cannot perceive what I need to know. I doubt. I have looked too much. I will have to start all over again. I have over-looked.

And yet, I am compelled to keep on looking. The looking holds me together.

Once upon a time, as a little child, they looked at me. They scrutinised my feet as I walked. They examined me. Decided my fate. I was looked at too much. I was over-looked.

Once upon a time, as a little child, they looked right past me. They did not see me. An absent gaze, a preoccupied gaze. They saw the foot. They saw the hand. I was overlooked.

Over-looking gaze, you punish me but I desire you. With you I may suffer the pain of being seen too much, but at least I am not overlooked.

I keep on looking. Everything must be over-looked. Nothing must be overlooked.

***

In this personal writing I coin the term 'being over-looked' to describe my own relationship with the Other's gaze, which pulls me in two directions at once. I hyphenate the term deliberately in order to highlight its double meaning. On the one hand, 'to be overlooked' implies that the object of the gaze is ignored and that there is a failure to see or notice it. On the other hand, 'to be over-looked' suggests that there is an excess of looking, that the object of the gaze is scrutinised. The visibly disabled infant's body is the object of 'too much looking'. The intensity of the gaze upon the impairment is matched by a lack of attention to other aspects of the infant's body and personality. In the absence of a gaze which 'looks after', there is no 'space free from intrusions' (Wright, 1991, p. 35) in which the infant can develop as a subject which has, but is not defined by, an impairment. The infant's subjectivity might thus be characterised in terms of an experience of being over-looked: this subject is, at once, both highly visible as a 'disabled infant' and yet invisible as an 'infant'. The body is an object of intense interest whilst the person housed in the body is unsure whether she too is of interest, as we saw in the writing at the start of this chapter. Perhaps many of us, with or without a visible impairment, have experienced some variation on this theme, yet I suggest that the scrutiny of the body for the signs of disability is a potent case study of this duality. Perhaps this dual experience of the gaze is especially powerful and confusing if the infant in question is pre-verbal, or if the gaze, unaware of its power, does not explain itself to the child.

In my personal writing, an experience of being made by the gaze – by being simultaneously over-seen and unseen – translates into difficulties in seeing the world 'as it really is'. The writing suggests a compulsion to keep looking that can never be satiated with certainty about what is being seen: I am never sure that the door is locked or the gas is off, no matter how hard I look. I continuously undermine my own capacity to connect seeing and knowing together. The act of looking is both comforting – my intense looking '*holds me together*' – and yet persecutory, because it has to be repeated over and over, so that nothing is '*overlooked*'. I suggest in the writing that this ambivalent relationship with looking repeats an early experience of being looked at. In my early years, my body was looked at a great deal, by those who cared for me, and by the doctors who sought first to diagnose and then to treat my hemiplegia. At first my hemiplegia barely showed upon my body, so there was a very real sense in which my body had to be scrutinised in order to find something 'wrong'. Indeed, when I was six months old, the doctors failed to produce a diagnosis and said there was nothing wrong with me. A second examination at eleven months finally identified hemiplegia. I cannot consciously remember the experience of being closely scrutinised by doctors in the early months of my life. Yet daily, in front of the closed gas taps, or when I am out and about, I am to be found in the act of intense scrutiny. The intensity and frequency of this compulsion has lessened in recent years – since I have been able to produce this narrative about it – yet it still threatens me at times of stress or difficulty. My looking fails, time and again, to find anything 'wrong' with the objects I am checking, yet I doubt and doubt, in a repetition of the trauma of (non) diagnosis. This is the first meaning of over-looking: the child is looked at too much, through eyes that search and doubt. It is reminiscent of Harriet Lovatt's agonised gaze in *The Fifth Child*: the ongoing lack of a diagnosis for Ben is lived as an ongoing imperative to look, yet the gaze is continuously thwarted in its attempts to find signs that will reach the threshold of being signs.

The term 'overlooking' is more commonly used when something gets 'missed', or passes unseen beneath the reach of the gaze. This is the second aspect of the idea that I want to emphasise. The medical gaze was preoccupied not with me, but with my impairment. My limbs were seen but I, Harriet, the person, was overlooked. This is the experience I describe in the passage of personal writing at the start of the chapter: the doctors who put on my 'plaster boots' (a rehabilitative technique) see my legs and my body but do not see me. I think we also see it at play in the representation of Colin and Mary in *The Secret Garden*, both of whom are shown to have had experiences of being unseen: in the case of Colin, his father's grief seems to block out the ability to see the son, except in relation to the deceased wife, while in the case of Mary, we learn early in the novel that she was an unwanted child, and that her mother sought to keep her out of view.

In another interpretation of this over-determined symptom of overlooking, we might read the early failure to diagnose the impairment, in spite of its presence on my body, as a form of anxiety-provoking overlooking. The signs of my impairment had been glimpsed now and again on my six-month-old body by my medically trained grandmother, who urged my parents to visit the hospital. Yet the doctors were reassuring: 'Go home: nothing is wrong with her, she's fine'. The response every parent wants to hear! Yet how does the revoking of 'fine', with the discovery, five months later, of 'not-fine' play itself out in the triad of doctors–parents–baby? What does the pre-verbal child learn about the desire to overlook, and yet the dangers of so-doing, through the affects transmitted via the gaze during these early months? And how might we connect up 'overlooking/ over-looking' with the reading practices which I engage in and distance myself from in this book?

I suggest that the trauma of the revoking of 'being fine' plays itself out later in my compulsive enactment of an oscillation between over-looking and fearing that I have overlooked something. Over-looking (looking too hard), and the fear of overlooking something important, operate simultaneously in such a way as to disrupt the so-called 'intentional arc' (Merleau-Ponty, 2002, p. 157; see also Fuchs, 2005, p. 101): they interrupt those activities that are, for most people, governed by automatic functioning – functioning that does not need to make itself known to the conscious mind. The act of looking is experienced as persecutory: it interrupts my train of thought, yet the feeling that I have overlooked (missed) something has the power to send me into intense anxiety and even panic. To frame this dynamic in Foucault's (1991) terms, I govern myself – I discipline myself – by subjecting myself to an overlooking/over-looking gaze. In spite of its intense attention to detail, this gaze continually *fails* to find the 'not-fine' thing it is seeking, and then, in the process, finds *itself* lacking – 'not-fine' – in its failure. I seem never to have looked hard enough for 'the thing'. Yet in terms of the process of repetition (Freud, 1958a), the failure to find the thing is the inevitable end point (and starting point) of the cycle: the 'thing' cannot be found in the present, for its proper location is in the past.

It is interesting to note that whilst the overlooking/over-looking gaze of diagnosing doctors and concerned familial figures had a very specific focus – my body and, even more specifically, the limbs on my left side – in the translation of the experience into a contemporary 'compulsion to repeat', the focus has broadened. As Michel Foucault (2003, p. 16) notes in the *Abnormal* lecture series with reference to the rise of a hybrid discourse he calls 'medico-legal opinion' (an adulteration of both psychiatry and justice), the use of '[e]xpert psychiatric opinion' in court pathologises a whole 'way of being' – a type of 'conduct' – as opposed to a particular 'action'. I want to suggest that the feeling of being 'wrong' and 'bad' at a global level of the self might be connected, at a psychological level, with pre-verbal experience – which is not to say that it is not also a function of discourse. Where language is not available for the purposes of drawing a distinction between 'myself' and 'my body', because such Cartesian dualism is itself a linguistic product, the over-looking gaze is felt to pathologise the subject as a whole.

The global nature of the 'not-fine' feeling might also be connected to the fact that the scrutinising look that fails to find anything wrong – to which I believe I was subject during the 'unsuccessful' diagnostic appointment at the age of six months – effectively has no identifiable object. If I use my eyes to check whether something is wrong, or out of place, or broken, but I find nothing, what am I looking at? I am looking at the whole scene. I have to broaden my gaze, and look at the entire panorama, and unless my gaze is immediately drawn to the 'wrong' object, I must keep looking until the entirety of the scene has been thoroughly checked.

***

You might think that the gaze without an object is a reassured gaze, but in fact, in this case, it is an impotent gaze. The medical gaze wants to be able to find and to diagnose, to reassure itself that when there is an inkling of something (and in my case there must have been an inkling), it can be given a name, brought out into the open, made to relinquish its hiding place. The gaze without an object feels mad. Not raving mad, but roving mad. It roves and roves and does not find, and everyone is staring at me with my checking eyes, asking: what's she looking at?

***

In this section I have proposed the term 'over-looking' to describe the doubleness of my personal experience of the look, which was an experience of being simultaneously over-exposed and yet not seen at all. I have sought to draw a link between the past and present, interpreting my own symptom as a product of the over-looking gaze. I am suggesting, through my personal writing, that my own obsessive looking 'got inside' me via the look. I reproduce, in my own gaze, the affect that was once transmitted from the Other into me.

The ambivalence of being seen

How might my experience of the double-ness of the gaze connect up with other theoretical work in critical disability studies, and have relevance to the field? The notion of the gaze as a site of ambivalence is by no means new. As Rosemarie Garland-Thomson (2005) has argued, there is a long history of staring at disabled bodies in Euro-American culture. Much of the writing on the gaze in a disability studies context focuses on the disabling effect of being subject to the glare of the look, or to the gaze that looks and then looks away out of awkwardness (Garland-Thomson, 2009; Reeve, 2008). The disability memoirs I have read tend to examine encounters with the look of the Other either as a stare or as the 'aversion of eyes' (Murphy, 2001, p. 119; see also Lapper, 2006). Even averted eyes can be read as a manifestation of an excessive or over-looking gaze, because, understood as a sign of curiosity thwarted by etiquette, they reveal an unsated desire to stare. To the extent that the averted gaze reveals an inability to really acknowledge what is there to be seen – as Murphy (2001) suggests when he recognises in this look a fear of being contaminated by disability – the gaze that looks away is excessive in that, in the process of looking away, it registers its object as a source of fascination and horror. The act of looking away is an act of refusing to engage, of refusing to know. Analysing the apparent need to both 'look at and look away' from disability, Goodley and Lawthom (2013, p. 169) read dominant cultural responses to the disabled body through the prism of the Freudian uncanny. The uncanny is disturbing – these authors note – because it not only represents that which is sinister but also that which is familiar; we are simultaneously fascinated by it and frightened, both at home and unsettled (Goodley and Lawthom, 2013). Goodley and Lawthom (2013) propose that the dominant cultural response to the sight of a disabled body is disavowal. This concept in itself might be thought of as bringing together a refusal to see with a refusal to know, a point that can be illustrated with reference to Freud's (1955a) discussion of the uncanny, which drew on Hoffmann's tale of 'The Sandman'.[11] There, the protagonist fears that he will have his eyes stolen, a terror that Freud aligns with castration anxiety: the eyes are linked with potency and the capacity to penetrate, and thus with knowing (1955a).

In these examples, 'looking away' is not the same as what I theorise as the 'overlooking' gaze, because looking away is still motivated by a fantasy of disability as contaminant, and the averted gaze still *wants to know something about disability*. What, on the other hand, does the overlooking gaze want to know? Can it even be thought of as a type of gaze, if it completely overlooks? Is it correct to theorise it as a presence, or is it instead an absence? It would be interesting for new work in critical disability studies to think carefully about the points of connection and disconnect between 'disavowal' on the one hand, which implies an active aversion of the gaze from *disability*, and overlooking, which refers to the way in which a *person* can be entirely *lost to the gaze*. The impairment comes to stands in for the person, a synecdoche for the person. In what ways do the politics of identity then cover over the pain of being overlooked? The feeling of being unable to define oneself except in relation to one's impairment has been a theme in disability studies as in other branches of identity politics (Reeve, 2008; Hughes, 1999; see also Fanon, 1986). However, here I want to read it as the more bearable counterpart of being subject to the over-looking/overlooking gaze. Garland-Thomson writes that 'the history of disabled people in the Western world is in part the history of being on display, of being visually conspicuous while being politically and socially erased' (2005, n. p.; see also Mitchell and Snyder, 2000). The construction of this sentence gives primacy to an active form of disavowal here, since 'erasure' implies agency on the part of those see-ers who do not want to see. Yet I think it is also the case that overlooking is at work in the exclusion of disabled people. Overlooking suggests a more profound failure of empathy, taking us to a place that is more passive and disengaged than disavowal. Whereas over-looking – the scrutinising gaze – requires animation, its obverse – overlooking – suggests that the object of the gaze might completely disappear, and is incapable of exciting scrutiny.[12] Although I am wary of aligning the 'overlooked' part of the self with authenticity, and with a notional 'real' self that could be uncovered, as though it were underneath disability (see, Lesnik-Oberstein, 2011, 2008), I nonetheless suggest that a diachronic theory of the look in disability studies should attend to the ways in which impairment animates attention. What happens, relationally, to parts of the self that do not animate attention? This leads me into a discussion of how the duality of over-looking/overlooking has relevance to the experience of passing as non-disabled.

Passing is '"a cultural performance whereby one member of a defined social group masquerades as another" in order to enjoy the privileges afforded to the dominant group' (Leary, 1999, p. 85, quoting Crutchfield, 1997).[13] To pass is to develop an ambivalent relationship with the gaze of the Other (on passing, see also Cooper, 2016). On the one hand, passing, where it is possible, shields the disabled person from the gaze and can thus protect this individual from persecutory scrutiny, as Susan Lingsom (2008) notes. However, possessing the potential to pass also leaves the individual with a choice about this, and '[d]ilemmas of concealment and disclosure are impairment effects' (Lingsom, 2008, p. 2). One key advantage of being able to pass is the ability to escape from oppression of the Other's gaze, however briefly (Lingsom, 2008). Yet the decision to pass can be accompanied by – as Ellen Samuels puts it – 'a profound sense of misrecognition and internal dissonance' (2003, p. 239). In this sense, while passing offers an escape *from* one aspect of the experience of 'overlooking' (being looked at too much), it is in fact an escape *into* the other side of 'overlooking' – to pass successfully means that part of oneself is overlooked. Thus, successful passing, whilst promising 'relief' for the disabled subject – in that it is a means of escape from the persecutory, scrutinising gaze of early childhood – actually *reproduces* the dynamic of the overlooking (misrecognising) gaze of early childhood in that the passer invites the Other to overlook a part of herself. In early childhood, the overlooked part may have been the self that identified only as a self, not a disabled self. In later experiences of passing, the part that the subject invites the Other to overlook is the impairment itself, which has become part of the subject's identity. If we are to understand some instances of passing as non-disabled as re-enactments of an early experience of being overlooked, this reframes the decision to pass as a psycho-social phenomenon rather than simply being a social one. For the individual who has had an impairment from birth, passing may be less a conscious choice and more an unconscious pattern of relating, which forms one aspect of internalised oppression. Individuals who are subject to this dual form of 'overlooking' in early childhood may be more susceptible to the desire to pass and to minimise the appearance of disability.

The psychic and social realms are both involved in any decision to pass, and, as Tanya Titchkosky (2003) has pointed out, it seems that society is often invested in enabling passing to happen. Titchkosky (2003) explores how friends and colleagues help her partner Rod Michalko, who is blind, to pass as sighted, although they know he is blind. Rod's friends work hard to ensure that blindness does not intrude in social interaction at an experiential level. For example, when, at the pub, Rod 'bumped someone's glass, which had been put into what would normally be regarded as his space at the table', Rod is teased for having 'butter fingers' but no reference is made to his blindness as the cause of this incident (Titchkosky, 2003, pp. 73–74). Rod's friends are happy to *talk about* blindness but not to *look at* it. Titchkosky articulates this paradox in the following terms: 'Give us blindness as an object for conversation, but do not give us blindness as a subjective state of affairs which reorganizes and influences our normal means of engagement' (p. 75). The friends engage Rod in conversation *about* the experience of blindness but they do not want to engage with blindness *as* an experience that intrudes upon social interaction. In the terms I have been proposing, we might imagine that the friends are seeking to eschew the reproduction of the scrutinising gaze that 'looks at' rather than 'looking after'. They are motivated by a wish to protect Rod. Yet, in the process of avoiding 'looking at' (or over-looking) Rod, they also, in a sense, 'overlook' what it means to be Rod. Whereas in *The Secret Garden* we witnessed an avoidance of the look as a means of avoiding the feelings of caring that it might provoke, here, in an intriguing reversal, the look is avoided as a means of *enacting care*. Yet it is an enactment of care that, in seeking to prevent or minimise the transmission of embarrassment and shame among friends, allows the societal existence of the 'shame of being disabled' to persist intact. Elsewhere, in relation to my own experience of passing as non-disabled, I have observed that the decision to 'come out as disabled' during a conversation could 'disrupt the conventions of small talk', especially if I think my interlocutor has not yet noticed my disability (Cooper, 2016, p. 128). These examples highlight how much can be compressed into the social dynamics of looking, and how much *speculation* can be generated by the liberal-tolerant overlooking/over-looking gaze, for all parties. I deliberately invoke the notion of liberal tolerance as a facet of a structure that promotes the care-full avoidance of looking, which should be distinguished from the avoidance of care-inducing looking seen in *The Secret Garden*. Although it is beyond the scope of this chapter to consider the relationship between liberal tolerance and overlooking at greater length, this may be a generative line of thought for future work. For me, the speculation associated with the look plays itself out in my head in new social situations with the question: *have I passed, or has my impairment been noticed? Should I say something? Is it okay to have this minor impairment in public, without saying? How will it be interpreted – as an impairment or as something that's just a little bit odd about me?* We have returned, once again, to Winnicott's (1971a) hall of mirrors, and the hermeneutics of reading the Other's face (and body).

In passing, then, the experience of being overlooked can be one that is solicited, as a way of avoiding the harsh glare of the over-looking gaze and the moments of awkwardness and embarrassment that interrupt the flow of social interactions. Yet this experience of not having been fully seen can leave the individual who passes successfully with a sense of inauthenticity – a theme that is explored further in Chapter 4, through the metaphor of skin. Passing could thus be said to involve the physical and psychological labour of concealment: Tobin Siebers uses the term 'overcompensation' to describe this type of work (2004, p. 10). Elsewhere, I have drawn on Bion's (1963) model of the container–contained relationship between caregiver and child to theorise this labour (Cooper, 2016; see also Cooper, 2010). As we saw earlier in this chapter, according to this model, the caregiver acts as a container for the infant's feelings. I have argued that this model may have significance for exploring how disabled people manage encounters with other people (Cooper, 2016, 2010).

The main characteristic of a 'container' is that it successfully holds something inside, preventing it from spilling out. Yet as Brennan (2004) argues, the self-contained individual is a fantasy – and one we might associate with liberal individualism, with its attachment to the concept of self-sufficiency (Cooper, 2010). Indeed, we might understand psychoanalytic narratives, which ardently pursue the goal of total self-containment, as governed by such ideology (see Brennan, 2004). For me, gaining the capacity to contain and regulate feeling in an imperfect and flawed way has meant, paradoxically, letting that container spill from time to time, and *not* shielding everything from view. Perhaps my very interest in the boundary between the 'inner' and the 'outer' – the Winnicottian psychesoma and the Foucauldian discursive formation – has arisen out of the conflicted experience of passing, in which the need to maintain the separateness of the two worlds is of paramount importance.

Conclusion: Looking and reading

The focus of this chapter has been on the constructive role of the look of the Other in the making of disabled subjectivity. I argued, drawing on Brennan's work, that in contemporary British culture there is resistance to the notion of the subject as unbounded. In Lessing's (2007 [1988]) *The Fifth Child*, the potential fluidity and relationality of subjectivity is perceived as a threat to the integrity of the family and even to bourgeois individualism, such that the indeterminacy of Ben's difference is intolerable. In a narrative mode that mimics the operation of ideology, the reader is initially drawn into colluding with the 'common sense' of individualism and then gradually exhorted to be sceptical. The narrator's shift away from depicting the couple's shared reality and towards Harriet's internal world is subtle at first, but later becomes increasingly pronounced, mirroring the cultural shift towards atomisation inaugurated by Thatcherism, but also reminding us of the gendering of the labour of early gazing relationships and of the attempts to 'know' a child. Meanwhile, in Hodgson Burnett's (1987 [1911]) *The Secret Garden*, the supreme power of the look undermines the physical reality of disability, but it also reveals the affective dynamics through which disability is internalised as oppression. Looking is associated with the arousal of (unwanted) affects – that is, with caring and with grieving.

I have suggested, via my personal writing that explored firstly the difficulty of distinguishing 'I' and 'you' and later the doubt associated with my experience of looking, that the experience of being disabled is formed relationally, in and through an exchange of gazes (including looking away) that may communicate confusion. In this chapter I have connected an ontology of (self-)doubt with a complex early experience of the gaze: *Am I disabled? Am I fine? Is there something wrong with me? Or is it okay after all?* As we saw, I suggested a connection between these questions and a questioning gaze, a gaze that was seeking to settle something indeterminate. I generated the term overlooking/over-looking, with its dual invocation of too much attention and too little, to describe the ambivalent experience of the gaze that seeks to find disability, and to dismiss it.

How might this searching gaze, this roving eye, relate to or be implicated in the choices I have made about my archive and the reading practices I have deployed in this chapter? I have been struck, whilst revising this material for publication, by the fact that my original version was very caught up in the narrativisation of my lived experience and in the need for both my narrative and the literary texts discussed here to be explainable within the terms of object relations psychoanalysis – as well as for them to augment, develop and repurpose these psychoanalytic theories for disability studies. This still strikes me as being the main contribution of this chapter to critical disability studies, but it also seems necessary to dwell briefly on some epistemological questions. What kind of knowledge is generated by the gaze that looks and looks without really seeing or allowing itself to know? How does an argument proceed when it is plagued by a dialectical sense of doubt, oscillating between 'fine' and 'not fine'? Can anything useful emerge here about the question of how we (should) read? Here I am drawn, again, to Sedgwick's brilliant essay on paranoid and reparative reading (2003), as well as to Wiegman's (2014) response, which takes issue with the move towards so-called surface reading that has become fashionable in some parts of the academy in recent years. Like Wiegman, I am suspicious of both the desirability and the possibility of abandoning hermeneutic reading practices in the humanities. But I also think that the terminology that Sedgwick (2003) adopts from Melanie Klein's psychoanalytic repertoire is suggestive; it has been incredibly generative in the development of a meta-theoretical discourse on reading in the humanities. Yet why stop at 'paranoid' and 'reparative'? I want to bring my anxious looking into the field of this discourse in order to suggest a place for reading practices that draw on, rather than disavow, the symptom. The book as a whole is seeking to grapple with this issue, or the question of what it means to do this – that is, the question of how, exactly, the psyche of the researcher is implicated in what emerges on the page. With regard to *The Secret Garden* (Hodgson Burnett, 1987 [1911]), I think its place in this chapter is very much connected with its presence in my childhood, and the fact that the novel is both *about* the intergenerational transmission of affect and *was an object of* intergenerational transmission (of social reproduction): it arrived in my childhood via parental figures or their proxies, even as my experience of the text was one of delighting in the escape to the secret space of the garden – another 'space free from intrusions' (Wright, 1991, p. 35), perhaps? I do not think these facts can be separated from my desire to undertake a naïve, childlike reading of the text, or from the reparative function of doing that reading – which gave me comfort (much as reading gave me comfort as a child)[14] and temporary *relief* from the need to be anxiously looking. With *The Fifth Child* (Lessing, 2007 [1988]), I think I was drawn to the device I discuss – the narrator's narrowing of vision and inability to see beyond what the central character (another Harriet!) sees – because of the intersection of this narrative structure with that of my symptom, which seems to isolate me with something I need to verify by looking. The opaqueness of Ben confirms the impotence of the gaze and the failure of the look, but the promise of transparency and of the finding of a connection between Ben and Harriet persists throughout the novel. In a sense this mimics my symptom, which continues to lurk for me by offering the promise of resolution with the next act of checking.

In using object relations psychoanalysis to theorise both how we internalise oppression and how we then reproduce it in our relationships with ourselves and with others, I am challenging an oversimplified dichotomisation of oppressor/ oppressed – an approach that is all too easy to adopt within disability studies. I am suggesting that the internalisation of a particular quality of gaze affects not only how one looks at oneself but also how one goes on to look at the Other, and at the world. As I have demonstrated via a discussion of my symptom, overlooking/over-looking is much more than a form of oppression that can be located in my childhood and then neutralised. Rather, it is what animates my own engagement with the world: for better or worse, it is there in my acts of looking and in the way I analyse. It is a mode of knowing myself, and a mode of knowing the world. As I move into Chapter 2, which seeks to 'know' the disabled child by using a very different set of conceptual tools, I take with me this ambivalent look, this doubting mode of knowing that is inclined to look and look again, and yet also, somehow, to overlook. As I move into a mode of analysis that is perhaps more 'proper' to cultural studies – historicising and contextualising a discursive formation – I nevertheless continue to unsettle my understanding as my argument proceeds.

Notes

1 For a discussion of ocularcentrism and the critiques to which it has been subjected, see Jay (1993).
2 During my close reading of this text, I use the acronym *FC* to refer to *The Fifth Child*.
3 During my close reading of this text, I use the acronym *SG* to refer to *The Secret Garden*.
4 Watermeyer (2013) is referring to Niederland, W. (1965) 'Narcissistic ego impairments in patients with early physical malformations', *Psychoanalytic Study of the Child*, vol. 20, pp. 518–534.
5 Lacan's ideas have informed the development of psychoanalytic literary criticism (see, for example, Felman, 1982). The prominence of Lacan in literary theory is evidenced by the frequency of references to his work, and the use of excerpts of his writings, in key introductory texts on literary theory: see, for example, Culler (2011) and Rivkin and Ryan (2004).
6 For Winnicott, the primary caregiver is always a mother. This is also a feature of object relations psychoanalysis more generally, and, as Rozsika Parker (1997) acknowledges, it has led many feminists to accuse psychoanalysis of 'mother-blaming' (p. 18).
7 See *The Secret Garden* (1993) and *The Secret Garden* (2020).
8 Sedgwick draws on Melanie Klein's terminology of psychic positions (paranoid-schizoid and depressive) to theorise critical reading practices as 'paranoid' or 'reparative'. She refers to a range of Kleinian writings rather than to one specific essay.
9 The relationship between the narrative and development comes under scrutiny in the next chapter.
10 In this era of a neoliberal economy of time – discussed further in Chapter 3 – the 'enough' in 'good enough mothering' might seem to take on a punitive quality. When do we ever feel that we have given 'enough' in this neoliberal economic order, for which we (apparently willingly) exploit ourselves (Han, 2017)? On the concept of the 'good-enough mother' in Winnicott's work, see Winnicott (1971b, p. 10).
11 Freud's editor references a translation of Hoffmann's tale in a 1952 edition, *Eight Tales of Hoffman* (trans. J. Cohen), London, Pan Books.
12 I would like to thank Emily Cooper for a conversation that helped me develop this idea.
13 Leary supplies the following reference for her quotation: Crutchfield, S. (1997) 'Color-blindness as "passing" fancy: Race and blindness in American cinema', unpublished manuscript, p. 1.
14 Elizabeth Freeman (2019) figured certain forms of reading as practices of *caretaking*, and explored their connections with care work, in a fascinating lecture at Birkbeck, University of London. Her focus on 'strategies of non-hermeneutic reading' (2019, quotation from my lecture notes) speaks interestingly to the ideas I am discussing here.

2 Making her better?

Denaturalising the notion of the 'developing child'

When I was growing up, there was a fantasy that I would become the normal child: the one who develops, goes forward, gets better. That my 'handicap' really would disappear if I practised the exercises enough. But this was a fantasy. Like when you dream that someone who's died is alive again, and you wake up and they're still dead. Perhaps the exercises did help in a certain sense, but they couldn't take away the brain injury. What had been invisible (or barely perceptible) when I was a tiny baby was becoming more visible. It was becoming clearer every day that my left hand was the hand of a spastic. That I limped when I walked. How does it feel to see your child becoming more visibly disabled day by day? To see the impairment emerging in the very texture of the body? To see the hand becoming stiffer, the Achilles tendon tighter? How much must you long to help the child to use those limbs?

To grow up is to be able to do more things. To grow up is to have a greater range of movement. To grow up is to become more autonomous.

***

If Chapter 1 posited a diachronic, temporal model of formative disabling gazes, this chapter focuses on an implicit strand of that thinking: the concept of development. It explores how a hegemonic notion of the 'developing child' governs our perception of the meaning of childhood. In what ways are the fantasies and desires for the child that develops part of a broader cultural narrative about what it means to grow up – about what it means to be a child and what it means to be an adult? The urge to rehabilitate the child, to do everything in one's power to try to 'make the impairment better', seems to be almost overwhelming in a situation such as the one described above. With my own impairment, hemiplegia, the signs of impairment are not visible on the body at birth, but become inscribed there over time through a lack of normative use of the limbs. Thus the impairment is only written onto the body gradually. This can be perceived as a deterioration, yet it can also be read as the visible manifestation of what has been known to the body since the birth trauma. The signs of cerebral palsy, as they emerge, are the signs of a body unfolding according to a logic that was inscribed there at birth.[1] What does it feel like to bear a child who, instead of developing as other children do, shows signs of 'deteriorating', 'getting worse', 'becoming more vulnerable'? What does it feel like to be that child who 'gets worse', to be the child whose impairment becomes more visible over time? These questions, among others, are the ones that interest me in this chapter. I will be exploring developmental logic and its impact on narratives of disability.

Physiotherapy is widely accepted as a treatment for hemiplegia, my impairment. In recent years, a new therapy – constraint induced movement therapy (CIMT) – has been being trialled, which involves intervening in the child's natural use of his or her body by restricting the use of the 'able' limb with a glove, sock or plaster cast, in order to encourage use of the disabled limb (see, for example, Boyd et al., 2017). A literature search I undertook revealed that the spotlight of medical attention focuses on the efficacy of the treatment in developing the child's use of the disabled limb; there appears to be less interest in the possible psychological effects of being prevented from using the body according to its own hemiplegic logic.[2] Whilst this is hardly surprising, perhaps the reason it is not seen as surprising has something to do with the cultural investment in a notion of the 'developing child'.

I begin this chapter by reflecting on my own ambivalence towards the concept of development. Whilst seeing this as arising from my own internally conflicted relationship with the notion, I also situate it within the broader methodological tensions that I grapple with in the book. This section is followed by a theoretical discussion considering the embedment of a notion of development in scientific and social scientific discourses about the child. Subsequently, these discourses of development are examined in action as I interrogate two cultural objects: in the first, development is desired by parental figures whilst in the second, a more unexpected relationship with the concept emerges. The first object is a text, the play *A Day in the Death of Joe Egg* (*DDJE*) by Peter Nichols (1967)[3] – a text which has enjoyed several contemporary revivals and which, I argue, is still representative of mainstream attitudes to profound disability in certain important respects. The second case study is a sample of texts exploring the controversial decisions made about an American child known as Ashley X, who was subject to a number of medical and surgical interventions that have meant her body will never assume its adult form. In both cases my analyses focus on the construction of development as implicitly 'good'. The discussion of the case of Ashley X is followed by a section that explores the relationship between narrative and development in the context of two recent children's novels that feature terminally ill children. I conclude the chapter by reflecting on resistance: how do we resist developmentalist narratives (if indeed it is desirable to do so)? I broach this question through personal writing that explores my own relationship with developmental time.

My discussion of the cultural objects in this chapter is partially organised via an engagement with Mikhail Bakhtin's (1981, p. 84) concept of the 'chronotope',[4] which highlights 'the intrinsic connectedness of temporal and spatial relationships that are artistically expressed in literature' and – I would argue – in other kinds of cultural representations produced in narrative form. Bakhtin argues that in literature, time and space are inseparable, and that time, infused with space 'thickens, takes on flesh, becomes artistically visible' (p. 84). The chronotope is, for Bakhtin, responsible for the 'representability of events' (p. 250); through it, the passage of time is transformed into narrative. In his long essay, which dates from 1937 to 1938,[5] Bakhtin identifies the chronotopes that operate in a range of different historical narrative forms. There is the 'adventure-time' of the ancient Greek romance, which does not engage with the maturation of characters and 'leaves no traces anywhere' (p. 91); it is 'controlled by one force – *chance*' (p. 94, emphasis in original). And there is the '*adventure novel of everyday life*' which combines 'adventure-time with everyday time' (p. 111, emphasis in original). Bakhtin also explores the 'chronotope of the encounter', and the related 'chronotope of the road' in relation to ancient stories (p. 243) – chance meetings are a key aspect of such narratives. In my chapter, a set of chronotopes referring to developmental and rehabilitative space-time emerge in response to my analyses: the 'developmentalist chronotope' to signal the imperative for space and time to line-up in normative ways; the 'chronotope of stasis' to highlight the problematic immobility of space and/or time and the 'rehabilitative chronotope' to denote activity taken to normalise embodied relationships with space-time. The conceptualisation of time as something made concrete by space – the idea that, representationally speaking, the two concepts are interdependent – is highly suggestive when it comes to speaking about development, which is otherwise an abstract notion. The temporal development of the child is often understood in terms of that child's growing ability to move through space. Thus spatial movement can come to stand for or signify a temporal or developmental shift, and vice versa.

Development: A concept I both desire and do not desire

What would it mean to think about a life as non-developmental? Is it even desirable to reject developmentalism, or is something important lost in the process? This book is about the cultural, discursive, ideological and psychosocial 'making' of disabled subjectivity. What is 'making' if not a developmental process, a laying down of foundations? Can we conceive of the 'making of the child' (indeed, the making of the adult), in terms that do not imply development over time?

Is it problematic to seek to deconstruct a monolithic notion of child development in a chapter that immediately follows one that has necessitated a conceptualisation of subjectivity as incremental and as formed through early relational experiences? Chapter 1 relied heavily on a developmental model of the self, drawn from object relations psychoanalysis. Psychoanalyst Stephen Mitchell is suspicious of placing too much importance on '[d]evelopmental [r]easoning' in psychoanalytic work (1988, p. 143). He argues that

> [w]hat makes genetic reconstruction so compelling (and so dangerous) is the ease with which one can attribute causation to structural parallels, can claim that the earlier phenomenon somehow underlies or causes the later one.
>
> (Mitchell, 1988, p. 146)

Although in Chapter 1 I was careful to draw attention to the speculative nature of the claims I made about earlier phenomena underlying later ones, my argument was nevertheless animated by the connections I drew out between the doubting scrutiny in the quality of a gaze that rests on the body of the disabled child, and the subsequent quality of the look of the adult who is compelled to check and check again. Even if the object relations psychoanalytic theory I relied on in the last chapter can be characterised as 'determinist' (Frosh and Baraitser, 2008, p. 354);[6] elsewhere in psychoanalysis the relationship between the past and the present is much less clear cut. The Lacanian idea that meaning is made with hindsight (a development of Freud's notion of *nachträglichkeit*) is a helpful mediatory concept (see Burman, 2008a; Frosh and Baraitser, 2008).[7] As Frosh and Baraitser put it, for Lacanians, 'narrative sense is always made *post hoc*' (2008, p. 355). When a trauma takes place, it does not make sense: in fact, Burman (2008a, p. 231) contends that in Lacan's work, it is only through the experience of a second trauma, which 'reanimates' the earlier one, that the first trauma can be understood as such. This notion troubles the linearity of the developmental narratives of object relations psychoanalysis, without suggesting that its narratives can, or should, be entirely dismantled.

Perhaps, in the same way that I have never been able to inhabit either a disabled or a non-disabled identity comfortably, I seek to maintain a kind of restless indecision about where to situate myself in relation to a notion of development. Moreover, although it was a (medical) developmental narrative that caused injury to me initially (at the diagnostic scene and then in the process of 'rehabilitation'), it is a (psychoanalytic) developmental narrative that has enabled me to understand why I long both to 'develop' and to 'be cured', and why I also reject these very processes as oppressively normalising.

To resolve the methodological disjuncture through which developmentalism appears as therapeutic on the one hand and as imprisoning on the other, is perhaps psychically impossible for me and also undesirable. Developmentalism is, genuinely, both of these things to me. My work retains this ambivalence about development: I want to suggest that it is most generative as a 'disagreeable' concept (Ahmed, 2010, p. 213), which resists categorisation as either wholly oppressive or wholly liberating. In this chapter, however, development will be seen mainly through a critical lens, as I attempt to show that it is the bedrock of our thought about what the child is and does. I want to dis-embed it, in order to understand its hegemonic power.

Discourses of development

This section focuses on developmental psychology, a discipline permeated by the idea that development is 'obvious to any with eyes to see' (N. Rose, 1999, p. 144). Development just 'is'. As Burman observes, '[d]evelopmental psychology seems to maintain its conceptual and political integrity in the face of the broader discrediting of developmental ideas throughout social theory and practice' (2008a, p. 43). Other disciplines, including other branches of psychology, have been influenced by postmodernism and deconstruction, but developmental psychology has 'remained relatively untouched by paradigm twists and turns' (Burman, 2008a, p. 42). What makes the notion of development so resistant to ideological critique? For Burman, '[t]here is something about the rhetorical power of "the child", of children, that renders claims and promises of developmental psychology seemingly incontestable' (p. 43). She notes that, whereas 'assumptions about gender, "race", class and sexuality are now being increasingly understood as social constructions that are historically and culturally contingent, age, and in particular "the child", seems particularly intransigent to this contextual analysis' (p. 43).[8] As noted in the Introduction, post-structuralist feminists have demonstrated the essentialism inherent in the category 'woman', yet developmental psychologists can still pronounce confidently about child development. In contemporary culture, as Burman, drawing on the work of Carolyn Steedman, has noted, the figure of the child has become synonymous with the idea of 'the "true" self, or even the [...] "lost" self' (2008a, p. 11; see also Steedman, 1995). Burman points out that '[n]ew age therapies mobilise notions of the "inner child"' (2008a, p. 11); contemporary cultural narratives tell us that if we can understand the child within, we can understand human subjectivity. Yet, as Steedman has written, 'children have not always [...] been used as emblems of the adult human condition' (1995, p. ix). Seeking to 'understand modern uses of childhood' (p. ix), Steedman (1995) suggests that a modern notion of history emerged alongside a deployment of the category of childhood 'to express the depths of historicity within individuals' (p. 12).

If Steedman (1995) historicises the contemporary resonances of the concept of childhood, Nikolas Rose (1999) performs a similar archaeological excavation of the notion of the developing child. Drawing attention to the emergence, in the nineteenth and twentieth centuries, of particular 'procedures of inscription' that made it possible to monitor the development of the child (1999, p. 153), he observes that:

> While children and their development, like persons and their peculiarities, have been the object of attention from philosophers, theologians, philan- thropists, reformers, and savants for centuries, the devices and techniques for visualization and inscription are not merely technical aids to intellec- tual processes. [...] Technological changes are simultaneously revolutions in consciousness. [...] In short, technical developments make new areas of life practicable.
>
> (N. Rose, 1999, p. 153)

By emphasising the role of new technologies in altering how the child is perceived, Rose denaturalises the notion of the 'developing child', grounding this concept firmly in a particular historical context. Certain ways of seeing are made available to us through particular technologies; this affects what we are able to know about the child and shapes our perceptions of what is normal and natural (N. Rose, 1999; see also Latour and Woolgar, 1986).

Furthermore, particular scientific metaphors may persist within a culture because they fit with prevailing ideologies (Bateman, 2012). In the provocatively titled *The Mythology of Evolution*, Chris Bateman (2012) points out that the notion that stronger creatures outlive weaker ones is not necessarily borne out by empirical evidence. For Bateman, the term 'survival of the fittest' is a metaphor that 'radically overemphasiz[es] the role and importance of competition' in evolution, with 'serious knock on effects on the way that natural selection is discussed' (p. 67); its persistence, he implies, may be at least partly ascribed to Victorian and contemporary political and economic ideologies. In this context, the tenacity of a developmental metaphor may explain more about a cultural investment in the notion of progress than it does about the scientific process to which it relates. Burman (2008a), too, makes an important conceptual link between the discourses of developmental psychology and those of economic development. Troubling the naturalness of 'development', she writes:

> [T]he faith in progress – that individuals and societies develop towards some 'better', more adaptive, more beneficial form of organisation – is one vital conceptual connection that ties developmental psychology in with the colonial and imperialist themes of (equally current) models of economic development.
>
> (Burman, 2008a, p. 42)

Thus, two disciplines that have hitherto been thought to be distinct and separate fields of enquiry can actually be seen to rely upon the same notion of progress, which is defined according to a model associated with the Global North (Burman, 2008a). Burman observes that 'current developmental research paradigms document what they find in relation to descriptive structures that are already shot through with assumptions about what development looks like, and who is more or less developed' (p. 31). This certainty about 'what development looks like' governs the discourse of development across disciplines, and, as will be seen later in the chapter, it structures perceptions about the development of the disabled child too.

Developmental psychology is invoked as a means of authorising discourses of child protection and children's rights: Burman notes that she herself has 'struggled to avoid being positioned as "knowing" what children "need"' (2008a, p. 47). Yet such discourses – exemplified by policy documents such as the *UN Convention on the rights of the child* (United Nations, 1990) – not only essentialise children as a unified and uniform group, but also impose a notion of child development associated with one part of the world on other parts of the world (Burman, 2008a). To critique liberal rights discourse is perhaps to occupy a position in which one is already distant from the kind of crisis of need that necessitates rights. However, it is important to explore what is either assumed or excluded when a rights discourse is mobilised as a norm or as a gold standard – whose voices are heard, and whose are overwritten? In relation to the child, some of these norms – for example, the idea that the child's place is in the home or at school – are deeply ingrained. Yet, as

Karen Wells (2009) suggests, it should not be assumed that it is necessarily better for children not to work. She writes:

> Campaigns on child labour take it as axiomatic that children should not be working. [...] Leaving aside what the ILO [International Labour Organization] has identified as the worst forms of child labour (bonded labour, illicit activities, armed conflict, prostitution, pornography and trafficking), the reason for targeting other forms of labour for abolition (rather than, say, regulating them) is that they affect children's long-term development – specifically work is assumed to compromise children's future health and employment and the formation of human capital. There is little concrete evidence on either of these outcomes beyond causal inferences that are made about the employment and health of adults.
>
> (Wells, 2009, p. 109)

To assume that home and school are the only spaces in which a child can develop is to assume a view of development that is particular to the Global North in the contemporary historical moment (Wells, 2009; Burman, 2008a, 2008b; Cunningham, 2005; Prout, 2005). To invoke the idea of 'a proper childhood' (Cunningham, 1991, p. 1) is to 'privilege the model of childhood associated with the Western world' (Burman, 2008a, p. 47).

The 'developed child' is thus inextricably linked with the 'developed world', but perhaps only because, to use Burman's terms, the 'developed world' defines what a 'developed child' looks like, as well as defining a 'proper' childhood. The liberal 'progressive' notion that the child should be at school rather than being at work might not stand up to scrutiny if we consider how it fits with the capitalist and patriarchal ideological investment in surveilling and safeguarding the child in order to protect the 'human capital' of the future. Compulsory schooling can be seen as a 'pedagogic machine that operates not only to impart knowledge but to instruct in conduct and to supervise, evaluate, and rectify childhood pathologies' (N. Rose, 1999, p. 124). Moreover, although we tend to think of the family as a '"private" domain' – as Rose observes, drawing on feminist thought – '[t]he language of privacy [has] disguised and legitimated the authority of men in the household over both women and children' (N. Rose, 1999, p. 126). Meanwhile, Viviana Zelizer (1994) observes that the child's removal from the sphere of work makes the child 'priceless':[9] whereas previously the child might have been regarded as a source of economic value, this is no longer a socially acceptable position in most cultures. Yet this shift has not entailed a concomitant de-commodification of the child; indeed, as Zelizer points out, it has instead led to 'the increasing monetization and commercialization of children's lives' (p. 15).

Developmentalist thinking might purport to describe, rather than construct, reality, but by recognising that '[d]evelopmentalism [...] is one of the hallmarks of nineteenth-century European thinking' (Burman, 2008a, p. 42),[10] it can be seen that this mode of thought contains within it the impulse to colonise and to dominate other ways of thinking about human life. While the techniques for measuring economic development construct a hierarchy of nations, the technologies of developmental psychology permit a hierarchical organisation of bodies. The disabled child, whose body registers at the low end of this hierarchy, is thus also marked by the imperialist tendencies of developmentalist thinking. Yet, to reframe this point drawing on Puar's (2017a, 2015) work, bodies that are understood as 'disabled' rather than 'crippled' are ones that have already been retrieved for subjectivisation via the human rights discourses that circulate within Anglo-American disability studies. '[P]art of what gels the disabled body that is hailed by rights discourses', writes Puar, 'is the availability of the process of rehabilitation' (2015, p. 11). Thus, the bodies of children that are seen as worthy of rehabilitation already exist within a paradigm in which disability is the exception, the effects of which must be mitigated in order to retrieve an 'empowered' disabled subject (Puar, 2017a, 2015).

Relatedly, it can be argued that it is in fact *payment* for children's labour that renders it offensive to liberal values, because the *transaction* exposes the commodification of something (someone – the child) who should not have a price-tag attached, according to the logic under discussion. I shall consider the notion of the child-as-commodity at greater length in Chapter 3. As long as the child's labour is not paid – as, for example, rehabilitative labour on the self is not paid – the child is retrievable as a 'developing child' of the 'developed world'. The same dynamics of value are operative, interestingly, when the labour of caring and cleaning is paid for and performed by someone from outside the family (often by underpaid migrant workers), rather than being done unpaid, and kept within a family. Another, related example, is sex work. It is the price-tag placed upon the thing or person that 'should' be priceless, in order to maintain a particular ideological illusion, that has the potential to disrupt a developmental order here. In her celebrated 1975 essay, 'Wages against Housework', Silvia Federici (2012) argues for wages for housework as the first step in a struggle to destroy capital. This is a struggle that begins by recognising how much capitalism owes to unwaged domestic labour – labour that has for so long been framed as a natural attribute of femininity, and as the priceless labour of love (2012). In another essay from the same period, Federici and Cox (2012, p. 39) write:

> we should not ask capitalism to change the nature of our work, but struggle to refuse reproducing ourselves and others as workers, as labour power, as commodities; and a condition for achieving this goal is that this work be recognised as work through a wage.

These authors also draw out connections between a particular view of development and the problem of characterising feminist struggle only in terms of the right to undertake waged work outside the home:

> In this sense, there is an immediate connection between the strategy the Left has for women and the strategy it has for the 'Third World.' In the same

way as they want to bring women to the factories, they want to bring factories to the 'Third World.' In both cases they presume that the 'underdeveloped' – those of us who are unwaged and work at a lower technological level – are backward with respect to the 'real working class' and can catch up only by obtaining a more advanced type of capitalist exploitation, a bigger share of factory work.

(Federici and Cox, 2012, p. 29)

This state of affairs is, as Federici and Cox (p. 29) observe, not a 'struggle against capital' but rather a 'struggle for capital'. Whilst this particular example may seem dated, it is nevertheless notable that what goes unquestioned in the vision of progress articulated by the Left in this discussion is the sense that 'development' is a stable concept, and that we can all agree on what it means. Yet as these feminist thinkers demonstrate, in fact it means something very particular about the way inequality is maintained under global capitalism, and is by no means neutral.

Not all disabled children in the Global North are seen as retrievable for rehabilitation, and my interest here is in exploring what happens discursively in these 'problem' cases, which might seem at first glance to defy colonial-developmental logic. Yet, even in these cases, the *notions* of rehabilitation and development are available: these children are understood to be exceptions (see Puar, 2017a, 2015, 2009). Following Puar (2017a, 2015), it should be noted that what causes offence is the *treatment* of the child as beyond the reach of liberal rights discourses, but that in order for such offence to appear at all, certain bodies must remain invisible; these are 'those bodies that are sustained in a perpetual state of debilitation precisely through foreclosing the social, cultural and political translation to disability' (Puar, 2017a, p. xiv). Although I cannot deny the fact that this chapter – and indeed the book as a whole – focuses on cultural contexts and objects in which disabled bodies tend to be regarded as retrievable for rights and empowerment (and, as previously discussed, this can be seen as a weakness of the work), I hope to suggest that such a focus can still contribute to a project of revealing the hierarchical structures that animate the politics of disability, debility and capacity. An investigation of the invisibility of the conditions of possibility for 'child development' can sharpen our understanding of what gets to count as 'disability', and how.

Desiring development: *A Day in the Death of Joe Egg*

A Day in the Death of Joe Egg (*DDJE*) is a black comedy by English playwright Peter Nichols, which depicts an evening in the lives of Sheila and Bri, a white,[11] middle-class, English couple in their mid-thirties who have a child with a severe physical impairment, and, it is implied, a severe cognitive impairment too. Written in 1967, the play has enjoyed several recent and contemporary revivals (*A Day in the Death of Joe Egg*, 2019, 2013, 2011, 2001). Watching a production of the play in 2013 at the Rose Theatre in Kingston, UK, I was struck by a sense of how the play spoke to certain current debates in disability studies, in spite of the fact that it is not a contemporary cultural object. The production was directed by Stephen Unwin, who observes in the programme (2013a) that the play's exploration of the experience of caring work had been of particular interest to him as the father of a disabled child. In showing Sheila and Bri's expectations for parenthood, which gesture frequently to a notion of the developing child, the play highlights the extent to which discourses about development and normalcy shape notions of childhood. Certainly, assumptions in the UK about disability and institutionalisation have changed since the play was written. However, it seems that expectations relating to development have only intensified, due, perhaps, to a variety of factors, including on the one hand the rise of pre-natal testing technologies to predict the likelihood of disability (a shift that impacts on the birth rate of children with disabilities),[12] and on the other hand the apparent normalisation of so-called '"intensive parenting"' in the Global North (Faircloth, 2014, p. 25). The latter describes a social status quo in which responsibility for child-rearing has been individualised, the 'social importance of the parent role' has been 'inflated' (Faircloth, 2014, pp. 26, 27), and a new norm for parenting (and particularly mothering) has emerged: that it should consume vast amounts of parental time, energy and money.[13]

After a subsection exploring how the spectator locates herself in relation to a play that can be read as using humour to offend and provoke, I analyse the naming of the disabled child, before proceeding with a series of subsections that examine how the play is in dialogue with discourses of (non)development. In particular, I consider how the play deploys a lexicon of space, time, mobility and immobility to figure non-development.

Locating ourselves in relation to the play: Disability, comedy and offence

The child's subjectivity is an empty space in *A Day in the Death of Joe Egg*, filled in by Sheila and Bri who impose a range of identities on their daughter. Bri notes that 'we've given her dozens [of personalities] down the years' (*DDJE*, p. 43). Paul Darke – a disability theorist – has observed in relation to the figure of the disabled child (called Joe Egg)[14] in the play:

> Joe Egg – the character – is quite literally speechless. She *has* to be, because to have given Joe Egg a voice would have put into doubt the whole point of the drama; it would have meant that she herself would have had a voice to be listened to.
>
> (Darke, 1999, p. 70, emphasis in original)

In Darke's terms, the play explores 'what *we* should do about *them*' (p. 70, emphasis in original). Broadly speaking, disability is understood – by the parental and societal 'we' of the play – as a tragedy: the title of the play frames Joe Egg's experience of the world as a 'death' rather than as a 'life'. It is true that disabled subjectivity has no voice in this play.[15] Yet the play could also be read as exploring 'what *we* should do about *them*' in order to *problematise* the fact that this was at the time – and remains to some extent – the dominant discourse about those with severe physical and cognitive impairments. The play asks – without necessarily answering – ethical questions about relating to a non-linguistic Other, demonstrating how this Other becomes a receptacle for parental and cultural projections.

A Day in the Death of Joe Egg is difficult to celebrate from a disability studies' perspective because of the way it discourages identification with the disabled character. It raises questions about the alterity of the Other. For me, the gap that the play leaves where Joe's subjectivity might have been is where I feel that important work around identification and difference can be done, but this work must be undertaken with sensitivity. The difficulties I have in approaching the play arise out of a sense that I do not know where to place myself in relation to those portrayed in it (indeed, as the reader will be discovering, the question of *placing myself* in relation a cultural object under discussion is a running theme in this book; I seem to be attracted to objects that bring difficulties of positioning to the fore). As I analyse the representation of Joe Egg, I find myself facing the following question: how can I practise a kind of Levinasian respect for the Other's unknowability,[16] and not a defensive 'she-is-not-like-me' disavowal of the possibility for identification?

Arguably, then, the play does not set out to explore disability itself, but the question of what it means to be the parent of a disabled child in a world in which disability is stigmatised. To say this is not to try to deny that there are aspects of the play that are problematic (and perhaps even offensive) for disability studies, but it is, I think, to ask that the play is read and produced not simply as a regressive representation of disability from a time when people were 'unenlightened', as if to contrast that with 'contemporary liberal values'. To do the latter is to run the risk of positing the play's comedy as an offensive historical artefact from which the spectator can maintain a critical distance, exiting the theatre with a self-congratulatory sense of 'how far we have come since the 1960s', but without in any way having had to engage with his or her own discomfort about what it means to raise a child such as Joe Egg. I contend that the play's challenging sense of humour is designed to implicate the spectator in the protagonists' ambivalence about parenting a child with a profound impairment. When the play's comedy is taken seriously as the vehicle through which an uncomfortable identification is created, the protagonists are no longer people who can be pitied from a distance, but people in whom we recognise our own human complexity. This is a delicate task and is by no means straightforward to achieve, as there is no denying that, on the page, many of the play's lines read as profoundly distasteful, or even as outright offensive.

By way of example, we might consider Bri's problematic tragi-comic rebuke of his daughter in response to her fits in Act One. He chides, '[h]ow are you to raise yourself above the general level if you keep having fits?' and goes on to demand what the 'council-house types' would say about Joe if they knew about her fits, suggesting that they would agree that 'she's no better than the likes of us' (*DDJE*, p. 19). The joke here is on the status-conscious middle classes (among whom Bri and Sheila would surely count themselves): the humour arises out of the brutal and shameless foregrounding of the (normally unspoken) narcissistic desire of middle-class parents for their child to excel, to surpass others – to develop. The concomitant anxiety that one's child might *not* exceed 'the general level' is also thematised: Bri's remark has the potential to discomfort an educated middle-class audience by drawing attention to a norm of social reproduction that many would prefer to try to ignore. Yet the function of the remark is to highlight the privilege that inheres in the state of being able to ignore or not notice something (Ahmed, 2012). Bri *cannot* ignore: his experience of parenting is one of continuously being brought up against his own longing for something other than what is. His comment contains an unfulfilled wish for a daughter who *does* develop and thus it gives voice to loss and yearning, even as it appears superficially heartless in its attribution of conscious control to an involuntary activity: the neurological condition of fitting. The line can be played in such a way as to make Bri seem a cruel and contemptible relic of the 1960s, or, if the actor introduces a certain wistful sorrow into the delivery of the line, it can make us feel that this character is articulating something of the complex entanglement of love, loss, grief and rage that is involved in parenting a child whose development does not follow a normative pattern.

Given the difficulties that the script presents to any director, it can be argued that a production of the play will succeed or fail on the basis of its sensitivity to comic timing. Comic timing is about using the time-space of the stage for maximum impact, so that, for example, the underlying vulnerability and despair of a character such as Bri is highlighted via the joke's delivery, where the same joke handled in a different way might instead draw attention to the character's cruelty and heartlessness. In this way, comic timing is the means through which the characters' complexity can be observed and is the vehicle for creating uncomfortable identifications in the audience. Developmental time and developmental space are important themes in the play, and come to stand in for each other, as my analysis will demonstrate. In a sense, a chronotope of stasis is developed on the stage via a black comedic chronotope, in which comic timing is used to highlight the couple's experience of the passage of time as having brought disappointment and alienation from each other. Through the black comedic chronotope, the stage becomes a space in which the parental imagination visits and revisits a normative developmental time-space that might-have-been, only to re-experience this time-space as being beyond their grasp, as being continuously knocked down like their daughter's unrepeated intentional knocking down of the tower of bricks, which Sheila recounts to the audience as a moment that had promised development during Joe's childhood. The 'jokes' that Bri and Sheila tell each other about the identities they imagine for their daughter discomfort the audience because of the liberties they seem to take with 'the possible', given Joe Egg's apparent impairments, yet they recall the existence of a time-space in which, we assume, the various imagined futures were all possible. As such, these jokes are a tender and painful tribute to parenthood as a state of keeping the future open. Of course, the construction of parenthood in this way depends on the existence of a norm of the capacitated, developing child in the cultural context in question.

Naming, identification and the developing child

The disabled child's name in *A Day in the Death of Joe Egg* has particular implications in terms of the representation of development in the play. Although the character's real name is Josephine, she is almost always referred to as Joe, for reasons explained as follows:

BRI: Joe Egg. My grandma used to say, 'Sitting about like Joe Egg,' when she meant she had nothing to do.

(*DDJE*, p. 51)

All stage directions referring to Josephine use the masculine form of her name, Joe. Why does the play engender confusion about gender? Is it implying that the character's gender is unimportant, gesturing towards her presumed lack of a sexual future? With reference to the case of Ashley X, discussed later in this chapter, Alison Kafer (2013, p. 57) observes that the doctors who carried out the surgery on Ashley's body refer to 'children' rather than girls when discussing the decision to perform a hysterectomy. Kafer argues that such a linguistic choice reflects a cultural tendency to see the disabled child as without gender. Arguably, then, the hailing of Josephine as Joe can be read as a disavowal of her existence as a gendered, sexual being. The use of the name Joe Egg betrays, on the one hand, a desire to bring playfulness into the life of the child, while on the other hand it closes down any possibility of subjectivity or agency because the child becomes the parents' plaything, their toy. In giving their daughter a name that connotes a toy, these parents reinforce their sense that Joe exists in a permanent, unmoving childhood time.

Doing development, being static

The desire for evidence of development in Joe Egg is on display in the scene in which Bri and Sheila re-enact the diagnosis of Joe's impairment. Sheila's questions to the consultant – '[w]hat can she *do*?' and '[w]ill she ever [do anything]?' – frame the normal human child as one who 'does', one who acts (*DDJE*, p. 36, emphasis in original). The doctor (enacted by Bri), whose strong German accent is written into the script, uses the incorrect verb tense – 'was' rather than 'is' – when he states, '[d]o you know vot I mean ven I say your daughter vos a wegetable?' (p. 36). The decision to portray the doctor as a German man suggests a deployment of xenophobia for comedy's sake that will almost certainly make a contemporary liberal audience uncomfortable. The mistake the doctor makes with tenses implies an uncaring detachment, although his self-correction frames him as incompetent instead:

BRI [AS THE DOCTOR]: Ach himmel! Still is, still *is*, always vill be! I have trouble vis Englisch werbs.

(DDJE, p. 36)

There is a poignant moment just prior to the doctor's self-correction when Sheila repeats what he has said, with hope seeming to rest on the past tense indicated by 'vos' [was]. The stage direction indicates that Sheila '*smiles*' at this point: her smile, perhaps, indicates her momentary hope that Joe's impairment might be a 'was' rather than an 'is' (p. 36). The emphatic present and future tenses of the doctor's answer seem to dash Sheila's hopes. Evoking an unchanged and unchanging state, his emphatic, repeated '*is*' conjures up the present as continuous and immovable. Qualified by the adverb 'still', the present is made to seem particularly monotonous and wearisome. Development is thus characterised in the play through the use of the verb 'to do' whereas stasis, or a lack of forward movement is associated with the verb 'to be'.

When Sheila asks, finally, '[i]sn't there *any*thing at all we can do?' (*DDJE*, p. 37, emphasis in original), the doctor's reply is framed not in terms of developmental outcomes but in terms of what Unwin (2013b, n. p.), himself the father of a disabled child, has described as the 'grindingly hard work' of 'dealing with [the] physical needs' of a disabled child. The doctor speaks of care: of feeding the child, washing nappies and keeping her warm. The fact that Sheila's question is framed in the negative, with the emphasis on the '*any*' betraying an escalating sense of despair, indicates that this is not the kind of 'doing' that she has in mind. Joe's circumstances are constructed as tragic because her existence cannot be conceived in terms of development.

Immobility and non-development

The characters' loaded references to Joe Egg's immobility contain their own projections. A fear of unplanned time(-space), and of the existential doubt it engenders in the self, is elucidated by the character Grace, Bri's mother, who observes that 'after you've been round with a duster, there's nothing much to fill in the afternoons and no one wants to *sit about* like a mutt', later adding that 'if you didn't have some diversion, you'd *sit around* like a blooming nun' (*DDJE*, pp. 65–66, my italics). Since Joe spends much of the play either seated in her wheelchair or lying on cushions, Grace's remarks can be interpreted as a commentary on her granddaughter's embodiment, and indeed Grace invokes 'Joe Egg' in her monologue on loneliness, presumably referring to both the proverbial character of her own mother's idiom and to her granddaughter (p. 66). The disabled subject is aligned with the non-human (the 'mutt') and with the contemplative mode (the 'nun'). When Grace poses the rhetorical question, '[w]ouldn't she be lovely if she was *running about*?' (p. 67, my italics) – which has by this point become a recognised refrain in the play – we must ask ourselves exactly *whose* tragedy is being articulated. For whom is movement a signifier of development?

Spatial phrases are deployed in the play as a means of reflecting on temporality. They work as examples of Bakhtinian chronotopes. The chronotope 'expresses the inseparability of space and time' (Bakhtin, 1981, p. 84). Thus, we could say that if spatial terms are being used to express time, it is because it is impossible not to conflate the two dimensions. 'Sitting about' (which is juxtaposed with 'running about') seems to be synonymous with failing to develop: to be stationary in a spatial sense is to be stationary in terms of development. The Oxford English Dictionary (2019) observes that the adverbial use of 'about' in this manner causes the 'sense of movement [to be] weakened or absent' and it also posits the following connotations of the construction: 'at large, freely; in an aimless, idle or frivolous manner; without any definite purpose'.[17] In the case of 'running about', a strong sense of motion (albeit without purpose) remains, yet the other associations listed apply to both phrasal verbs. Does the formal paralleling of these two terms suggest that *both* modes of existence – unproductive stillness and manic activity – are being depicted as ultimately futile? It seems significant that the term 'running about' has quite different associations when used to describe the action of a child, and that of an adult. In the case of the adult, the term implies a manic, hectic and perhaps chaotic mode: it is relatively pejorative, since its implicit purposelessness implies non-productivity. When used in relation to the child, however, it can imply carefree play, as well as spontaneity and engagement with the world. Perhaps these positive connotations arise out of conceptualisations of the child as a figure who does not 'work' and so is not to be judged in terms of capitalist productivity. Having said this, might there not be a sense in which the term 'running about' – which, operating as a lament in the play, appears to pass moral judgement on the character of Joe Egg – implies that the child's 'work' is precisely the *work of development*, which takes place, ironically enough, through play, not labour? I am back to the issue of playing versus being trained, which I invoked in relation to reading practices in Chapter 1, and which I shall be revisiting in Chapter 3 as I explore how the future-time of the child may come to be associated with rehabilitation rather than play.

Development as a sign of goodness

Joe Egg's developmental stasis and physical passivity are interpreted by Sheila as a judgment upon her own moral status, and even on her sexual history. In a poignant speech at the end of Act One, Sheila recalls a time when she began to believe that her daughter was showing signs of 'improvement', which did not last (*DDJE*, p. 44). Signs of physical ability in her daughter are read as evidence of maternal and filial moral status. The dominant cultural alignment of physical 'doing' with 'that which is good' is a trope that Nancy Mairs has observed in her writing about living with multiple sclerosis. She remarks:

> But is a woman for whom any action at all is nearly impossible capable of right action, or am I just being morally cocky here? After all, if I claim to be a good woman, I leave myself open to the question: Good for what?

The most straightforward answer is the most tempting: Good for nothing. I mean really.

(Mairs, 1996, pp. 60–61)

Mairs poses an important question about the cultural construction of morality: is it possible to *be* good without *doing* good (see also Cooper, 2013b)? In *A Day in the Death of Joe Egg*, there are plentiful references to the idea that the disabled child is a punishment for the mother's 'sinful' behaviour, specifically to the fact that prior to her marriage Sheila was, in her own words, 'promiscuous' (*DDJE*, p. 28). The child who does not develop thus problematises a naturalised relationship between morality and activity. Although the concerns around promiscuity and goodness locate the play in a particular cultural and historical moment, making it momentarily seem dated, arguably the strength of the connection between productive 'doing' and moral worthiness has only become more marked since the play was written.

This is a theme that emerges in Sara Ahmed's (2010, pp. 208–211) meditation on the work performed by the terms 'active' and 'passive', and which I have also explored elsewhere (Cooper, 2013b). Noting that '[p]assivities tend to be located in the bodies of those on whom we have given up', Ahmed goes on to observe that '[t]o give something up can be not to see the quality of an action' (2010, p. 209). Joe Egg exemplifies the body in which passivity has been located, but it is the other characters that position the Joe Egg character as such. Ahmed turns to grammar, and to the grammatical positioning of certain bodies as subjects and others as objects to illustrate the idea of failing to see the 'quality of an action'. The phrase 'the chicken crossed the road' is never articulated in the passive voice as 'the road was crossed by the chicken', which – Ahmed argues – arises out of our need to 'preserve the fantasy that the subject, even the animal-subject, is the one who acts' (p. 209). Yet the road does not 'do nothing in the event of the crossing' – it is a 'provider' (p. 209). Using this example as a means of defamiliarising objects we consider ourselves to know, Ahmed concludes that the object that 'has been deemed as passive, as just there doing nothing, is doing something and even provides the conditions of possibility for doing something' (p. 209).

Non-development and non-humanity

On a number of occasions, Joe Egg is compared, either directly or obliquely, with non-human entities: the terms 'mutt', '[v]egetable', and 'a kind of living parsnip' are all used figuratively to describe her subjectivity (*DDJE*, pp. 36, 39, 66). Mel Chen (2012, p. 40) has referred to an 'ordered hierarchy from inanimate object to plant to nonhuman animal to human, by which subject properties are differentially distributed (with humans possessing maximal and optimal subjectivity at the top)'. The language that compares Joe Egg with a 'mutt' or a 'vegetable' relegates her to a less-developed state and to a lower place in this hierarchy.

Not all of the characters in the play subscribe to such a hierarchical view of the natural world. Yet Sheila's capacity to 'embrace all living creatures' (in Bri's terms) is represented in pejorative terms in the play (*DDJE*, p. 26). Her attention to her many pets and pot plants is a point of comedy:

SHEILA: [...] Oh, and all the wild-life's fed – the cats, the guinea-pigs, the goldfish, the stick-insects –

> [*Pause.*]

BRI: The ginger-beer plant?

SHEILA: All the plants.

(*DDJE*, p. 15)

The accumulation of animals listed by Sheila here seems hyperbolic, and is thus comedic. Comedy is also in evidence when Bri interrupts with the bathetic reference to '[t]he ginger-beer plant'. The humour derives from the fact that we are descending Chen's (2012, p. 40) 'ordered hierarchy [of animacy]', with the implication that one should not care as much about a ginger-beer plant as a cat (indeed, a ginger-beer plant is not, strictly speaking, a plant at all, but rather a mixture of a yeast and a bacterium). Sheila's care, conceptualised as indiscriminate, is connected with being 'simple' (*DDJE*, p. 26). The joke about Sheila's love of animals resurfaces later in the play, when an infestation of fleas from one of the cats is once again framed in terms of Sheila's failure to use reason in the attribution of care. Moreover, the main reason given by Bri for his decision to leave the family at the end of the play is his experience of being 'one of the menagerie' (p. 85).

Although the play continually unsettles any attempt to let our sympathies rest with one particular character, I read it as articulating a particular hatred of Sheila's tendency to care for (and about) all things equally. The critique of her undiscriminating capacity to care is also, of course, an implicit critique of her seemingly unlimited energy to care for her disabled daughter. Sheila is portrayed as failing to understand the supposedly natural order of 'animacy' (Chen, 2012, p. 2), an order that dictates that individuals like Joe Egg 'wouldn't have survived in nature, it's only modern medicine [...]', as the character Pam puts it, echoing a eugenicist position (*DDJE*, p. 63). Indeed, Sheila is linguistically aligned with her daughter in Bri's comment that '[s]he sits there embracing all live things' (p. 26). Here the phrase 'sits there' is reminiscent of the phrase '"[s]itting about like Joe Egg"', one of the play's key refrains, which captures the perceived passivity of the Joe Egg character. The semantic echo here implies that Sheila's love of all living things is not a praiseworthy self-chosen activity, but rather is a mark of weak character – of passivity, simplicity, slowness. Thus, although Joe Egg is problematic as the child who does not develop, Sheila is criticised as the adult who has not developed the capacity to discriminate between 'the developed' and 'the undeveloped'. This portrayal of Sheila's caring labour chimes with Baraitser's (2012a) characterisation of maternal time as unproductive and non-developmental, which is discussed in more detail in Chapter 3.

Staging non-development

The play potentially poses 'developmental' challenges for the audience at the level of meta-narrative, and in relation to staging. In what ways does Joe Egg, who has no apparent developmental trajectory through the course of the play, frustrate our expectations of the 'development' implicit in narrative form? Can Bri's seemingly impulsive decision to leave his daughter out in the car, to die of cold, be read as a response to a need for narrative, a need for improvement or deterioration, as a need for something to *change*? Are such needs located in the character, or in the spectators of the play? The play's embrace of what might be called a chronotope of stasis is part of its challenge, both in terms of its content and its form: it poses the question of how apparent non-development is to be managed, in a narrative as well as in life.

What effect do decisions about staging and casting have on the framing of issues of disability and development? The role of Joe Egg gives rise to both political questions about who has the right to play a disabled character in a mediated context and ethical issues around the on-stage representation of a child with an intellectual and physical impairment. It is beyond the scope of the chapter to explore these questions in detail, but it is worth briefly observing that the licensing team that originally reviewed the play recommended using a doll or dummy to play the character of Joe Egg (Nichols, 2013). What might the effect of such a casting decision have been? The presence of the inanimate dummy would, I think, prevent us from confronting the anticipated animation of the developing child. According to Masahiro Moto's (2012) hypothesis of 'the uncanny valley', humans are capable of identifying with humanoid figures such as robots, as long as they retain a degree of morphological difference which distinguishes them from a real human. Figures that mimic the human too closely are experienced as being uncanny. Following Moto, it could be argued that the figure of the dummy would actually provoke more empathy than the figure of the inanimate child, which would be felt to be uncanny.

As the antithesis of the developing child, Joe Egg reveals the extent of our investment in this concept and its shaping of our expectations about what a child 'is' and 'does'. Having introduced these ideas, I will now be considering their relevance to a discussion of the controversial case of a young American woman known only as Ashley X. The decision to write about Ashley raises certain ethical issues in itself, which make me uncomfortable. I shall be exploring these in the next section, alongside my thoughts on the place of developmentalism in the case.

Desiring non-development? The case of Ashley X

Ashley X is a young, profoundly disabled, white woman living in the USA, who was administered surgery and growth attenuation treatment in the early 2000s (Pilkington, 2007). This treatment ensured that her body would never reach its adult size or form (Pilkington, 2007). Her parents state that she 'had a normal birth, but her mental and motor faculties did not develop' (Ashley's parents, 2012, p. 1). The doctors who treated Ashley write that

> her development never progressed beyond that of an infant. At the age of 6 years, she cannot sit up, ambulate, or use language. [...] The combined opinion of the specialists involved in her care is that there will be no significant future improvement in her cognitive or neurologic baseline.
>
> (Gunther and Diekema, 2006, paragraph 1 of 'Case Report')

When in 2004, Ashley began to show signs of early puberty, her parents approached doctors to explore 'options to minimize her adult height and weight' (Ashley's parents, 2012, p. 4). Following consultations with an ethics committee, a number of hormonal and surgical interventions were performed on Ashley's body. Ashley was given hormone treatment, a mastectomy and a hysterectomy. As Kafer observes, the rationale for these interventions was made in terms of 'Ashley's future quality of life: they would reduce her pain and discomfort [...] and would enable her parents to continue caring for her at home' (2013, p. 47). The case has attracted much attention from disability activists and bioethicists debating the ethics of the treatment. My own focus here is on the positioning of rehabilitation in the discourse of development; my analysis owes a lot to Kafer's discussion, which recognises the case as a 'stark illustration of how disability is often understood as a kind of disruption in the temporal field' (pp. 47–48).

My discussion of the case will be in three parts. Firstly, I want to consider a series of ethical questions that arise from any decision to write about the case and its protagonists. Secondly, I will explore how Ashley's imagined adult body poses a challenge to a 'developmentalist chronotope'. Thirdly, by reflecting on the way in which this case sits rather uneasily within the rhetoric of rehabilitation that characterises much medical discourse about disability, I argue that the Treatment is controversial precisely because it cannot be straightforwardly assimilated into a discourse of rehabilitation. This leads me to explore how rehabilitation comes to be defined in relation to development, and how development is, by the same token, defined in terms of the potential to be rehabilitated. This, I suggest, leads us back to a very narrow, highly medicalised definition of 'what development looks like, and who is more or less developed' (Burman, 2008a, p. 31).

Unsettling questions

I am conscious that an analysis of the representation of a living child – as opposed to a literary character – raises certain ethical questions in itself. Kafer writes, in relation to Ashley's case: 'In thinking about crip futurity, I find myself haunted by Ashley X' (2013, p. 47). I too feel haunted by Ashley X; relatedly, I feel uneasy about the ethics of juxtaposing a 'real-life' case study with a literary one, and of analysing both in terms of discourses of the 'developing child'. One of my goals in this book is to examine the work done by the distinction drawn between the discursive, on the one hand (as the 'non-real') and that which is posited as 'real', on the other, as something that escapes discursive intervention (Lesnik-Oberstein, 2011). Indeed, my interest in this thorny issue should be seen not as a way of eliding the ethics of this juxtaposition, but rather as being *prompted by* the very ethical and epistemological questions raised by the decision to write about the life of a living person (even if – perhaps especially if – that life has already been highly mediated and discussed). Indeed, the ethical dilemma to which I am alluding might best be articulated in relation to the question of voice and agency in the case. As Jake Pyne observes:

> [...] we can note that Ashley herself, her will and her views, do not feature in this story. [...] The silence of Ashley's perspective is not a mere footnote or methodological dilemma in attempting to study her situation; it is entirely emblematic of it. Thus I acknowledge my unease at contributing to the commentary about Ashley, and hope to draw attention to her silencing, rather than reproduce it.
>
> (Pyne, 2017, p. 100)

I share Pyne's discomfort about the reproduction of 'silencing', but I also wonder how far it is possible to avoid such a reproduction. The production of academic discourse about the case – even academic discourse that is invested in a politics of emancipation – involves a degree of 'speaking for'. It cannot (and perhaps does not always want to) disentangle itself from historically specific notions of what emancipation looks like. We are back with the question of 'voice', and with the 'speechlessness' of a protagonist: in this sense, the juxtaposition of this case study with *A Day in the Death of Joe Egg* is illuminating. There I argued, in dialogue with the work of Darke (1999), that the play itself both reproduces *and* problematises the dominant discourse of 'what *we* [i.e. non-disabled people] should do about *them* [i.e. disabled people]' (p. 70, emphasis in original). My hope here is that in my reading of the case, I can highlight the role of an attachment to rehabilitation in the shaping of bioethical discourse, whilst also remaining conscious of how my own political investments give form to my analysis (Wiegman, 2012). There is not a straightforward resolution to the ethical dilemmas around 'speaking for' or around the decision to discuss a 'real life' case study. For me this is not a reason to avoid speaking altogether, but rather a reason to do so whilst simultaneously attempting to remain aware of, and open about, my own desires and commitments (Wiegman, 2012).

A further ethical issue is the question of how we understand the role of Ashley X's parents. Bioethical discourse often assumes an oppositional structure (Tremain, 2006), and is expected to proceed by reaching a moral judgement. The idea that there is a 'right' and a 'wrong' – and the attachment of these labels to individual actors – can be understood as a function of this discourse. One of the unfortunate side effects of this approach is the tendency to individualise and decontextualise decisions which take place in a particular cultural, social and economic environment – in this case, one that places great emphasis on the fantasy of the adult as a self-sufficient individual (Cooper, 2010). Pyne notes that his observations about the case are 'not meant to imply that [Ashley's parents] do not love and care for her [...] [and they are] not meant to imply that Ashley's parents made choices in isolation' (2017, p. 101). He writes: 'The abysmal lack of support for families with disabled children and the pervasive devaluing of disabled life situate this Treatment in a profoundly ableist context' (p. 101). These are important points about context, which should be borne in mind in any analysis of the case.

As disability theorists, I think we have a duty to open ourselves to such questions, let them unsettle us, and not expect to be able to answer them. Nevertheless, I hope that an analysis of the figure of the 'developing child' in the context of the case of Ashley X might tell us about how we invest this figure with value and meaning. An analysis of the relationship between language and ideology as articulated in relation to living children can be an ethical activity, and is, moreover, a necessary activity – but only as long as we continue to respond to these cases affectively as well as cognitively.

Ashley X and the 'developmentalist chronotope'

Kafer (2013, p. 53) argues that in the case of Ashley X, what was experienced as disturbing was a lack of synchronicity between the development of Ashley's body ('en route to "adulthood"') and that of her mind ('mired in "childhood"'). The child's occupation of space is out of kilter with her existence in time:

> Ashley's disabilities rendered her out of time, asynchronous, because of this developmental gap between mind and body; her development needed to be arrested to correct this mind/body misalignment.
>
> (Kafer, 2013, p. 53)

This view of disability as misalignment fits with a 'developmental model of childhood', as Kafer (p. 53) suggests: 'in classical child development theory, children move through a defined sequence of stages toward adulthood, a one-way and linear march "upward"' (p. 53); we might say that the Treatment circumvents this trajectory at the level of the individual, in order to preserve the hegemony of the idea of alignment. Arguably, then, a developmentalist *aesthetic* is at work here, governing the desire for 'mind/body misalignment'. This perceived misalignment will, it is anticipated, lead to a body that is understood as being 'grotesque' (Kafer, 2013, p. 55). Kafer (2013) quotes the bioethicist Norman Fost (2007, n. p.), who uses the term 'aesthetic disconnect' to describe the relationship between the 'developmental status' of a learning-disabled adult and her body.

The justification for the Treatment is highly gendered (Kafer, 2013), and Pyne (2017) refers to the significance of whiteness. The language used by Ashley's parents in their article idealises her physical appearance: 'Ashley is a beautiful girl; see photos below' (2012, p. 1). Ashley's childish beauty is invoked as one of her most significant attributes; it is seen as one that can and must be protected by the Treatment. Time and space will be realigned via the Treatment. Alongside physical beauty, characteristics that are associated with Ashley in the article are sweetness and innocence (Ashley's parents, 2012). Ashley's parents note: 'we call her our Pillow Angel, since she is so sweet and stays right where we place her – usually on a pillow' (p. 1). As Kafer observes of the term: '[it] paints a picture of infant-like dependency and passivity; it makes it difficult to imagine Ashley as a teenager or a woman-to-be' (2013, p. 55). The term also refers to Ashley's stasis in space; the need to halt the temporal forward movement of her bodily development is seen as a function of this stasis. Ashley's 'pure, innocent and angelic spirit' is mentioned, as well as 'her aura of positive energy' (Ashley's parents, 2012, p. 3). Here, the spiritual, non-bodily qualities of the child are emphasised in such a way as to construct Ashley as an ethereal being, as one for whom being in her body is not important, or for whom the need for a light body appears self-evident. Further, as Pyne (2017, p. 109) explains, the representation of Ashley as an angel 'deriv[es] significance from racialized notions of whiteness and purity'.[18] Whereas in *A Day in the Death of Joe Egg* it seemed that there was *no action to be taken*, in this case action is being taken to *prevent* development in order that body and mind *appear to be* in synchrony, in accordance with the terms of an aesthetic that determines what development should look like. The developmentalist chronotope is in play here: there is an expectation as to how the body's occupation of space should correspond with a developmental timeline for the mind.

Ashley X, non-development and the rhetoric of rehabilitation

Ashley's parents have received 'fierce criticism' for deciding to pursue the Treatment (Pilkington, 2012, n. p.), as well as much 'support' (Ashley's Dad quoted in Pilkington, 2012, n. p.), which they document on their website (Ashley's parents, 2018). Why are some procedures that are performed on the bodies of disabled children uncontroversial and routine, while others are the subject of intense discussion? How far is the level of scrutiny of this case study a product of the fact that the child in question is a white American girl? How is the discourse of medical ethics itself structured according to a developmentalist norm associated with the Global North? Are procedures interpreted as acceptable if they subscribe to a developmentalist logic? How far does the impetus to rehabilitate come to the assistance of, and shore up, developmentalist norms? Does a rehabilitative chronotope work in tandem with a developmentalist chronotope? I shall now explore some of these points.

In the bioethical literature, the Ashley case is controversial because there is a lack of agreement about whether the Treatment should be characterised as benefiting or harming Ashley, and because Ashley cannot speak her wishes in relation to the Treatment. However, it is also controversial, I would argue, because it cannot be cast as being rehabilitative. In fact, it *prevents Ashley's body from developing* as it would have done. By contrast, physiotherapy apparently enables or facilitates the 'normal development' of the child's body. Through physiotherapy, development is said to be achieved rather than being stunted. However, treatments that are cast as rehabilitative do not necessarily benefit the child in question, if viewed from a particular standpoint. What if definitions of development are too narrow; what if they are too focussed on instilling a sense that only normative development is to be valued? How does the notion of the 'developing child' affect how some cases are selected as fitting subjects for the medical ethics committee, while other cases are already closed because they are seen to be, purely and simply, facilitating the child's development? The notion that some forms of treatment are already bracketed as 'acceptable' in relation to biomedical ethics arises, in my view, from a narrow, highly medicalised view of what constitutes the 'developing child'.

According to Kafer (2013), what is intolerable about the case of Ashley is the asynchrony between body and mind. I agree. Yet it is also interesting that medical intervention or rehabilitation may actually *achieve* asynchrony as its outcome. A disabled body can be in tune with itself – it is only out of tune in relation to a normative standard. An intervention is disruptive insofar as it generates asynchronicity. Physiotherapy was, in my early experience, a way of telling the body to 'speed up', to 'catch up' with my mind. But my body (according to its own logic) *did not need to catch up because it was already there*. In fact, the physiotherapy caused its own asynchrony, its own disharmony, by making me feel that my body was out of time with its existence in space.

A 'rehabilitative chronotope' might thus be set alongside a 'developmentalist chronotope' and a 'chronotope of stasis' in relation to these case studies of (non) intervention. The developmentalist chronotope represents a normative model of time-space relations in contemporary narratives of childhood. The chronotope of stasis dominates in *A Day in the Death of Joe Egg* (Nichols, 1967), with a lack of forward-movement in the narrative mirroring the disabled character's physical immobility and the seeming irrelevance of 'intervention' in this case. This irrelevance is experienced as a tragedy by the parents, who long to see development in their child. They long for the relevance of the rehabilitative chronotope, which uses up time (and resources) to restore the child to the 'correct' occupation of space. It is arguably the emptiness of time – the impossibility of using it in the service of rehabilitation – that prompts Bri's departure and his attempt to make something happen. In the case of Ashley X, the time-space of rehabilitation is also irrelevant, and this seems to prompt a reversion to the aesthetic of normative development, in an attempt to reclaim the cultural and social status bestowed by the developmentalist chronotope. Meanwhile, my own disability was seen as responsive to rehabilitation, and as a result the demand on me was to come to occupy the time-space of the normally developing child. I was left feeling that my body's occupation of the spatial world was too slow, or not quite right in ways that were hard to understand. In *A Day in the Death of Joe Egg*, Joe's development was desired; in the case of Ashley X, a particular kind of development was stopped. Yet in both cases, the category of normative development *per se* stayed intact. These examples therefore serve to 'reify an (human) exceptionalism that only certain privileged disabled bodies can occupy' (Puar, 2017a, p. 14), and in this way to allow a normative narrative of child development and rehabilitation to persist in the dominant culture of the Global North.[19] In this section I have sought to show that the embedment of such concepts makes it almost impossible to conceive of rehabilitation outside of a medical model of child development. Fisher and Goodley (2007) have emphasised the linearity of such models, which – they argue – can be oppressive for the parents of disabled children, precisely because their children's lives do not always unfold according to developmental norms. In the next section, I turn to the issue of narrative structure to reflect further on the connections between linearity and developmentalism.

Development and lives as narratives

Disability is almost always required to mean something more than, or in addition to, itself: it is a 'symbolic vehicle for meaning-making' (Mitchell and Snyder, 2000, p. 1). Often, a change in disability status over time may be used in the service of a narrative that develops – a trope that Keith (2001) has explored. When illness and disability cannot be overcome, but are destined to end in death, does this 'queer' the notion of the 'developing child'?[20] What happens to narrative when it has to contain deterioration? To explore these questions, I turn to two novels for children that feature children dying of cancer: Morris Gleitzman's (1989) *Two Weeks with the Queen* (*TWQ*) and Sally Nicholls' (2008) *Ways to Live Forever* (*WLF*).[21] The former is strongly narrative-driven whilst the latter is composed in the style of a diary or scrapbook. My reading of the two texts problematises the idea of an inherent connection between the linear narrative form and an endorsement of developmentalism on the one hand, and the diaristic form and a radical rejection of 'development' on the other. It is more complicated than this in these cases. The text that evades a conventional narrative form cannot escape developmentalist thinking, because it creates the expectation of deterioration as a means of feeding the reader's interest. Meanwhile, the text that deploys a linear narrative – *Two Weeks with the Queen* – is critical of the developmentalism of the guardians of the central character, celebrating instead the acceptance of 'the terminal' displayed by a gay man who supports the protagonist as he comes to terms with his brother's illness, and who ultimately takes up the role of guardian in relation to Colin.

Desiring development? *Two Weeks with the Queen*

Morris Gleitzman's novel, a third person narrative told from the point of view of twelve-year-old Colin, tells the story of Colin's quest to find the 'best doctor in the world' to cure his younger brother's cancer (*TWQ*, p. 36). Colin's legal guardians in the novel – his parents, and later his aunt and uncle – avoid addressing the issue of his brother's imminent death with him. Luke's diagnosis even precipitates a parental decision to send Colin away to England (from

Australia) to stay with his aunt and uncle, the idea being that in this way Colin will be protected from knowing about death. In the chronotope of terminal illness, it seems that there is no place for the child. Colin's aunt in particular is portrayed as studiously maintaining a taboo around the subject of death; she also perceives her own son as vulnerable to sickness and is depicted as an over-protective and overbearing mother. In the context of this persistent disavowal of imminent death and a refusal to speak openly about the realities of his brother's condition, it is perhaps not surprising that Colin resorts to elaborate schemes to find a cure for Luke: breaking into Buckingham Palace to discuss doctors with the queen; travelling to South America to meet the 'ancient tribes' who will have 'discovered a cure for cancer' (p. 98). The remedy sought by Colin is imagined as having a dual curative function in that it will also restore his parents' interest in him, perceived as lacking even prior to his brother's diagnosis. Colin's manic scheming is eventually contained by an encounter with a young man who is crying in the street outside the hospital – a man whose partner, Colin later learns, is dying of AIDS. Through the encounter with Ted and his partner Griff, Colin is finally helped to feel the rage and grief that his brother's diagnosis has evoked in him. Ted is Colin's true '[g]uardian', the novel suggests (p. 125): when his aunt and uncle refuse to let Colin travel home to Australia to be with his dying brother, Ted steps in to sign the relevant papers. The novel's title plays on the double meaning of 'queen', with 'the' queen of England proving to be disappointingly elusive and unhelpful. Even someone who signifies power and authority in the mind of the child is unable to defy death.

The child whose condition is deteriorating, Luke, is almost entirely absent from the novel, although he figures as the damaged object that must be repaired in order for Colin to be allowed to return to the bosom of the family as an object of love and pride. Colin's removal from the family at the moment of his brother's diagnosis seems almost to frame him as responsible for his brother's condition. His mother goes from sleeping beside him, when she is anxious about his brother's condition, to packing his case for him the following morning and announcing his departure for England. Yet even when Colin is spatially removed from the scene of illness, the theme of deterioration and repair continues to haunt the time of the novel in the protagonist's obsession with finding a cure for his brother. It is as if the attempt to separate out space and time, to break open the chronotope (as though Colin could un-know his family's pain by being spatially distant from the scene of it) has failed, mirroring the failure of a parental attempt to protect the child from suffering.

There are different ways of reading the novel; I will firstly elaborate one possible reading, and then explain why I feel that it is insufficiently attentive to some of the more radical aspects of *Two Weeks with the Queen*. One could argue that rather than focussing on the 'queerness' of the deteriorating child, this novel maintains a more conventional and conservative focus, being, in structural terms, a *Bildungsroman*. According to this logic the developing child is, in fact, Colin: he develops in the course of the novel – as a 'good' liberal subject – by coming to terms with the vulnerabilities and limitations of adults. He learns that no one is omnipotent (not even the queen). Meanwhile, whilst the deteriorating body of the child remains absent, the deteriorating body that *is* presented in the novel is that of Griff, the homosexual AIDS victim. Thus the 'queerness' of youthful deterioration – one might contend – is embodied only in the figure of the male homosexual and in this way the novel reiterates the dominant order's marginalisation of this figure, to use Edelman's (2004) terms. I return to these terms in the next chapter, in the context of a discussion of the parallels between the figure of the disabled child and Edelman's figure of the queer, both of which can be read as disrupting the uncomplicated unfolding of 'the future' (see also Mollow, 2012).

In the context of children's literature about AIDS, Robert McRuer (1998, p. 136) identifies an 'immune/implicated' binary opposition – first discussed by Richard Goldstein (1991) – to argue that mainstream culture is invested in maintaining the fantasy of the child as immune to AIDS, a position that in turn arises out of a belief in the child as a non-sexual being, and the social construction of the child as innocent. Following this theory, one could propose that *Two Weeks with the Queen* locates immunity and development in Colin, and that in so doing, it preserves a dominant cultural status quo in which the child develops into a liberal subject who views the deteriorating AIDS victim with compassion: for McRuer, such an outcome exemplifies responses to the 'the liberal reinscription of AIDS [...] as "everyone's disease"' (1998, p. 134).[22] Although McRuer's reading is surely a compelling one with regard to many texts from the period, the representation of the gay man in *Two Weeks with the Queen* as the only 'grown up' who really deserves that epithet leads me to feel that this novel is not afraid of going to some queer places.

I am persuaded that this children's book goes beyond liberal tolerance in its treatment of the Other. The novel was written at the height of the AIDS crisis and can be read as challenging dominant cultural fears of contamination in its representation of a young boy visiting a dying man with AIDS alone in hospital, and confidently sharing fruit with him. In this encounter, Colin is not *immune* but rather is *informed*, acting on rational knowledge about how the disease is transmitted. Through his encounters with Griff and Ted, Colin is in some way inducted into their way of being, which is the time-space of AIDS, of anti-gay rhetoric and stigma. Colin is already 'contaminated' by the chronotope of terminal illness through the early events in the novel; yet it is in his two weeks with *these* queens – whose ability to share their own grief and loss with him contrasts with the avoidant tactics of the other parental figures in the novel – that this 'contamination' comes to be processed and understood. In this sense the novel queers developmental time and rehabilitative time: it is this pair of queers who help Colin to develop towards an acceptance of 'the terminal'. Although the form of this story is a conventional linear narrative, we might ask whether, in a certain sense, this convention is contaminated by the chronotope of 'the terminal', which dispenses with rehabilitation.

Another expression of the 'chronotope of terminal illness': *Ways to Live Forever*

The 2008 children's novel *Ways to Live Forever* by Sally Nicholls approaches the figure of the deteriorating child using a rather different narrative technique. The story (such as there is) is recounted by eleven-year-old Sam, who is dying of leukaemia. The tale of a dying child told in the first person presents a number of problems for a narrative: most importantly, the question of how it will deal with the event of Sam's death (which would seem to be the natural conclusion of the story), when this cannot be related by Sam himself. Perhaps the unresolved question of how the text will handle what we imagine to be its conclusion is part of the draw of the text. It is a conundrum that is hinted at in the opening to the novel. Sam's early statement, '[b]y the time you read this, I will probably be dead' (*WLF*, p. 3) draws attention to an uncanny temporal relationship between writer and reader, and between the mortal body of the author and the immortal body of the text he produces, which might be read as a Derridean 'supplement' or substitute for the human body that cannot go on.[23] Indeed, the very fact that this text is less a narrative than a document – as Sam's epigraph states, '[i]t is a collection of lists, stories, pictures, questions and facts' (p. 1) – gestures to the status of this text as a substitute for a self that will die. The aspects of the text that bear resemblance to narrative – Sam's diary entries – are frequently interrupted by other kinds of writing, presented as though on notepaper or index cards, in the handwriting of a child. These are Sam's lists, examples of which include, 'Five Facts about Me' (p. 3); 'Favourite Things' (pp. 42–43); and 'Ways to Live Forever' (pp. 89–90). Sam's ongoing list of 'Questions Nobody Answers' – the difficult questions about death and dying – also interrupt the flow of the narrative.

In its documentation of Sam's gradual decline, *Ways to Live Forever* is the more naturalistic of the two novels, but I found it less gripping because it simply moves towards what – we presume – will be its inevitable conclusion: Sam's death. The novel does not chart the central character's emotional development, unlike *Two Weeks with the Queen*: Sam knows only too well, right from the beginning, that '[g]rown-ups' give you a 'waffly answer' on the subject of '[g]oing to die' (*WLF*, pp. 8–9). Thus *Ways to Live Forever* challenges developmental norms: the protagonist seems to have already reconciled himself to the inevitability of his own death at the start of the book. By contrast, the adults around him are depicted as struggling to come to terms with this fact – in an intriguing parallel with the parental figures of *Two Weeks with the Queen*. Sam's father, for example, observes on one of his son's better days: 'I don't think that doctor knew what he was talking about [...] Sam's doing great' (*WLF*, pp. 29–30). Structurally, the novel mimics the suspension of forward movement in Sam's life. Rather than being structured as a narrative, it is more of a snapshot of a child in the months before his death – a written record of a life that will, as previously stated, soon have to stand in for the life itself. Yet the formal qualities of this anti-narrative leave the developmentalist chronotope intact by implying that development equals narrative equals life, while terminal illness equals diaristic snapshot equals death. The chronotope of stasis is not applicable here, as it was in relation to *Joe Egg*, mainly because the text's anticipation of the child's death sets up an almost voyeuristic fascination with the question of how the text will deal with this event, and this has a propulsive quality that drives the reader onward (even if the lack of a conventional arc makes the body of the text less compelling, as I am suggesting). Techniques are thus deployed to create forward movement even here: notions of narrative and of development are never completely dispelled from the text.

I have sought here to complicate the idea that if narrative is deployed, a developmentalist chronotope is inevitable. Efforts to avoid the conventions of linear narrative may not necessarily result in the queering of the deteriorating child depicted in the text: *Ways to Live Forever* (Nicholls, 2008) arguably memorialises Sam as a very 'normal' eleven-year-old boy. Sam's deterioration is rendered sentimental by emphasising features of his personality and development that make him 'normal' and universal. Whilst this might apparently enable identification with Sam's character, in some ways the blandness of the protagonist makes it easier not to identify with him, to see him as at once 'every child' and 'no child', and thus to dismiss deterioration as something which 'never touches my life'. By contrast, the linear narrative of *Two Weeks with the Queen* (Gleitzman, 1989) arguably confronts the difficulties posed by the deteriorating child unflinchingly; it is not afraid to explore how a family deals with (or rather fails to deal with) the affective impact of a child's imminent death, nor to think about how the unprocessed emotions triggered by these circumstances play themselves out in terms of fear of contamination (by AIDS *and* by childhood cancer).

I want to end the chapter by turning back to the personal, and to the endlessly self-repeating symptom as a feature of experience that fails to respect the norms of either linear narrative or developmental time. As it happens, the symptom I will foreground is doubly significant in this context in that its purpose (as I have gradually come to understand it) is to comment on the oppressive nature of developmental time.

To conclude ...? Resisting developmental time

I must not be slow. I must show them I am just as fast as all the rest. If I am slow, I am falling behind. I must do it right and I must do it quickly, efficiently.

In their time. Never in my time.

I must show them I am getting better. Developing. Learning. Improving. All of these things are the good things I must show the doctors.

I pay the price now for having lived according to someone else's time. Living with anxiety is like rewinding again and again. Anxiety is trying to catch me up and slow me down all at once, trying to get me back into MY OWN TIME. So time-consuming! Over and over again I check. Trying to get my time back. I enact lost time in my search to re-find a time snatched from me. I play it over.

The time that could never be mine. I enact the losing of time. Once upon a time you snatched time from me, now I endlessly snatch time from myself.

Time is always imagined as someone else's. I never knew until now that I wanted my own time. I thought I could do without, thought I could make do, living inside someone else's clock. But it turned out I was only making do. And it turned out that making do wasn't enough for me after all.

I'll tell you what it's like. When you're a very small child with a disability, when your embodiment isn't valuable just as it is, in the end you internalise a sense that having a life, a life-TIME of your own, is something other children get, but not you. For you, time is exercises. The exercises stretch out your body, but they also stretch out into the future, the interminable future. That's what no one notices. The way time dies inside you because none of it is yours. And none of it ever will be yours, as far as you can understand. Time stretched out, flattened, homogenous, into the distance.

No point in resisting the compulsion to check because there is nothing good to put in its place, for time belongs to the exercises, not to me. Time is the exercises. Time is the moving through space of the physiotherapy. Time is checking. Checking is time. Time passing.

It's time.

***

In this angry piece of writing, rehabilitative time is experienced as the time of the Other. In submitting to this timeframe, the recreated child-self in this piece loses her own time. Perhaps, to some extent, this is always the fate of the child, whether or not she has a disability, yet perhaps this experience is intensified when disability is around. This child is caught inside a rehabilitative chronotope, in which time is used up in order to 'correct' the body's movement through space. If activities take her longer than they 'should', this feels shameful: she understands herself as being 'slow'. My writing theorises anxiety as an alternative use of time, an alternative chronotope that is designed to resist the strait-jacket of developmental time. Checking behaviours (visited in Chapter 1 as the look which can never satisfy itself) seem only to waste time (and are certainly conceptualised in this way by the dominant culture). Yet they might actually be understood as seeking to find a 'time of the self' – a time that is not governed by a developmentalist logic. The endless repetition of persecutory thoughts and behaviours, which can at one level be understood as a repetition of the physiotherapy exercises, also 'replays' time at my pace, rather than at the pace of the Other. The circularity of the anxiety structure might be read as resisting the linearity of developmental time.

If, as Baraitser (2012a, p. 234) points out, the time of global capitalism is 'a commodity that can be lost and saved', my own anxious time is time lost as a means of resisting the 'continuous working time' of both capitalism and developmentalism. Anxious time both repeats and resists the working time of the child 'labourer', whose plight I explored earlier in the chapter. A developmentalist position is highly compatible with a capitalist one – indeed, the infant of developmental psychology can be seen as a baby assembly worker, atomized parts of mind and body in the service of an adapting intelligence, itself at the service of an evolving hierarchical structure. Infancy, in this treatment, is the business of building structure, building habits of thought and consumption, as well as goal-directed behavior in the service and in the guise of technology.

(Harris, 1987, p. 41)

No wonder the child who fails to develop 'normally' must have her time appropriated by a developmentalist regime – if she is to become a 'baby assembly worker', she has additional work to do.

It is paradoxical that a symptom that persecutes me and that *wastes* time should also be a mechanism of resistance. Moreover, my account – which draws on insights from my experience of psychoanalysis – raises the question of whether I am endorsing a highly individualised model of resistance to developmental time. On the one hand, this is a model that locates the problem inside me, and that does, therefore, underscore the liberal individualism of the project of psychoanalysis. On the other hand, I would argue that the radicalism of psychoanalysis is demonstrated here in the sense that the transference releases forces that have their *own* directional power and that might unite against the developmental teleology of cure.[24] The celebration of the symptom *for itself* is hardly an outcome that could be allowed in medical models of disability. Yet, if the analyst can interpret, rather than enact (or, at least, as well as enacting) the counter-transferential demand to rehabilitate, there is the potential to turn the tables on developmental and rehabilitative teleology – to see it as part of our past as (disabled) children but not necessarily as part of our present as (disabled) adults. This realisation has, for me, entailed a painful acknowledgement of my own normalising investment in the fantasy of cure.

'Anxiety time' is not so much a way of *thinking* non-developmentally (since it takes place outside of thought), as it is a way of *existing* non-developmentally. Whilst I would, on the one hand, want to defend it as a non-developmental practice that prevents my reincorporation into a normalising agenda, its incompatibility with thinking – indeed, *its traumatic interruption of thinking*, which I discuss in more detail in later chapters as I seek to develop my theory of resistance – makes it difficult to embrace fully as a technique of liberation. At this point, then, I must re-invoke my ambivalence about development, because *thinking itself* relies on a concept of development, of change over time. Here I am drawing on psychoanalytic thought – in particular that of Wilfred Bion (1962) – which proposes that thinking comes about in the absence of the object (see also Freud, 1958b). Thinking is the act of fantasising the object's return at a future point, and thus a notion of development inheres in it. Development is a concept that I rail against, but one that I cannot do without.

Even if we cannot do without developmental thinking, it is nevertheless vital to ask: *who* defines development, and in the service of *what* (Burman, 2008a)? By denaturalising this notion, we might reduce its capacity to act as an impediment in the lives of children who do not develop according to conventional developmental norms. In this chapter, I have sought to do this through an interrogation of objects that reveal development as desired, and others that seem to reject it, but are still, ultimately, operating within its logic. In the next chapter, I continue to be preoccupied with the question of the disabled child's relationship with time, as I probe the issue of the child-as-commodity, and as an investment for the future.

Notes

1 In Chapter 4, I reflect in more detail on the embodied experience of having one's own bodily logic thwarted by the 'rehabilitation' process.

2 I undertook a literature search using the terms 'constraint induced movement therapy', 'hemiplegia' and 'child' in the databases Web of Science and PsychINFO, with the date parameters January 2014–September 2019. I retrieved 11 articles in PsychINFO and 48 in Web of Science. The focus in the vast majority of papers was on physical/functional outcomes, with very little attention given to the acceptability of the treatment. Virtually all papers used quantitative outcome measures (of which almost all measured functional improvement), and only two papers mentioned using qualitative methods to explore the acceptability of an intervention. There were a small number of papers that documented seeking the opinion of therapists – such as occupational therapists – on intervention design and/or the experience of implementing such therapy.

3 During my close reading of this text, I use the acronym *DDJE* to refer to *A Day in the Death of Joe Egg.*

4 I am grateful to Davis (1995) for leading me to the concept of the chronotope.

5 See Bakhtin (1981, p. 258) for the date of the essay.

6 Relatedly, we might want to consider how the increasing hegemony of the neurosciences (Abi-Rached and Rose, 2013) emphasises a kind of determinism associated with parental nurture, which positions 'poor mothers as architects of their children's deprivation' (Edwards et al., 2015, abstract). Neuroscientific approaches to emotional life started to gain traction beyond the scientific community in the late 1990s and early 2000s via the work of authors such as Damasio (2000) and Gerhardt (2004): these works draw out connections between psychoanalysis and neuroscience.

7 The notion that understanding may not coincide with experience, but may be deferred (*nachträglichkeit*) is explored at various points in Freud's work, for example in the discussion of the so-called Wolf Man – see Freud (1955b).

8 See also the work of Lesnik-Oberstein (2011, 2008), Caselli (2010) and J. Rose (1984), discussed in the introduction.

9 This word is used in the title of Zelizer's (1994) book.

10 Burman (2008a) references Morss, J. (1990) *The Biologising of Childhood*, Hillsdale NJ, Lawrence Erlbaum Associates and Morss, J. (1996) *Growing Critical: Alternatives to Developmental Psychology*, London, Routledge.

11 We are not given any explicit markers about race in the play. Whiteness, as Frankenberg (1993) notes, is usually unmarked.

12 See, for example, the British documentary *A World without Down's Syndrome?* (2016), which examines the effects of the rise of pre-natal testing for Down's Syndrome, from the perspective of the mother of a child with this diagnosis.

13 I revisit these debates in Chapter 3.

14 I discuss the naming and gendering of the character in an upcoming section of my analysis.

15 One only has to think of the anti-discrimination campaigns which use the slogan, 'nothing about us, without us' to realise how problematic this is. But then, if we

think of children more generally, to what extent are *they* included in decisions about their futures? Is the disabled child thus doubly voiceless in contemporary culture?

16 Here I am referring to Emmanuel Levinas' ethics, in which the notion of the 'face' stands for the Other's alterity and irreducibility (Hand, 2009; Levinas, 1985). According to Seán Hand, the face, in Levinas' work, 'emerges as the emblem of everything that fundamentally resists categorisation, containment or comprehension' (2009, p. 42). Levinas states, of the face, '[i]t is what cannot become a content, which your thought would embrace; it is uncontainable, it leads you beyond' (1985, pp. 86–87). This concept reminds us of the complexities involved in writing about the Other.

17 'about, *adv., prep.*1, *adj.*, and *int.*' (section A.2.b of entry), Oxford English Dictionary (2019).

18 Pyne cites Berthold, D. (2010) 'Tidy whiteness: A genealogy of race, purity, and hygiene', *Ethics and the Environment*, vol. 15, no. 1, pp. 1–26.

19 Indeed, as Puar observes, this focus on disability as exception is endemic within Anglo-American critical disability studies and it no doubt features in my own conception of disability in this chapter, although I always seek to question my own assumptions with regard to this issue.

20 Nikki Sullivan (2003) has explored the use of 'queer' as a verb.

21 During my close readings, I refer to these two texts using the acronyms *TWQ* and *WLF* respectively.

22 McRuer (1998) laments that a politics of compassion has displaced the politics of community for which AIDS activism originally fought. Is the developing child thus a child in the process of becoming-liberal? And in what sense, following McRuer and drawing on Eve Lacey's (2016) discussion of these ideas, do the formal qualities of a narrative position not just characters but readers too as immune or implicated?

23 In *Of Grammatology*, Derrida (1997) explores the way in which writing has been perceived as a supplement to speech in Western philosophy, so that writing is understood as mediated whereas speech is associated with immediacy.

24 I am indebted to Hocking (2014), which has helped me to think through these knotty issues of teleology.

3 (Un)making the child, making the future

On gifts, commodities and diagnostic speech acts

'Harriet has a condition called hemiplegia. It's a form of cerebral palsy. She might never learn to swim, might never ride a bicycle, might never play a musical instrument', the doctor told my mother.

I imagine my mother trying to process this information, her arms tightening around me in her lap. How does one take in words like these?

If I had had language, I would have perhaps wanted to say:

'Nothing about me changes in this moment!'

And yet this is me in the now, seeking to talk back to that diagnostic scene, to make it other than what it was. What did this speech act filled with modal verbs, hanging overhead like a foreboding raincloud, feel like to the little girl who had no words?

***

The theme of 'time' has been resonating through the previous chapters – in the temporality of the gaze that looks and looks again, and in the time of (non) development. In this chapter, it becomes even more central to my discussion, which focuses on its role in the creation, the perception and the spoiling of value in the life of the child. What does the arrival of disability in childhood do to 'the future'? The first half of the chapter considers the (veiled) commodification of the child under advanced capitalism, which frames the child as an 'investment for the future'. The second half of the chapter explores what happens when the diagnosis of impairment intervenes, intruding upon an imagined future for the child.

If, as Guy Debord wrote (1994, p. 12), the spectacle is not a 'collection of images' but rather a 'social relationship between people that is mediated by images', how does the image of the child, and its particular significance in early twenty-first century Anglo-American culture, mediate a particular relationship with the real child? How do the images of children that circulate in contemporary Euro-American culture alter how we see the figure of the disabled child? In the early part of the chapter, I examine the commodification of the child and the role of liberal individualism in shaping perceptions of both the mother's labour and the 'product' she generates. The concept of the 'child as commodity' is not, in itself, a new idea, nor indeed one that has remained within the academy, but rather, with the advent of new reproductive technologies, it has become a locus of cultural anxiety (Lesnik-Oberstein, 2008; Scully et al., 2006).[1] What is perhaps problematic about the wider cultural uptake of the idea is the sense that we might be able to undo the commodification of the child: as Lesnik-Oberstein argues, there is often an unspoken assumption that one can be a 'privileged viewer of the baby's selfhood', and can have unmediated access to an un-commodified version of the baby (2008, p. 84). Where ideology is under discussion, the notions of both the privileged viewer who can see through hegemony and its obverse, the dupe, are never far away (Blackman and Walkerdine, 2001).

In the context of my discussion of commodification, I ask how discourses that construct the child as a gift complicate the arrival of the disabled child. I draw on Derrida's (1992) work on the gift to explore this question. In the Foreword to a book that examines the relevance of the notion of the gift to experiences of 'nonnormative [...] family making', Rayna Rapp (1999, p. xi) asks: '[c]an the rhetoric of gifts [...] transform the cultural oppositions set up between matter and spirit, love and money, social solidarity and market contract in U.S. consumer culture?' If the disabled child is seen as a gift, is this conceptualisation simply 'rhetoric', or might it have the capacity to enact transformation in the life of the child? I will suggest, following Gail Landsman (2004), that the arrival of the disabled child draws attention to the commodification of the child precisely because the disabled child is *not* the desired 'commodity'. Drawing on the idea that certain bodies 'bear the promise of happiness' (Ahmed, 2010, p. 45) and on the concept of 'reproductive futurism' (Edelman, 2004, p. 2), I develop the idea of the 'normal' baby as an 'investment for the future'.

In the second half of the chapter I consider the relationship between the disabled child and the future in more detail, with reference to my own experience of being diagnosed with an impairment at the age of eleven months. What is the relationship between medical diagnosis and the 'promise' that the child represents? With reference to the concept of 'rehabilitative futurism' (Mollow, 2012, p. 288), I argue that the disruptive body of the disabled child, which threatens futurism's hegemony by reminding us of human fragility and mortality, has to be re-appropriated into the dominant order. I reflect on diagnosis as a speech act, using Judith Butler's (1997a) reflections on what the speech act does as a starting point for exploring the pre-verbal child's experience of (per)formative language. I conclude by considering, in more detail, the (disabled) child's relationship with time and with the gift.

Bodies and selves as commodities

In his 1923 essay 'Reification and the Consciousness of the Proletariat', Georg Lukács distinguished between a society in which the 'commodity form' is 'dominant, permeating every expression of life' and a society where 'it only makes an episodic appearance': it is only under the conditions of 'modern capitalism' that the commodity form comes to dominate all aspects of human life (1971, p. 84). What is so powerful about the 'commodity form'? For Karl Marx, writing in the mid-nineteenth century, commodities 'come into the world in the form of use-values or material goods, such as iron, linen, corn' (1976, p. 138). However, they can only be regarded as commodities 'because they have a dual nature, because they are at the same time objects of utility and bearers of value' (Marx, 1976, p. 138). It is the exchange value of material goods that is central to their identity as commodities. Thus the commodity form causes the 'sensuous characteristics' of different 'products of labour' to be 'extinguished'; concepts such as time and labour are objectified because they become 'congealed' in the commodities they produce (Marx, 1976, p. 128). This is the process of reification, which takes place when a society 'learn[s] to satisfy all its needs in terms of commodity exchange' (Lukács, 1971, p. 91). Through the process of reification, 'a relation between people takes on the character of a thing and thus acquires a "phantom objectivity"' (Lukács, 1971, p. 83). For Lukács, the 'commodity relation' mediates our understanding of our labour, our bodies and ourselves: it possesses a 'dehumanising function' because, through it, we relate to ourselves as objects (p. 92).

The commodity relation has become hegemonic in the contemporary politics of the body (Katz Rothman, 2004; Diprose, 1994). It has been observed that '[i]n capitalist society, where the emphasis is on private ownership, the body is viewed [...] as private property, a personal resource' (Katz Rothman, 2004, p. 21). Indeed, this view has become so naturalised that is hard to imagine the body otherwise. It is inscribed within the project of biomedical ethics (Diprose, 1994). But phenomenological accounts of the embodied self problematise the idea of the body as a possession: as Rosalyn Diprose (1994) has argued, the major problem with biomedical ethics is its conception of the self as stable, continuous and unaffected by bodily change.[2] Barbara Katz Rothman (2004, p. 22) suggests some alternative metaphors for the body – 'the stream of life, the gene pool, the evolutionary chain, the fatherland or motherland, the family' – but laments that whilst 'we may be able to talk about and think about the body in all of these ways', 'legal recognition goes only to the view of the body as individually owned'. Before I turn my attention to the body of the child, I will consider the effects of reification on the pre-maternal subject. In order to understand the commodification of the child, we must first explore how the contradictions of capitalism are inscribed upon the pregnant body.

Liberalism and the pre-maternal subject

As Katz Rothman (2004, p. 23) notes, 'intelligent feminist use of the individualist ethos has been invaluable in assuring women's rights in procreation'. Such rights are necessary in a liberal, capitalist society, but they are not unproblematically positive (Katz Rothman, 2004). The construction of pregnancy in terms of a series of choices taken by an individual needs to be critically examined (on this, see Salecl, 2010). If the child herself is the end 'product' of all these choices, how does this construct and situate the child? If the child is the product of maternal labour (understood at least in part as the liberal maternal subject's decision-making labour), she is surely a commodity to the extent that she, in a very literal sense, makes concrete – makes flesh – the results of those decisions. This also means that the child-commodity can – to borrow Landsman's (1999, p. 148) phrase – be judged 'defective'.

If the pre-maternal subject is interpellated as a decision-maker who must make the 'right' choice in each situation for herself and for her unborn child, she is 'free' to make choices but she is also held responsible for making 'bad' choices or for 'failing to choose'. As Renata Salecl (2010, p. 97) notes, 'the question of choice in reproduction' was opened up 'for women in the West' by the invention of the contraceptive pill. Yet where choice appears to exist, there is greater potential for a binary opposition to arise between the 'good' pregnancy and the 'bad' pregnancy, a distinction that often masks racist and classist assumptions (see Salecl, 2010). Women who have unplanned pregnancies are demonised. The notion that the 'good pregnancy' is a chosen pregnancy is pervasive, informing even sympathetic media coverage.

Even before she conceives, a woman is expected to ensure that her body offers the most hospitable environment for a prospective foetus: she must make 'good' choices in order that her reproductive labour makes a 'good' commodity. In practical terms this pre-maternal labour involves considerations not only about diet, vitamin intake and exercise, but also about the use of medication and alcohol (Landsman, 1999). Kim Hall (2014, p. 179) argues that the naturalisation of a discourse of 'food as medicine' – the notion that healthy eating prevents the onset of illness and disability – has potentially oppressive effects and may stigmatise those living with disabilities and chronic illnesses. The effect of this discourse is to re-inscribe a liberal notion of personal control over the body – the idea that, as Salecl puts it, 'I am free to make whatever I want out of my life' (2010, p. 1). This not only implicates mothers in questions of responsibility for a disability, but also produces the disabled baby as an undesirable object, as 'damaged goods'. At the same time, this discourse reifies the 'normal baby' as a desirable commodity that can, theoretically, be obtained through careful maternal labour.

The normalised use of technologies such as pre-natal scanning and testing also plays a role in the construction of pregnancy in terms of choice. As Tremain (2006) has argued, we need to attend to the role of reproductive technologies in the production of new objects of discourse. Contending that debates on the ethics of pre-natal testing serve to produce impairment as an object for discussion, she suggests that disability activists who oppose testing contribute to the constitution of impairment as 'the embodiment of some natural defect, deficit or lack' in their opposition to the use of such technologies (2006, p. 39). Such a position, which relies implicitly on the social model of disability, fails to see how 'impairments are *naturalized* as an interior identity or essence on which culture acts in order to camouflage the historically contingent power relations that materialized them as natural in the first place' (Tremain, 2006, p. 39; emphasis in original). Tremain (2006) argues that the very concept of bioethics invites us to be 'for' or 'against' a certain policy. Instead of framing our discussion of pre-natal testing in terms of being 'for' or 'against' – that is, in the terms of bioethical discourse – Tremain (2006) advocates for the importance of understanding how the very practice of pre-natal testing as a technology *produces* the notion of impairment. As she puts it, 'the liberal governmentality that facilitates the birth of the practices of biopower also spawns reactions to that apparatus, some of which have been articulated in the language of reproductive freedom' (Tremain, 2006, p. 49). In this reading, the pre-maternal subject is not a free agent, but rather operates within a biopolitical network. The decisions she faces are represented to her in the terms of reproductive freedom, yet they should rather be understood as regulated by the practices of biopower that will categorise her foetus as a particular kind of body.

It is not surprising that the occurrence of foetal impairment is understood in terms of a maternal 'failure to exert control', if a successful pregnancy is constructed in terms of 'good' decision-making (Landsman, 1999, p. 139). In her interviews with mothers of disabled children, Landsman (1999) found that women often blamed themselves for their babies' impairments, ruminating about how the intra-uterine experience they had provided for the child might have been less than perfect: in two accounts, for example, the baby's impairment is linked by the mother to her consumption of alcohol during pregnancy. In another case, 'a mother of a boy with spina bifida tried to remember what she was doing on the twenty-eighth day of her pregnancy, when, she had heard, the spinal cord closes' (p. 138). What form could resistance take in this context, where failure has been internalised as a personal lack of vigilance? Can the concept of the child-as-gift offer some sort of counter-discourse?

The child as gift?

In *Transformative Motherhood: On Giving and Getting in a Consumer Culture*, Linda Layne (1999, p. 2) writes that 'in contemporary North American culture, children are commonly understood to be "a gift"'. Meanwhile, in a study exploring the views of 'lay people' on 'social sex selection', Jackie Leach Scully et al. (2006, p. 753) found that one of the key themes that arose in discussions was the 'idea that children should be a "gift" (and not a "commodity" [...])'. This was one of the arguments that those interviewed used to oppose pre-natal sex selection for social reasons.

Is it possible for the child to function as a gift under neoliberalism? Can the gift even exist in these conditions? As Diprose (2002, p. 2) suggests, 'generosity is difficult to distinguish from parsimony when understood in terms of an exchange economy where virtue is subject to calculation'. Diprose (2002) seeks to move beyond a conception of generosity predicated on 'the logic of an exchange economy' (p. 2), to one that involves 'an openness to others that not only precedes and establishes communal relations but constitutes the self as open to otherness' (p. 4). She is critical of Tibor Machan's (1990, p. 61) contention that 'there cannot be any generosity involved in a polity in which one is forced to share one's wealth'. Such a position assumes that '[g]iving […] is exercised *subsequent* to individual sovereignty and property ownership as part of the means for establishing communal relations of contract and exchange' (Diprose, 2002, p. 4). I find Diprose's project to reframe generosity compelling. Yet, in the spirit of Lesnik-Oberstein's (2008) aforementioned analysis of texts that invest in the idea of undoing commodification, it seems important to ask whether, under capitalism, it is ever possible to give a gift *prior* to individual sovereignty? Can our concept of generosity ever escape reification? Doesn't our conception of generosity rely on a notion of the individual as capable of giving, even when the gift in question is an intangible, abstract one? In *Given Time: Counterfeit Money* – to which Diprose refers – Derrida (1992, p. 6) argues that as soon as a gift is recognised as such, either by the donor or by the recipient, it becomes caught up in the circular, reciprocal movement of 'economy', and is thus no longer a gift. The gift, for Derrida, is 'the very figure of the impossible' in that, in order to function as such, it must not be understood as a gift by either giver or receiver, because recognition 'gives back, in the place, let us say, of the thing itself, a symbolic equivalent' (p. 13). Recognition itself thus has a kind of 'phantom objectivity' here, to use Lukács' (1971, p. 83) term – it has become a commodity in itself. Derrida thus diagnoses a 'madness' in the insistence on the gift's distinctiveness – a madness that 'manages to eat away at language itself' and 'ruins everything that claims to know what gift and nongift *mean to say*' (1992, p. 47, emphasis in original). The gift cannot remain if it is to be outside of economy, but how can it be immediately forgotten, erased?

Derrida seeks to problematise what he perceives as Marcel Mauss' tendency, in his celebrated anthropological study of gift-giving,[3] to posit the gift as 'originary', to use Derrida's term (1992, p. 42). In Mauss' text, Derrida reads a desire to position the gift as prior to 'cold economic rationality' – to see it as that which is behind, or at the start of the circle of economy (1992, p. 42). Ventriloquising Mauss' position, Derrida summarises: '[t]he difference between a gift and every other operation of pure and simple exchange is that the gift gives time', since it does not have to be returned immediately (p. 41). Yet this distinction is shown to be unstable. We need think only of forms of exchange governed by time-bound contracts – indeed, Derrida suggests that paradoxically the gift, in order to be understood as such, must be governed by an 'unsigned, but effective contract' (p. 11), but equally that 'it is necessary […] that the donee not give back, amortize, reimburse, acquit himself, enter into a contract, and that he never have contracted a debt' (p. 13). The giving of the gift is necessarily both a contractual and a non-contractual event. Thus, for Derrida, the gift 'demands, and takes time' (p. 41) because, once the gift is recognised as such, it requires a counter-gift after a certain amount of time has lapsed. In this way, the gift as conceived by Mauss is not, in fact, outside the circle of economic relations (Derrida, 1992).

What would it therefore mean for the child to function as a gift in contemporary Anglo-American culture? If we figure the child as a gift, is this to elide the way in which reification touches us all? As Carolyn McLeod queries in a review of Layne's book, 'does gift language truly elevate [women whose mothering experiences are devalued] or does it merely mask inequalities, or mask their devalued status?' (2001, p. 70). The troubled nature of the notion of the child-as-gift does not go unacknowledged, either by Layne (1999) or by Scully et al. (2006). In both texts, there is a recognition that '[t]he claim that "children are a gift" is [...] a metaphorical one' (Scully et al., 2006, p. 753). As Layne (1999) puts it, women who have 'nonnormative mothering experiences' use the 'rhetoric of the gift' as a way of 'creatively meet[ing] the challenges' they face (p. 1), and as a way of showing 'discomfort with the commodification of life' (p. 3). In both cases, there is a sense that the child 'should' be a gift, but not a conviction that this is how the figure of the child actually functions.

The instability of the idea of the child-as-gift is underlined by the findings of the research by Scully et al. (2006). The researchers emphasise that the gift was associated by participants with the inability to control what arrives: we do not 'quibble about its specifications' (Scully et al., 2006, p. 754). Derrida (1992, p. 122, emphasis in original) notes that the gift must '*remain* unforeseeable' (even as it must not remain): it is associated with chance. Study participants regarded the child as a gift because 'the notion of the gift implies a lack of control over what is received': we do not control what kind of children we have (Scully et al., 2006, p. 754). It is in this sense that sex selection was seen as morally dubious. It is not so much the 'role of market forces' implied by the 'metaphor of commodity' that is troubling but the sense of '"exceeding an appropriate level of choice"' (Scully et al., 2006, p. 754). For example, one focus group participant from the study is quoted as saying: '"I just don't think it's right that people can actually just sit down and choose what colour hair they want [for the child]"' (p. 754). As I have shown, the pregnant subject is expected to make the 'right' choices in relation to her body and her health, in order to produce a healthy child. However, when the choice under discussion is the sex of the child, choice is regarded as wrong because the child should be understood as a gift: something that 'you accept [...] unconditionally, with gratitude' (Scully et al., 2006, p. 754). The incongruence here between neoliberal narratives of choice, self-control and self-surveillance on the one hand and a more archaic, religious concept of unconditional acceptance on the other, is only thinly veiled by the rhetoric of the child-as-gift. Yet this rhetoric *does* conceal the commodification of the child, at least from those who produce children whose bodies *do* 'bear the promise of happiness', to use Ahmed's terms (2010, p. 45). The process of reification does not become visible unless a child with an impairment is born: 'the normal baby in contemporary North American culture is considered a person and is decommodified; rather than being salable, the child itself is now "priceless"' (Landsman, 2004, p. 105).

This pricelessness, or gift status, renders the reality of reification obscene and unspeakable, as the focus group participants revealed. If the child is perceived as a gift, there can be no public acknowledgement of the process of reification that differentiates between bodies. There is a disparity, therefore, between the interpellation of mothers as responsible, autonomous subjects who should have made 'better' choices during pregnancy (and must now make the 'best' rehabilitative choices for their child), and their interpellation as subjects who should accept their children, as they are, as 'gifts'. On the one hand, mothers are required to participate in the processes of social reproduction that effectively commodify themselves and their children, whilst on the other hand they are expected to disavow the existence of these inescapable processes of commodification in order to pronounce their children unconditionally loved 'gifts'. The discourse that posits the child-as-gift seeks to retrieve the child from contamination by a clinical, debasing notion of economy – to draw again on Derrida's (1992) critique – but in the process it places an unbearable contradiction on those families whose children are designated 'gifts'. For Derrida (1992, p. 42), Mauss' rendering of the gift attempts to suppress its deconstructive logic, by simultaneously banishing associations with 'cold economic rationality' (which must be seen only as secondary and subsequent to the gift), and by reifying the gift as sacred and archaic. In the discourse of child-as-gift, it is as if the deployment of this word – 'gift' – could in itself somehow re-mystify a damaged commodity, and could, by sheer word-power – by sheer 'stubbornness', to refer to Derrida's (1992, p. 42) characterisation of Mauss' essay – expel economy from the scene. Later in the chapter I will be giving word-power its due, when I examine the performative potential of diagnostic language; for now, it is perhaps worth noting that, if we were ever sceptical of the capacity of deconstruction to stay with the 'real', with the referent, here we can see it reminding us of the 'madness' in obstinately insisting on an imposed structure that does not match the reality of what has to be lived (Derrida, 1992, p. 35).

Staying with irreconcilable contradictions, in the next section, I will draw on Edelman's notion of 'reproductive futurism' (2004, p. 2), Ahmed's work on the attribution of happiness to particular cultural '"scripts"' (2010, p. 59), and recent feminist work (McRobbie, 2013; Baraitser, 2012a; Quiney, 2007) on parenting in the twenty-first century to consider in more detail how the demands of neoliberal capitalism shape practices of child-rearing. My discussion will crystallise around the fraught question of time: whose time matters? Who is able to take enough time to raise a child? What happens when it takes too long to raise a (disabled) child?

Child-rearing as future-oriented work

In *No Future: Queer Theory and the Death Drive*, Edelman argues that politics is always caught up in '"fighting for the children"' – a struggle which is synonymous with the 'fight for the future' (2004, p. 3). Indeed, it is the so-called 'fascism of the baby's face' that is, for Edelman, behind all political actions and demands (p. 75). It reproduces the current social order. As Edelman puts it:

> [f]uturism thus generates generational succession, temporality, and narrative sequence, not toward the end of enabling change, but, instead, of perpetuating sameness, of turning back time to assure repetition – or to assure a logic of resemblance [...] in the service of representation.
>
> (p. 60)

The baby's face here operates as a signifier that demands succession but conformity, futurity but homogeneity: the reproduction of the norms of today.

Although Edelman rejects politics *per se*, reproductive futurism could, I think, be seen as a facet of advanced capitalist hegemony. Reproductive futurism demands that we propel ourselves into the future, make ourselves (re)productive and defer gratification, reaping the rewards of our reproductive labour through our 'child-commodities', which are the objective manifestations of that labour. The commodity relation is, in a sense, always a futural relation, in that exchange value only has meaning in terms of a notional future commodity that it might purchase: exchange value is anticipatory value. Edelman reads Charles Dickens' *A Christmas Carol* (1843) as a tale of the re-incorporation of a queer figure into normative reproductive futurism: Scrooge is the queer who is finally persuaded to embrace the 'communal realization of futurity' (Edelman, 2004, pp. 44–45). As Edelman (2004) notes, the miserly Scrooge that we first encounter in *A Christmas Carol*, regarded in popular culture as the ultimate capitalist, stands outside of reproductive futurism. By refusing either to give or to receive, he remains beyond the circular relations of the exchange economy, and untouched by the futural demand of the gift to be returned. In order to rescue Tiny Tim, Scrooge engages in an act of philanthropy – an act that signifies not only a relinquishment of 'queer negativity' (Edelman, 2004, p. 6), but also an engagement with an economy in which generosity is an attribute of an individual, a liberal subject (Diprose, 2002; Machan, 1990). Thus reproductive futurism can be understood as a capitalist ideology insofar as Scrooge's philanthropy effectively purchases a future for Tiny Tim (Edelman, 2004).

Dickens' character Tiny Tim is read by Edelman (2004) as an example of reproductive futurism's child. Yet Tiny Tim is hardly futurism's typical child, as Mollow (2012) has noted. Rather than seeing Tiny Tim and Scrooge as divided by reproductive futurism, mightn't they instead be regarded as united in queer negativity (Mollow, 2012)? Whilst remaining attentive to the differences between 'disabled' and 'queer' identities, mightn't we then ask, following Mollow (2012), whether the figure of the disabled child *disrupts* the hegemony of reproductive futurism, and in this sense *shares* in the negativity that Edelman (2004) associates exclusively with the figure of the queer? Indeed, the disabled child 'might not even have a future at all' (Mollow, 2012, p. 288). Admittedly, Scrooge's gift appears to secure Tiny Tim's future, but the novella does not suggest that Tiny Tim is cured (Dickens, 1843). His body may continue to act as a reminder of the ephemeral nature of able embodiment and indeed of life itself. In what ways does the arrival of the disabled child therefore disrupt an imagined future, and an imagined connection between the child and happiness? I turn to Sara Ahmed's (2010) work *The Promise of Happiness*, and then to some reflections on twenty-first century childcare discourses, to discuss these questions.

Ahmed proposes that the association of happiness with particular objects 'not only precedes our encounter with things but directs us toward those things' (2010, p. 28). She asks whether the notion of having a child in order to secure one's future happiness happens by chance, or because that idea had already been 'judged to be good' (p. 28). Happiness, Ahmed notes, has become unmoored from its etymological link to a notion of chance and contingency – it is now seen as 'an effect of what you do', as 'a reward for hard work' (p. 22). The pregnant woman labours to ensure a happy future, by making particular lifestyle choices. This labour is rewarded by the arrival of the child, whose body promises happiness. Yet not all bodies bear this promise equally. The smooth unfolding of the narrative of happiness is unmasked as a script – to use Ahmed's (2010) terminology – by the arrival of the disabled child. In thinking about scripts, it might also be necessary to return to the stage before pregnancy, to explore the naturalisation of the '"own", "biological" child' within our culture, following Lesnik-Oberstein (2008, p. xii). As Lesnik-Oberstein (2008) asks, why does having a child always mean having one of our *own*?

The body of the disabled baby does not carry the *promise* of happiness, even if it brings happiness in reality. A test result or diagnosis of impairment disrupts this narrative of promise. For Ahmed, since '[h]appiness scripts could be thought of as straightening devices', a disruptive body is in fact one that holds great political potential (2010, p. 91). In Ahmed's terms, 'a revolution would not simply require that subjects be revolting; it would demand a revolution of the predicate, of what gets attached to the subjects of the sentence' (p. 192). In the moment of a diagnosis or a positive test result, the baby's body is uncoupled from one signifier – the promise of happiness – and 'gets attached' to another. In these terms, we could say that it is not enough to revolt against the disabled child's diminished personhood; first we must understand how twenty-first-century childcare discourse – as well as, later in the chapter, diagnostic speech – works to construct the child in terms of futurity and promise.

Recent maternal scholarship highlights a renewed imperative for enjoyment and fulfilment in relation to child-rearing in the twenty-first century (Wilson and Chivers Yochim, 2015; McRobbie, 2013). Angela McRobbie argues that:

> The professionalisation of domestic life forcefully reverses the older feminist denunciation of housework as drudgery, and childcare as monotonous and never-ending, by elevating domestic skills and the bringing up of children as worthwhile and enjoyable.
>
> (McRobbie, 2013, p. 130)

This shift is seen as part of the formation of a new liberal – but regressive – post-feminist consensus around the family. McRobbie's thinking chimes with that of Faircloth (2014, p. 25), who recognises the increasing dominance of 'intensive parenting', as we saw in Chapter 2. This is parenting as project management – there is an intensification of expectation surrounding the child and her progress (the project) because of the ways in which this reflects on the mother's performance of her role as project manager.

The re-imagining of motherhood needs to be seen in the context of an overall cultural shift in terms of how work is performed, recognised and made visible as such. The boundaries between what counts as work and what counts as leisure have been dismantled; these categories have become intermingled (Han, 2017). In the era of social media, work has been reframed as work-on-the-self, and as activity that is no longer distinct from enjoyment (Han, 2017). In her novel *Motherhood*, Sheila Heti's narrator – whose decision-making process about whether to have a child is placed at the centre of proceedings – realises that '[her] inclinations towards motherhood' take the form of '*the idea of a feeling* about motherhood' (2018, p. 41, emphasis in original). Heti (2018) characterises this feeling as a form of sentimentality in the novel, detaching it from the actual day-to-day toil of parenting. Such a gesture feels transgressive: it works against the grain of the interminglement of love, work and enjoyment that are invoked under the sign of the maternal. The ideology of professionalisation, and of enjoyment, makes maternal labour vanish into a form of entrepreneurial, narcissistic, self-improvement activity – with the child as an extension of oneself (Han, 2017; Wilson and Chivers Yochim, 2015; McRobbie, 2013). It becomes not work, but an activity that is undertaken willingly. There is a collocation of happiness, choice and work. This returns us to Ahmed's (2010) point about the decoupling of happiness from chance: today happiness is supposed to be an effect of work, of the things one does, the choices one makes. It is imbued with a futural logic – the 'promise' that Ahmed (2010) invokes in the title and throughout her book. This has also been framed in terms of 'cruel optimism' (Berlant, 2011),[4] the idea that, as we perform our (often underpaid or unpaid) activities in the present, we invest these with futural hope, led on by the (often illusive) sense that the future will deliver something better.

A notion of the promise of happiness – to draw again on Ahmed's (2010) lexicon – is mobilised by the childcare manual, as it is by the reams of online advice that now exist about child-rearing (see, for example, Babycentre UK, 2019), as well as by social media platforms, which 'actively incite mothers to participate in the affective structure of family happiness, to document, display and organize a "horizon of likes"' (Wilson and Chivers Yochim, 2015, p. 243; quoting Ahmed, 2010, p. 24). The economies of competition, envy and display that have perhaps always animated child-rearing practices are now ever-present in one's pocket – at the touch of a button on one's smartphone. I want now to turn briefly to a bestselling childcare manual that slightly precedes the social media era, if not the professionalisation of motherhood that McRobbie (2013) describes: Gina Ford's *The Contented Little Baby Book* (1999). I shall argue that whilst the manual clearly invokes a relationship between the arrival of the child and the promise of (futural) happiness (Ahmed, 2010), the parenting model it promotes – against which advocates of 'attachment parenting' (Sears and Sears, 2001)[5] have reacted (Freeman, 2016) – unexpectedly helps to make visible some of the contradictory demands of contemporary Anglo-American parenting practices.

The Contented Little Baby Book emerged at a time when 'attachment parenting' was gaining in popularity in the UK (Freeman, 2016; Sears and Sears, 2001), and, although the book was a bestseller in the UK (Bamford, 2010), Gina Ford's method has been seen as controversial, with broadsheet newspapers including the *Guardian*, the *Independent* and the *Telegraph* covering the emergent culture war between the different approaches to child-rearing (Freeman, 2016; Bamford, 2010; Jardine, 2010; Benn, 2006; Hickman, 2005). Attachment parenting has, over time, gained increasing prominence in the UK policy context, seemingly because of the ways in which its norms intersect with those of the ascendant neuroscientific paradigm of child development (Abi-Rached and Rose, 2013). Edwards et al. (2015) have shown how uncritical policy engagement with this emergent field of brain science is re-naturalising class prejudice in relation to child-rearing practices. The shift towards attachment parenting can and should be seen as coeval with the 'professionalisation' of middle-class motherhood and the intensified denigration of the welfare-dependent working-class mother (McRobbie, 2013).

As the title suggests, in *The Contented Little Baby Book*, the pursuit of happiness and contentment are key features of the method. The manual is hardly unusual for its genre, even if Ford's (1999) method itself is controversial. The arrival of the child is understood as the first stage in the unfolding of a script that promises happiness (Ahmed, 2010): '[o]bviously a new baby always brings much joy and excitement' (Ford, 1999, p. 37). The central concept in the book is the idea that a routine is best for babies. Ford avows that if you follow the routines, you will create a 'contented little baby', like the child mentioned in the Foreword – 'a true Gina baby who sleeps 12 hours every night, has always eaten well and is happy and content in all ways' (p. 8). The author's mantra that '[t]he one thing that parents comment on time and time again is how happy their baby is on the routine' (p. 49) interpellates parents as followers of the routine by naturalising the pursuit of the baby's so-called 'happiness'. What exactly is this 'happiness' and *whose* happiness is actually at stake? In Ford's example, 'happiness' is set up in binary opposition to the crying of the baby: the routine is seen as making the baby happy because the 'true Gina baby' hardly cries at all. Ford thus seems to define happiness as 'not crying'. Here we might ask how we know that the baby who does not cry is a 'happy' baby, and whether it may actually be the parents' contentment that is sought via the method, rather than the child's? We might ask, following Ahmed, why is it taken for granted that happiness is the goal? Ahmed valorises difficult feeling and suffering as having an important place in 'heighten[ing] the capacity to act' (2010, p. 210). Yet, in *The Contented Little Baby Book*, difficulty is what is to be avoided: '[m]any parents who have followed the demand method with the first baby, and my routines with their second baby, would *confirm wholeheartedly that my methods are by far the best* and, in the long term, the *easiest*' (Ford, 1999, p. 49, my italics). The routines make 'the bonding process a *happy and more enjoyable one*' (p. 51, my italics). Happiness is thus aligned with future ease in this manual. It is, furthermore, interesting that the baby that cries too much is aligned by Ford with another non-normative baby: '*[u]nless your baby has a medical condition*, I would be very surprised if you experienced much crying from him, provided of course you are following the routines to the letter' (p. 50, my italics). Both the baby with a 'medical condition' and the baby that displays too much feeling are characterised as disrupting the routine; it is implied that their needs *take up too much time* (on this, see Baraitser, 2012a, to which I now turn).

I draw attention to the assumptions made in the book about achieving happiness and minimising difficulty not to single out this manual, but rather to show how far this affective landscape is normalised and taken for granted as what it means to be oriented (Ahmed, 2006) in the world of child-rearing. I want to make a further point, which is that it is entirely to be expected that Ford should prioritise ease and the need for childcare to be manageable within the time available: her advice speaks to the material reality of family life for most people under neoliberalism, in which a routine that fits around the working day is essential. Ford's focus on routines puts her method at odds with the child-centred approach of attachment parenting. Child-rearing advice that is based around concepts from psychoanalysis and attachment theory often casts the mother as someone who has the luxury of spending time alongside her child, yet such ideas tacitly and uncritically frame a highly privileged version of maternity as universal (see McRobbie, 2013; Baraitser, 2012a; Quiney, 2007). Thus, although the aspiration for contentment (parental and child's) is shared by both Ford and advocates of attachment parenting, we might say that on the subject of difficulty and on attitudes towards the consumption of time, they appear to part company. For the attachment parent, *unless* childcare feels as though it 'takes too much time' (Baraitser, 2012a, p. 236), the parent may feel as though it has not been carried out with the requisite intensity, so the 'ease' that is so valued by Ford would be seen as somehow suspicious. But – as Baraitser (2012a) and Quiney (2007) observe – where else is the neoliberal subject exhorted to take too much time? In this sense I think that *The Contented Little Baby* book draws attention to a contradiction that remains unspeakable in dominant middle-class British culture: the temporal incompatibility of intensive mothering with advanced capitalism (Baraitser, 2012a; Quiney, 2007). Ford's insistence that there are ways of making the process easier might – we could speculate – attract rage and class-based condescension because time-saving techniques are precisely what most parents feel they need, but they are deemed damaging to children's wellbeing by increasingly dominant intensive models of parenting. The project to hegemonise intensive parenting is thus jeopardised by any reminder of its participation in the circle of economy: we are supposed only to see the 'gift' (of time) that all parents give to their children but, in fact, parenting *takes time* that most people without a private income simply do not have (Baraitser, 2012a).

Commenting on confessional writing by mothers who have dared to speak out about the intensity of parenting as a contemporary cultural practice, Quiney remarks: 'from its class-privileged vantage point, [this writing] demonstrates a new consciousness of childbearing as barely compatible with the goals of the capitalist consumer or with the life-course of the highly trained "symbolic-analytic" worker of the new global labour elite' (2007, p. 31). This incompatibility can lead to an experience of motherhood – in a particular social class context – as trauma and loss (Quiney, 2007). Authors who have spoken openly in these terms about the experience of motherhood, such as Rachel Cusk, have been roundly condemned

(Cusk, 2008; Quiney, 2007), suggesting that the articulation of this temporal clash, and its psychic fallout, is still taboo outside of feminist academia. Drawing on Quiney's (2007) essay, Baraitser describes the experience of middle-class motherhood in terms of a '*traumatic loss of productivity*', which is then denied via the 'uptake of this maternal career-vocation', which 'defers lost productivity onto the future citizen who must, in this psychosocial economy, come first' (2012a, p. 229, emphasis in original). This is the child as investment for the future, as the (impossible) gift that will one day give back. Middle-class motherhood is a '*practice of waiting*' (p. 235, emphasis in original), yet it takes place in a sphere in which no time can be uncommodified, hence it is difficult for it not to be experienced as a kind of waste. Thus, for Baraitser (2012a), the child develops and has a future, whereas the mother is involved in a project of waiting for the child, which places her on the side of Edelman's (2004) queer, in a temporal sphere that deviates from neoliberal 'chrononormativity' (Baraitser, 2012b, p. 119, citing Freeman, 2010).[6] If, as Cusk (2008, p. 5) suggests, the childcare manual is an 'emblem of the new mother's psychic loneliness', then this loneliness might be conceptualised as an experience of being at odds with dominant time. Might we see it as a time of waiting for the gift's return (we are not supposed to be waiting for the gift's return, as it will negate the gift)? If neoliberal time always has to be put to good use, and if maternal time must be expended on the child even as this is experienced as a loss for the mother, how does this intensify expectations placed on the unfolding time of the (middle-class) child, and perhaps especially on the time of the disabled child?

Thus far in the chapter, I have been exploring how twenty-first century imperatives around pregnancy and parenting focus attention on the child as a locus of future-oriented promise, whose potential can be maximised through adherence to methods, routines and advice. I have also explored the ways in which the arrival of the disabled child disrupts the promise of happiness. The chapter now changes course to focus on the shock of diagnosis – the traumatic interruption of the diagnostic speech act. Although different approaches are being brought into play in this section (speech act theory, as well as phenomenology), I remain focussed on interrogating the disabled child's place in time, and in relation to the future.

Diagnosis: Re-imagining baby's future

For most of the remainder of the chapter, I explore the performative qualities of diagnostic speech. Firstly, in the section 'The shock of the diagnosis', I return to the personal writing at the start of the chapter, and start to consider how the language of diagnosis alters parents' orientation towards the future. Then, in the next section, 'The diagnostic speech act: Unmaking the subject', I speculate on the phenomenological effect of the diagnostic 'pronouncement' on the pre-verbal child. I use the term 'pronouncement', with its connotations of the marriage ceremony, deliberately, as I want to think about diagnosis as a speech act, and I draw on Butler's (1997a) reading of J. L. Austin's (1975) work on performative language to do so. What does the diagnostic speech act bring about through its pronouncement – that is, through the '"illocutionary"' aspect of performative speech (Austin, 1975, p. 99)? I explore language as both a discursive entity and in terms of its 'semiotic' component (Kristeva, 1984, p. 24), as a transmitter of affect, in order to think about how the diagnostic speech act alters the child's future by re-ordering her embodied relationship with language. In this section, taking care to attend to difference and specificity as well as analogy, I also draw on Frantz Fanon's (1986) graphic account of how it feels to be hailed as a black man, which helps to theorise the physicality of the experience of the offensive call (Butler, 1997a). The third section, 'Un/re-making the subject' explores the 'perlocutionary' effects of performative speech (Austin, 1975, p. 101); that is, what follows as a result of a speech act. In this case, I consider how the demand to rehabilitate oneself is internalised by the child, and changes her lived experience of futurity.

Diagnosis has been discussed from a range of perspectives in the burgeoning field of the sociology of diagnosis (see, for example, Jutel, 2015; Jutel and Nettleton, 2011). The field – as Jutel and Nettleton (2011) note in their introduction to a special issue of *Social Science and Medicine* on the subject – has drawn on influential terms from canonical papers in medical sociology from the 1980s, including: 'biographical disruption' (Bury, 1982), 'loss of self' (Charmaz, 1983) and 'narrative reconstruction' (Williams, 1984).[7] In these studies (in which diagnosis is not the specific focus), the onset of illness is broadly characterised as a process that disrupts a person's understanding of themselves, or as an experience that necessitates the 'reconstruct[ion] of a sense of order from the fragmentation produced by chronic illness' (Williams, 1984, p. 177). Meanwhile, the work of Michael Balint (2000) on the psychodynamics of the doctor–patient relationship and the patient's desire for a 'name' for the illness – on which I draw in the next chapter – presents diagnosis as an act that gives form and shape to something previously chaotic and undefined. In a wide-ranging and much-cited article, Brown (1995, p. 39) refers to the way in which diagnosis offers 'control', both to patients and to medical practitioners (in different ways). In these accounts – to generalise greatly – illness is broadly characterised as a disruptive experience, and diagnosis provides a way of understanding or ordering it. The account I shall be providing is informed by this thought, in particular by the prominence of narrative and temporality therein. Yet my account is also divergent, in that I focus on a childhood diagnostic scene (my own) in which the diagnosis itself, rather than the impairment, caused disruption. I speculate about how diagnosis *feels* when it happens for a pre-verbal child who has not sought it.

The diagnostic scene to which I refer could and should be situated within a wider cultural context of the prominence of what David Armstrong (1995, p. 395) has called '[s]urveillance [m]edicine', in which there is a focus on 'the constant threat that proper stages [of development] might not be negotiated' (p. 396). As we saw in the previous chapter, in contemporary Euro-American culture, children's development is subject to monitoring: developmental milestones must be met at the appropriate times. And yet, as Puar (2009, p. 165) emphasises, the perception of 'normativity and pathology' involves operating within a 'self-other' arrangement that claims universality whilst being particular to a given time and place, and that tends to maintain a focus, within disability studies, on the 'individual subject that is Euro-American, white, middle-class and neo-liberal'. Puar uses the term 'prognosis time' (p. 166) in order to reframe debates about the diagnosis of disability in terms of risks and probabilities that affect whole populations, rather than in terms of the tragic events taking place within the life of an individual whose cultural setting renders disability visible as such. One of the limitations of identity-based models of disability is – as Puar notes – the reification of 'exceptionalism', whereby 'claims to exceptionalism are loaded with unexamined discourses about race, sexuality, gender and class' (2017b, p. 11). In acknowledgement of this, it feels important to recognise that in the account of the diagnostic scene that follows, which draws on personal experience, exceptionalism *is* at work: it is about what the diagnosis of disability means in the life of a white, middle-class, British girl, born in the 1980s, where disability was framed and perceived as the exception.

The shock of the diagnosis

How does diagnosis make for a traumatic re-evaluation of the future of a baby? Whereas the process of monitoring the 'normal' child might be said to produce generalised, ongoing, 'ordinary' anxiety (scrutiny), diagnosis is shock. It takes place in one moment of time, and arguably cuts through time, creating a 'before' and an 'after', a past and a future. In this sense, diagnosis lives up to its etymology: the Greek word *dia* means 'through' or 'asunder' (Oxford English Dictionary, 2019).[8] Diagnosis brings knowledge that cuts through time, traumatically sundering the 'before' from the 'after'. There can be no return to the 'ordinary' anxiety of the past, once diagnosis has been spoken.

When my disability was diagnosed, it was accompanied by the prognosis that I 'might never learn to swim, might never ride a bike and might never play a musical instrument', as the writing at the opening of the chapter showed. What is the effect of this speech act on the parents of an eleven-month-old baby? A contradictory duality arises when the modal verb 'might', with its sense of possibility, is juxtaposed with the adverb 'never', which connotes negative certainty and closure. What is given with one hand is taken away with the other, but neither hand succeeds in giving or in taking. Hope is not completely dashed; a glimmer remains: taunting, tantalising. The taunting duality of the 'might'/'might never' focuses parents' attention on the future as a kind of glittering prize that is just out of reach. We might also note that the activities discussed – swimming, riding a bike, playing a musical instrument – immediately transport parents into a futural temporal mode. As noted, Austin (1975) distinguishes between the illocutionary and the perlocutionary speech act: with the former, the pronouncement itself makes something happen; the latter type is performative to the extent that certain deeds will follow as a result of it. The speech act of the consultant who diagnosed my impairment had both qualities: it was illocutionary in the sense that the doctors words 'made' me disabled in the moment they were spoken (of which more in the next section), and perlocutionary in that particular consequences followed from the words: a programme of rehabilitation and an uncertain future. Whilst most parents probably do imagine their baby's future, a prognostic speech act such as this calls upon parents to imagine their baby's future in terms of specific, concrete activities. In Ahmed's terms, we might think of the prognostic speech act as one that 'orientates' or 'turns' parents towards the future in a very specific way (2006, pp. 13, 15). In being 'turn[ed]', by diagnosis, towards a specific kind of future, is it possible that a 'turn[ing away]' from the baby may also be enacted?

When doctors put specific childhood activities into the category of the 'might never', they invoke an actual future made up of concrete activities such as learning to swim, potentially casting such activities as goals. In the disorientation that the diagnosis creates about the future, perhaps the thought of enabling the child to learn to swim (for example), can provide a point of orientation for parents, who might themselves be feeling lost at sea, and as though they need to relearn to swim. The baby's future may thus be imagined in terms of specifics.

Whereas for the 'normal' baby, the future is encountered, for the newly diagnosed baby it has to be constructed, for fear that it may not otherwise happen. The (queer, disruptive) disabled baby who, in Mollow's terms, 'might not even have a future at all', has to be rescued for futurist agendas (2012, p. 288). Mollow coins the term 'rehabilitative futurism' to describe this process (p. 288): the disabled child has to be rehabilitated, through therapy programmes and other measures, to ensure that she too has a future. Rehabilitative futurism thus claims the child for a normative future. In acting as a reminder of mortality and fragility, the figure of the disabled child provokes a kind of manic reclamation on the part of the dominant order. This figure threatens the fabric of reproductive futurism in representing human fragility, and as a result has to be fiercely reincorporated into the dominant order through a rehabilitation programme that will orientate her towards the future not less than other children, but *more* than them. In the aftermath of diagnosis there could be a coming-to-know-loss, yet, as we have seen, this may be covered over by the discourse of the child-as-gift, whose coercive properties we begin to see more clearly here.

***

Your child is a gift – you did not choose disability, but we can celebrate her gift-ness now because she's on a different schedule from other children.

This child is not a gift! She is a burden! She has no future.

(If she were truly a gift, she would have no future – the gift must not remain).

But look, her future is there for the taking. Reclaim it.

***

In the place where loss would have been, the idea of the gift. In the place of no future, the future reclaimed – a carefully planned future, a schedule. The excessive focus on the future disavows the way in which the disabled child symbolises the lack of a future. My own experience of physiotherapy was that it was entirely future-oriented. By using my muscles, I would, in future, have a greater range of movement and more control over them. Somewhere, I think there was the unconscious fantasy that, if I performed the exercises, I would become the same as ('as good as') other children. I could and would resemble reproductive futurism's poster child. In a strange paradox, then, the disabled child both seems to have *no future* and exists *only in relation to a (particular kind of) future*.

I have been arguing that the figure of the disabled child disrupts the dominant ideology of reproductive futurism by being aligned, like the figure of the queer, with death. Yet I have suggested that, given that the disabled child acts as a reminder of mortality, this figure must be forcefully reincorporated into the dominant order, so as not to pose a threat. The disabled child is 'given' a future, rather than being allowed to encounter her future. What kind of giving is this? Before returning to this question, I want to think further about the diagnostic speech act, but now I want to interrogate its meaning in, and its effects on, the life of the pre-verbal child. What does a pre-conceptual experience of diagnosis feel like? How far is it possible to really *be present* in this experience, as that child?

The diagnostic speech act: Unmaking the subject

When trauma happens, 'the most direct seeing of a violent event may occur as an absolute inability to know it' (Caruth, 1995, p. 89). As a pre-verbal child, present at my own diagnostic scene and yet without words to make sense of it, how might the 'inability to know' the trauma of the diagnostic speech act have nevertheless played itself out in and on my body, with the kind of 'belatedness and incomprehensibility' that Caruth describes (p. 89)? In 'Remembering, Repeating and Working Through', Freud writes of early childhood events 'that were not understood at the time', noting that 'the patient does not *remember* anything of what he has forgotten and repressed, but *acts* it out' (1958a, pp. 149, 150, emphasis in original). This patient 'reproduces it [i.e. the experience] not as a memory, but as an action; he *repeats* it' (p. 150, emphasis in original). In this subsection, I draw on the work of Butler (1997a), as well as on that of Fanon (1986), to develop a theory of the unremembered diagnostic speech act, which, pronounced over the body of the pre-verbal disabled child, fixes her future in her body: it becomes part of her embodiment.

In *Excitable Speech: A Politics of the Performative*, Butler emphasises the 'ambivalence' of the act of naming, exploring the different directions in which it moves (1997a, p. 163). 'One is not simply fixed by the name that one is called' she notes (p. 2), complicating Althusser's (1971) uni-directional model of interpellation – the process through which the subject is called into subjectivity. Her argument continues:

In being called an injurious name, one is derogated and demeaned. But the name holds out another possibility as well: by being called a name, one is also, paradoxically, given a certain possibility for social existence, initiated into a temporal life of language that exceeds the prior purposes that animate that call. Thus the injurious address may appear to fix or paralyze the one it hails, but it may also produce an unexpected and enabling response. If to be addressed is to be interpellated, then the offensive call runs the risk of inaugurating a subject in speech who comes to use language to counter the offensive call.

(Butler, 1997a, p. 2)

Perhaps my voice in this book could be understood in precisely these terms: if the diagnosis of my disability is understood as an injurious speech act, it is one that has nonetheless created 'a scene of agency from ambivalence' and 'a set of effects that exceed the animating intentions of the call' (Butler, 1997a, p. 163). The diagnostic speech act that 'subordinate[d]' me is also the one that 'enables' me to speak of this experience (Butler, 1997a, p. 163). However, over the course of this chapter and the next, I want to probe this conceptualisation of the speech act, via what might be thought of as a speculative, phenomenological investigation of the performative power of diagnostic speech on the body of the disabled child, which is informed by the narrative I have pieced together of my own unknowable lived experience of diagnosis.

Can a parallel be drawn between the kind of speech under discussion in Butler's (1997a) book – injurious speech – and the diagnostic speech act? Diagnosis, as sociologists of this subject attest, can perform a range of functions, some of which are experienced as helpful or even emancipatory by the patient. By juxtaposing diagnostic speech and injurious speech, I am seeking to defamiliarise a routine part of the medical encounter, to ask that we look afresh at it, and to ask, *what is it like* – and especially, what is it like if one cannot understand it rationally, in words? I am also drawing attention to the way in which we might think of diagnosis as a practice of naming, and thus as an activity that evokes and reproduces a particular history:

The name has, thus, a *historicity*, what might be understood as the history which has become internal to a name, has come to constitute the contemporary meaning of a name: the sedimentation of its usages as they have become part of the very name, a sedimentation, a repetition that congeals, that gives the name its force.

(Butler, 1997a, p. 36, emphasis in original)

In my own history, the naming of my impairment as 'cerebral palsy' has stood out as something indigestible. Diagnosis, here, is a form of citation, to use Butler's term, in that the utterance cannot help but join with, and be made meaningful by, a field of previous utterances. In the context of racist speech, Butler describes citation thus: 'only because we already know its force from its prior instances do we know it to be so offensive now, and we brace ourselves against its future invocations' (p. 80). The term 'cerebral palsy' is given force by its prior instances, by its historicity, and in this sense it performs something when it is used for the first time to describe another individual.

I now intend to probe a little further into Butler's characterisation of the act of naming, which, she claims, does not necessarily 'fix or paralyze' a subject, in spite of appearances (1997a, p. 2). How can we be sure that a speech act does not 'fix or paralyze' a subject? From where do we obtain the capacity to use terms 'against [their] originary purposes' (p. 14)? What if the speech act is delivered in a moment prior to the subject's coming into language – what if it is indeed her inauguration into language, but that in constituting her, it also *unmakes* her? What if the founding speech act, the speech act that interpellated me as a subject, was also one which *interrupted* my being? What if the pre-verbal child can make neither head nor tail of the inaugurating speech act, which only makes itself known in its 'belatedness', through 'repetitive phenomena' (Caruth, 1995, p. 89)?

I am especially interested in Butler's choice of the term, 'paralyze', given its connotations of impairment. In choosing such a term, but in suggesting that it is *not* in fact sufficient to encompass the effects of the injurious speech act, Butler frames language as a tool that enables as much as it disables, and which, moreover, mobilises – rather than immobilising – the subject. Yet – by the logic of Butler's own argument – the very deployment of the terms 'fix' and 'paralyze', which cannot fail but to conjure the disabled body, also fails to *dispel* the disabled body from the mind of the reader purely by conjuring it in the negative. It stays there. Indeed, the body and physicality are very much present in *Excitable Speech*, in spite of the fact that it is often regarded as a text about performativity as a property of discourse. Drawing on Shoshana Felman's work, Butler pauses, in the first chapter, on the incongruous relationship between the body and its speech; here the body comes to stand for 'unknowingness precisely because its actions are never fully consciously directed or volitional' (1997a, p. 10).[9] Somehow, this image reminds me of cerebral palsy – of the body that jerks and wobbles, and for which there is a disconnect between the neural messages and the muscular activity.

Metaphors of (im)mobility, circulation, life and death persist throughout *Excitable Speech*, almost as if the 'speech' under discussion is a homeostatic organism, regulating itself so that every movement in one direction is matched by a symmetrical one in the other direction. A threat of death is also an incitement to life; the wounding effects of hate speech cannot be simply immobilised via censorship, pedagogy or legal proceedings, because such proceedings require that the language be revived and reiterated and '[t]here is no way to invoke examples of racist speech, for instance, in the classroom without invoking the sensibility of racism, the trauma and for some, the excitement' (Butler, 1997a, p. 37). We may be reminded of the language of the circle and of reciprocity invoked by Derrida (1992) to speak of 'economy'. And yet, the images of circuits and of movement, however, are not permitted to proliferate endlessly in Butler's text. They encounter blockages. For example, they seem to come to a stop in and through the name: 'the name carries within itself the movement of a history that it arrests' (Butler, 1997a, p. 36). Here Butler overtly references Foucault's discussion of power as an *arresting* force (as well as one that derives its force from movement),[10] but it is surely also significant that this discussion takes place within the context of a section on Althusser's (1971) policeman who interpellates the subject. Furthermore, as we have seen, the name is associated with 'sedimentation' – a term with connotations of layering, laying down, of the static. The pronouncing of the infant as 'well-attached' or 'shy' or 'handicapped' or 'as a gift' fixes that child's commodity value. Named as the unasked-for gift, the disabled child is rhetorically positioned as beyond the reach of linguistic and monetary economies, as if this would exempt her stock from commodification, and yet this proves impossible, as we have seen. To be associated with the gift is to be weighed down in another way; it is to be simultaneously 'liberated' from economy's movement whilst being painfully inside of it and aware of it. Although I hesitate to make a case for where emphasis lies in *Excitable Speech*, a text whose function is to describe performativity at work, I cautiously suggest that tropes of mobility and agility are inflected with optimism, while tropes of stasis are associated with a model of subject formation (Althusser's) that is seen as problematically unidirectional, and, paradoxically, stasis is shown always to give way to mobility again – it is impermanent. Stasis is homeostasis – it might seem *like* stasis,[11] but movement is taking place to maintain this stillness. Where does this leave us in terms of disability politics?

Whilst I find Butler's (1997a, p. 163) argument about the 'redeployment' of '[t]he word that wounds' in the service of 'resistance' highly persuasive, does it work for thinking through the experience of being diagnosed with a disability in early childhood? I want to move into a more phenomenological mode now, as I think through the implications of this model with the pre-linguistic child's diagnostic scene in mind. Butler speaks briefly about what it might mean to be 'named without knowing that one is named' (pp. 30–31), which, she notes, is 'the condition of all of us at the beginning' (p. 31). As she observes, '[o]ne need not know about or register a way of being constituted for that constitution to work in an efficacious way' (p. 31). Yet what if one does not know, consciously, that one is named, but one nevertheless knows this pre-consciously, affectively? I want to suggest that that the 'injurious' diagnostic speech act that is delivered upon the pre-verbal child can indeed 'paralyze' that emergent subject: its effects play themselves out across and through the body in wordless affect. I do not think this hypothesis is necessarily at odds with Butler's argument in *Excitable Speech*, which recognises the capacity of the name to operate via 'an encoded memory or a trauma' (p. 36). She notes:

> The force of the name depends not only on iterability, but on a form of repetition that is linked to trauma, on what is, strictly speaking, not remembered, but relived, and relived in and through the linguistic substitution for the traumatic event.

> (Butler, 1997a, p. 36)

Here, as in Caruth's (1995) analogy, it is the connection between trauma and the belatedness of language, or its incongruity, that intensifies the power of the name. We might also say that the name of *the gift* functions as a linguistic substitution for the loss associated with diagnosis. I will be returning to these ideas in more detail in Chapter 4, in the context of a discussion of the relationship between pre-verbal trauma and language; before that, I want to think further about the question of how exactly diagnostic language signifies for the pre-verbal child, if not symbolically.

It could be argued that the infant is in some ways more susceptible to injury by language than the verbal subject – or at any rate, susceptible in a different way. As Brennan notes, there is a physical aspect to words – to 'the quavering notes of language' – and it is the physicality of language which affects the pre-conscious baby (2004, p. 32). Julia Kristeva's term, 'the semiotic' (1984, p. 24), can also be invoked here to conceptualise the baby's experience of language: the semiotic is the 'psychosomatic modality of the signifying process' (p. 28). It refers to the sensual, rather than the symbolic properties of language. If '[f]reedom from the affects means freedom for the feelings to be known to consciousness' (Brennan, 2004, p. 139), then the baby who lacks the apparatus for making something known to consciousness also lacks the capacity to free herself from the affects of the speech acts that take place around her. Brennan notes that through processes such as psychoanalysis, '[l]anguage releases us from the affects [...] via words that express something occluded and thereby releases the energy deployed in this occlusion' (p. 140). To the baby, however, the speech act is *only* affect. Through the process of projective identification – one of the processes that transmits affect intersubjectively – the baby may come to harbour, in her body, the very 'energy' to which Brennan refers. Is there a contradiction here, in that I am suggesting that the child is at once the site of projected, affective energy and is also potentially 'paralyze[d]', in Butler's (1997a, p. 2) terms, by the diagnostic speech act? In this case, the paralysis and the energy coexist: the paralysis is a state of *trapped* energy – energy that cannot be released in words, in a speech act that would 'counter the offensive call' (Butler, 1997a, p. 2). This energy may then be employed (unconsciously) by the subject to enforce the paralysing effects of the injurious speech act, in an act of 'introjection of the aggressor' (1999, p. 299), to use Ferenczi's terms, which shall be revisited shortly.

***

Yes, it's true, I was partially paralysed once, in the moment of my birth. This diagnostic speech act paralyses me twice!

***

Thus far I have argued that the diagnostic speech act can have paralysing effects, but I would go further, to suggest that it performs an *unmaking* of the emergent subject in the moment of its pronouncement. By unmaking, I mean that the words of the diagnosis cut through, and cut into, the child's experience of herself. It is an interruption. Here diagnosis enacts its etymology. Diagnosis makes the child 'Other' in the eyes of those who see her, and in this sense it unmakes her. Once again, for the pre-linguistic child, this experience of unmaking, of becoming Other to oneself can only be understood in bodily terms. In Chapter 1, we encountered the disabled child becoming Other to herself through a phenomenology of the gaze and its alienating potential – in Sartre's 'The Look' (2003). Here I want to think further about diagnosis as an act that brings about alienation for the pre-verbal infant. I theorise diagnosis – in these circumstances – as an interpellation of the subject into an embodiment that cannot be borne.

In the process of theorising my present-day suffering as a repetition of something from early childhood that could not be experienced except belatedly, I began to read Frantz Fanon's (1986) *Black Skin, White Masks*. I was utterly gripped by Fanon's phenomenology of internalised racism in 'The Fact of Blackness' (pp. 109–140). This essay remains, for me, peerless in the searing precision of its juxtaposition of an 'intellectual understanding' of racism on the one hand, and the phenomenology of *how racism feels* as an already-internalised structure of oppression that is awakened through the black man's encounter with 'the white man's eyes' (p. 110). Given that my own focus is on a different form of marginalised embodiment, my reference to this work is not unproblematic: I do not want to suggest that one kind of oppression is analogous with another; to do so is to risk losing something of the specificity of each. Furthermore, it troubles me that in putting these figures (the black man, the pre-verbal (white?) disabled child) alongside each other I might seem to be infantilising the black man, repeating the very Othering that Fanon describes. And yet, I cannot get away from the fact that when I read this essay I identify profoundly with it; it speaks to me. Its valency for thinking through the shock of the diagnostic speech act arises, I think, from its focus on the relational encounter, on the violence experienced in the moment of being named as a 'Negro' and interpellated as the black subject (p. 111). As in Butler's (1997a) account, to be named is to be hailed within the terms of a particular set of fantasies and imagined histories of blackness; interestingly Fanon uses a word that Butler also emphasises – he refers to 'legends, stories, history, and above all *historicity*' (1986, p. 112, emphasis in original). Further, it is intriguing that for Fanon, the interpellation disrupts a physical experience of himself: '[i]n the white world, the man of color encounters difficulties in the development of his bodily schema' (p. 110); '[...] assailed at various points, the corporeal schema crumbled, its place taken by a racial epidermal schema' (p. 112). Here Fanon is surely drawing on the rich tradition of phenomenological thinking about 'the bodily schema' (which includes the work of Sartre), to explain how the black man's experience of his bodily being in the world fragments via the objectification of the racist gaze, which places all of its attention and expectation at the level of skin. The language of racial Othering enacts a certain kind of violence on the body, evidencing the performative properties of language.

It is fascinating to me that Fanon describes this experience of how racism feels in terms of the *debilitation* of the body. Disability enters the frame:

> On that day, completely dislocated, unable to be abroad with the other, the white man, who unmercifully imprisoned me, I took myself far off from my own presence, far indeed, and made myself an object. What else could it be for me but an amputation, an excision, a hemorrhage that spattered my whole body with black blood? But I did not want this revision, this thematization.
>
> (Fanon, 1986, p. 112)

This is the language of dissection, of losing a limb, of losing an organ: it is the body in deficit, the disabled body figured as loss, negativity and deprivation of agency. It is notable that both Butler and Fanon have recourse to metaphors of disability as they seek to describe the performativity of injurious language. Yet I think it is valid to ask how far we should think of Fanon's language as metaphor. Of course, at one level it is – and it is significant that the disabled body is invoked as analogy – but at another level, he is describing a phenomenological experience of *physical debilitation* transmitted via the word (and the gaze) that is reminiscent of the 'transmission of affect' (Brennan, 2004, p. 1). Fanon is also making reference to an act of reification of the self ('made myself an object'), in response to injurious speech. (Nor do I think that Butler is uninterested in the 'violence' of language conceived in these terms, as we shall see shortly).

Fanon's (1986) use of the imagery of disability for exploring the phenomenology of racism itself suggests that, whilst we must continue to remain sensitive to difference, there may be scope for exploring parallels with the diagnostic scene. Furthermore, like Fanon, my use of the disabled body in this context is arguably somewhere between the figurative and literal; I am talking about the nature of an embodied unmaking that the undigested diagnostic speech act performs, in pronouncing disability. In that moment, were my body and my identity wrested from me, subjected to a 'revision' that was also an 'amputation' (p. 112), to use Fanon's terms? Fanon writes that '[his] body was given back to [him] sprawled out, distorted, recolored, clad in mourning in that white winter day' (p. 113). Did I undergo a similar experience of having my body 'given back to me [...] distorted' on that day? Did I suddenly feel myself to have been cast out as different, as the object of medical scrutiny? And yet, how can a pre-verbal child feel these things in these terms, without language to symbolise them? How do these words affect – formulate, regulate, give order to – the phenomenology of the impairment itself? Fanon's essay provides a compelling set of images with which to begin to theorise these experiences, which, as pre-verbal ones, I can never access directly. The question of whether the injurious call can be countered is unresolved in Fanon's essay, although the conclusion of *Black Skin, White Masks* is a rallying cry, urging its readers to step outside of oppression and to embrace freedom. For my part, I turn to the question of resistance in Chapter 4. For now, having explored the illocutionary aspects of the diagnostic speech act – its capacity to paralyse and to unmake – I turn now to its perlocutionary effects (Austin, 1975). The reader will recall that whilst an illocutionary speech act makes something happen in the moment of speaking; with perlocutionary speech, certain deeds result from it. What comes about as a result of diagnosis? If the emerging subject is unmade by the speech act, is it also 'remade'? And if so, how, and by whom?

Un/re-making the subject

'Remake thyself!'

Did the doctor then speak of the programme of rehabilitation through which I could begin to approximate the 'norm' of other children?

'Harriet will need to have weekly physiotherapy to learn to use the muscles in her left arm and leg. The more she uses her left side, the more the neural pathways in her brain will develop. She'll need to practise the physiotherapy exercises every day at home: the more the better!'.

The contents of my future, and its discontents, spelt out. My future as a programme. My future envisioned as a time of being measured, and of trying to measure up. Will I ever manage the task in hand? How can I take this task in hand, into my hands, and throw it back to the Other, say that it is unwanted? My hands are tied, it seems. Did my hands feel literally tied, when they were manipulated by the physiotherapist?

***

For Toni Morrison, language is something which is 'in [our] hands' (1993, n. p.). The text of Morrison's (1993) Nobel Prize acceptance speech, to which Butler (1997a) refers, tells the folkloric story of some children who attempt to trick an elderly wise woman, who is blind, by asking her whether the bird they hold in their hands is alive or dead. The woman replies that she does not know, but that it is 'in [their] hands' (Morrison, 1993, n. p.). Morrison reads the bird as a metaphor for language, which is 'in [our] hands' to the extent that language is 'an act with consequences' (n. p.). It is a parable about the 'violence of representation' (n. p.). This is demonstrated by the blind woman's refusal to make a choice – an act which, Butler argues (1997a, p. 8, quoting Morrison, 1993, n. p.), 'calls attention to "the instrument through which power is exercised," establishing that the choice is in the hands of the interlocutors she cannot see'. In a sense, this is a story about refusing to diagnose – and about choosing instead to highlight the consequences involved in delivering that diagnostic speech act. It is interesting that, with this tale, we are back with metaphors of embodiment, as if there is an inevitability about the entwinement of the body and language. The blind woman, whom Morrison reads as a practised writer, cannot see but is shown to have a depth of insight – a trope that is quite commonly associated with blindness in literature and mythology (Hass, 2011). Meanwhile the children, who fail to humiliate the woman because of her ability to reframe the issue, are, as far as we know, able-bodied children with two hands. Responsibility in language is figured as something that is 'in our hands'; it is left in the children's hands via the woman's *refusal to engage with the issue on the terms in which it is posed*. In this example, then, the ability to 'counter the offensive call' is drawn from an ability to analyse the very terms of that call. But what happens when the emergent subject does not have such an apparatus? In the case of my own writing above: how does the doctor's speech act, detailing what my future holds, come to be felt as an (impossible) task that is in my hands, as the child? How does this peculiar act of translation occur? How is it that, instead of seeing the doctor's language as an act with consequences, the child comes to feel somehow that she is taking the consequences of his words into her own hands, becoming responsible for her own ability (or inability) to approximate the norm?

The figure of holding something 'in our hands' also takes us into the realm of the gift, which has woven its way through this chapter. Etymologically the term 'present' connects with an idea of *placing* something in front of someone (Oxford English Dictionary, 2019);[12] the idea of *placing* evokes gift-giving as a simultaneously temporal and *spatial* act, as well as referencing the movement of the object from the one person to another. The bird is not being offered to the woman, it is a parody of the gift in that it is placed before her in order to mock her. Partly because of the woman's response, the bird never actually leaves the hands of the children, she does not allow herself to become indebted to them, by taking it. By contrast, in my personal writing, attention is drawn to the transfer into my hands of the task of rehabilitation, which could be seen, in Derrida's terms, as the 'poisonous' gift, which 'amounts to hurting' by creating a debt (1992, p. 12). I cannot 'throw it back' to the Other as 'unwanted' because it has already been internalised by me as 'good' (rehabilitation is good, it is doing me good, I am indebted to those who are doing me this good). Is rehabilitation in early childhood a manifestation of the gift that must stubbornly proclaim its gift-status?

***

My powerlessness to resist the programme is unbearable. If I too coerce myself, I have the power to decide how I am measuring up. I too shall want this kind of future for myself – one in which I am going to become like you. I shall shed the skin of the present, the loving, gentle, present that is just about itself and nothing more. That is for other children, but not for me. If I try hard enough, I can believe that it is not because I have been cast out, but because I am special, that the present is not for me. The present is not a present – a gift – it is a distraction, which makes other children less focussed than me. I am focussed, I am productive, I have a goal. Look at them, as they play! They really believe that it is just fine to relax into that present, to grasp it in both hands. I am being taught to grasp things with both hands – rather than one: that is why I don't get to play like they do.[13] But I know better than those children do. I am grown up before my time. Before my time? As though I had a time, in the future, that would have been MY time? What a strange thought – my time. I grew up before it, I grew up before my time could get to me, before I could have it but before I could lose it, before you could take it from me. How does playing teach us to be productive? I shall not mourn. I shall not feel.

***

Here, it is as if I, the child, am seeing through the gift as it masquerades before me. I see that it takes time, even if the other children do not. Rehabilitative futurism undoes the gift, reveals the demand made by 'the future' on time, even as it seems to give time.

One of the features that emerges in the passage of imaginative writing above is the child's sense of superiority over other children who value playing. Here she enacts what the psychoanalyst Ferenczi calls *'precocious maturity'*, which he compares to the 'precocious maturity of the fruit that was injured by a bird or insect' (1999, p. 301, emphasis in original). Rather than being able to grieve the loss of playtime, the rehabilitated child experiences the desire of the Other – the wish to be rehabilitated – as her own desire. This might be understood as a form of Ferenczian 'introjection of the aggressor' (p. 299). The child identifies herself entirely with the 'adult' values of work, productivity and deferred gratification. The futurist agenda is taken up as *her* agenda. In this sense, then, the diagnosed child becomes an active participant – perhaps *the* most active participant – in her own rehabilitation. Her remaking in the terms of the dominant order is not something she experiences consciously as something that is 'done to' her, rather she willingly remakes herself in the image of the Other. This subject experiences herself as *one and the same* with the one who makes the demands (1999). Yet strangely this personal writing undoes the very oneness and sameness that it is alluding to: there is something odd about the narrator's insight into a state that, in order to have existed, could not have been known. Is there a parallel here with Derrida's impossible gift, which simultaneously must be recognised as such, and *cannot* be recognised as such? The knowledge of a programmatic future, daunting and weighing down the present, is what deprives the gift of its present-ness. Yet the disabled child in this writing is also signalling the present's taking of time from all children with her apparently rhetorical question, laced with condescension, about how playing teaches us to be productive. Is this a rhetorical question? Whilst it might *seem* as though it is only the disabled child whose future is determined by her present productivity – and whilst it might *seem* as though contemporary middle-class modes of parenting give the child a childhood that is entirely for playing – in fact, as we saw in Chapter 2, 'play' is, ironically, what the child does to develop and is thus the child's work. Play, too, reproduces Capital.

To conclude these reflections on the internalisation of the remaking-agenda, if the Other's injurious speech act – the imperative to 'remake thyself!' – is in fact experienced not as issuing from the *Other* but *from the self*, how can that self even begin the process of attempting to 'counter the offensive call'? In order to wish to 'counter the offensive call', *there must first be an offended self.* In Chapter 4, I will seek to grasp hold of this offended self. I complicate the notion of rehabilitation as a form of 'remaking' by suggesting that it is only for the rational adult that it is such – for the child, the term 'unmaking' is more apt. Before turning to the question of how to resist being unmade, I will seek to draw together the disparate strands of this chapter with some thoughts on the fraught status of time in non/disabled childhoods.

Conclusion: Making childhood time productive

During the process of writing this chapter, I was working one day in a café and I found myself watching a grandmother playing peek-a-boo with a baby in a pram. It seemed to me like the ultimate moment of unproductive time, a moment in which both people were existing in the present, for the present. The game had no purpose except to be a game. There was nothing futural about it. Mightn't we expand Wright's aphorism about the Winnicottian good-enough mother who provides 'a space free from intrusions' for the baby (1991, p. 35), to think also in terms of a *time* free from intrusions? But, we might ask, informed by the gift's impossibility (Derrida, 1992) and by the queer negativity of maternal time (Baraitser, 2012a): isn't this 'free' time an illusion within the logic of the circle of economy, in which every act of giving demands reciprocity, and every moment of time must be put to good use? Rehabilitative activity might be disguised as a game in the present, but is its purpose ever to be *about* the present? And yet, although I do want to argue for the specificity of rehabilitative time, I am also arguing that it tells us something about time in the life of children more generally.

The idea of something being *about* the present, or *for* the present, is shattered in the moment of diagnosis and in the effort to reclaim the child for reproductive futurism. The diagnosis is heavy with foreboding, but there is one way to ease the uncertainty that has become attached to the idea of the future: rehabilitation. Suddenly, there is not a moment to lose: rehabilitation needs to start now, in order that the child does not 'lose out' later, or so the logic goes. In my case, it was said that the neural pathways in my brain were open to manipulation while I was young, making it important for me to do as much physiotherapy as possible at an early age, in order to maximise my physical development – to make me as 'able' as possible, in physical (medical) terms. It was a race against the clock. I was put to work on my body in order to guarantee a certain kind of future for me, but a future decided by doctors and parents. The time of the present, and the labour and suffering of the present, was unimportant, was unrecognised, because it was helping me to have a 'bright future' and that was all that mattered. The present was, in this way, *evacuated of meaning.*

The diagnosis of a disability, with its futural but uncertain mood exemplified by the anxiety of the 'might'/'might not' dichotomy, fragments and disperses the 'unqualified time' of mother and baby (Baraitser, 2012a, p. 235). Yet, as Baraitser notes, such temporality is itself is an impossibility: 'in capitalist terms, *motherhood simply takes too long*' (p. 235, emphasis in original). For the small child whose time has been taken over by rehabilitative futurism, the concept of the present becomes unmoored from any association with 'unqualified time' – she sees through unqualified time's mask. Present time that presents itself simply as such – to be enjoyed in itself, for itself – is an illusion. It is not Mauss' gift, giving time, except in the sense of the shrouded demand it makes on time (*taking* time), to which Derrida (1992) points. As I think of the small child – myself – performing physiotherapy exercises in the studio for the Other, being rehabilitated for the Other, giving my time to the Other, I am reminded of Marx's figure of the labourer working for the capitalist factory owner, a figure who owns neither his time nor his skills, who is alienated from both. As in Chapter 2, I am drawn to making comparisons between the child who rehabilitates herself, and the child labourer. But we should not exclude the child who plays, since she too is making childhood time productive as she enacts social reproduction – it is in appearance only that she is *given time*. For Marx, the labourer's enjoyment of his own time could only be understood as what Friedrich Engels (1893, n. p.) called 'false consciousness' – as a trick. The child who undergoes rehabilitation is – in the scene of my personal writing – the one who sees that the playing child is a dupe (Blackman and Walkerdine, 2001), as she (the self-rehabilitating child) attempts to erase her own traumatic loss of the present through the mastery of exposing the Other's naïveté.

In highlighting the closeness of the two alienated figures – the factory worker and the child who labours to make her body like that of the Other – I have sought to bring my argument full circle: I have returned to where I began the chapter, with Marx. When I read the following description of the worker's experience of labour under capitalism, it resonated with my childhood experience of the 'hard labour' of physiotherapy:

> [...] [all means for the development of production] [...] distort the worker into a fragment of a man, they degrade him to the level of an appendage of a machine, they destroy the actual content of his labour by turning it into a torment; they alienate [...] from him the intellectual potentialities of the labour process [...]; they deform the conditions under which he works, subject him during the labour process to a despotism the more hateful for its meanness; they transform his life-time into working-time, and drag his wife and child beneath the wheels of the juggernaut of capital.
>
> (Marx, 1976, p. 799)

The experience of physiotherapy alienated me from my body in the sense that I was instructed to use two hands to perform tasks that I could perform perfectly well with one hand; I became an 'appendage' to the 'machine' of rehabilitation. Just as the labourer is alienated from the 'intellectual potentialities' of his work, so the larger project of rehabilitation was beyond my comprehension as a small child. Certainly, my 'life-time' was transformed into 'working-time'.

In drawing a parallel between the alienated labourer and the disabled child undergoing rehabilitative therapy, I am not suggesting that the disabled child is unique in her alienation, but rather that she bears the weight of alienation on behalf of society, in a way that resonates with Edelman's polemic about the figure of the queer. Earlier in the chapter I argued that it is the disruptive body of the disabled child that both unmasks the commodification of *all* children and draws attention to human mortality. I suggested that in conceptualising the child as a gift, as something we accept without question, we disavow the power of reification. I have proposed that the 'hard labour' of rehabilitation both *deprives* the disabled child of an open future and yet makes the child's life *only* about the future. The disabled child is doubly disruptive: on the one hand she brings death and fragility to mind; on the other, she shows us commodification in places we would rather not see it. She is made to bear the full weight of the futurist project upon her shoulders as she is brought 'in line' with the dominant order through a programme of rehabilitation (Ahmed, 2006, p. 15). If, as Derrida (1992, p. 35) argues, there is 'madness' in insisting on distinguishing the gift from other operations of exchange by mistakenly referencing the *singularity* of the gift's giving of time, then we should be wary of the rhetoric of the disabled child as gift. The gift can never escape being contaminated by the connotations of contractual relations. What manner of loss is being covered over by the *idea* of the gift? The arrival of the disabled child puts us in contact with the madness that is needed to keep this unstable notion of the gift intact, by drawing attention to the ways in which her time is *given over* to rehabilitation; she is the gift that demands and takes time rather than giving it. She also fails to be the desired-thing, which in a curious way aligns her with the gift (the gift as surprise, as unchosen), even as it makes it impossible for her to be the gift (which must be desired and yet simultaneously forgotten). The (non-disabled) child for whom the mother waits (Baraitser, 2012a), gives time in the sense of being an investment for the future, thereby highlighting the fundamental imbrication of social relations and economic relations. In a certain sense, then, every child is being prepared for a future in which time is given over to the Other, because of the sense in which social reproduction is also the reproduction of Capital. And if I seem to be ending here on a pessimistic note without promise of agency, I invite the reader to turn to Chapter 4, in which the question of resistance will take centre stage. How does the disabled child come to find her voice, in spite – or perhaps *because* – of the injurious speech act which has become lodged in her body?

Notes

1   Lesnik-Oberstein (2008, p. 81) cites two books in particular to highlight a cultural focus on the child as commodity, offering the following bibliographic details: Greer, G. (2003) 'Afterword', in Haynes, J. and Miller, J. (eds) *Inconceivable Conceptions: Psychological Aspects of Infertility and Reproductive Technology*, Hove, Brunner-Routledge, pp. 207–216 and Wolf, N. (2001) *Misconceptions: Truth, Lies and the Unexpected on the Journey to Motherhood*, New York, Anchor (2003).

2　A phenomenological approach will emerge in the later stages of this chapter and will feature in Chapter 4 of the book. As Diprose (1994) suggests here, the insights of phenomenology help to problematise the hegemony of the notion of body as possession, enabling a reconceptualisation of the body as something we inhabit, or indeed as something that is part of a larger whole.

3　Derrida cites Mauss, M. (1990) *The Gift: The Form and Reason for Exchange in Archaic Societies* (trans. W. Halls), London, Routledge.

4　This term is the title of Berlant's book.

5　The term 'attachment parenting' was coined by the authors of the book cited here – (see Sears and Sears, 2001).

6　Baraitser is citing Freeman, E. (2010) *Time Binds: Queer Temporalities, Queer Histories*, Durham, NC, Duke University Press, which introduces the term 'chrononormativity' on p. xxii.

7　These terms all appear in the titles of the articles mentioned, and are key terms for each author's argument.

8　'diagnosis, *n.*' in the Oxford English Dictionary (2019).

9　Butler cites Felman, S. (1983 [1980]), *The Literary Speech Act: Don Juan with J. L. Austin, or Seduction in Two Languages* (trans C. Porter), Ithaca, NY, Cornell University Press.

10　Butler cites Foucault's *History of Sexuality*, p. 93 – Foucault, M. (1981 [1976]) *The History of Sexuality, Vol. 1*, London, Pelican.

11　The Greek term *homo* from which *homeo-* derives means 'of the same kind, like' (Oxford English Dictionary, 2019).

12　'present, n1': The etymological discussion (Oxford English Dictionary, 2019) refers to classical Latin terms, as follows: '*in rē praesentī* on the spot, *in rem praesentem* into the place itself, to the very spot'.

13　Micheline Mason's (1992, p. 27) poignant rhetoric on this theme chimes with my writing here – she writes: 'Other children play, but you do "therapy". Other children develop, but you are "trained"'. My own creative piece was written a long time after reading Mason's essay, and I did not consciously draw on these words, but they suggest that my experience is shared by others who have grown up governed by a medical model of disability.

4   Making, unmaking, remaking?
Finding a position from which to resist

There is no place for doubt in the rehabilitative regime, but not because there is none. Doubt is literally everywhere. Moving across the physiotherapy studio, carefully treading the path of insoles laid out before me, I know that there must be certainty about this course I tread.

The physiotherapist, after all, exudes certainty.

In her stride, in her stockiness, in her stance, her two feet so firmly on the ground in those trainers.

She isn't the type to fall over.

Unlike me.

A little child who feels so unsteady, who is not ready for balancing on one foot ... I am wobbly.[1]

Her voice confirms it. She is telling me again to try to stand for longer on one foot, not to put out my arm for support, that I can do it if I would only try. But I am wobbly. I am so wobbly and she doesn't see! She keeps on telling me. She won't let me stop. If only I could be the one with the two feet planted firmly on the ground, in the grown-up's shoes, standing at the side with that certainty.

I can't know it with my mind, but what I know with my body is this: as I wobble across the room, I am hoovering up all the doubt that can't be kept inside her.

I wobble because I'm wobbly.

Physically unsure of myself. But there's another dimension to the uncertainty in this room too. There's no place for 'wobbly' in her body. Wobbliness sticks perfectly to my body though.[2] Perfectly.

***

Towards the end of Chapter 3, I posed a challenge: how can the 'rehabilitated' child subject 'counter the offensive call' (Butler, 1997a, p. 2)? What does resistance look like in this context? This is the question I take up here, via a focus on the wobbly body of the child in the space of the physiotherapy setting. The narrative of this chapter will take me both beyond that space and back into it, as I pose three questions. Firstly, I ask: how did I become that wobbly body? In this part of the chapter I am focussed, in temporal terms, on my early childhood. I then turn to the question of how I stopped being – and dissociated from – that wobbly body, rescuing myself from the space of so-called 'rehabilitation'. This discussion relates in temporal terms to my recent past. In the final part of the chapter, I ask: what happened when I later returned to the wobbly body of my childhood, and what did I gain and lose in so doing? I associate this part of the narrative with a contemporary self that has emerged in and through psychoanalysis. I align the journey associated with the first question with a process of 'unmaking', the second question with a process of 'remaking' and the third question with a process that I call 're-unmaking'. In the context of the third question and the idea of 're-unmaking', I return to the unanswered question from Chapter 3 about resisting internalised oppression.

When I began work on the final chapter of this project, I was certain that the chapter would be dealing with the notion of 'remaking'. In contrast with earlier chapters, which had been preoccupied with the ways in which the child is 'made' through psychosocial, discursive, ideological and economic structures, the last chapter would focus on the more *literal and physical acts of making* that shape the body of the disabled child. It would examine rehabilitative therapies and surgery, exploring how it feels to be physically 'remade'. Rehabilitation has been subject to some, although not a huge amount of, critical attention within the disability studies community (see, for example, Abberley, 1995; Oliver, 1993). Recently, rehabilitative norms have started to come under scrutiny from health professionals who consider themselves to be part of a sub-discipline of 'critical rehabilitation studies' (Critical Physiotherapy Network, 2019; Gibson, 2015). Engaging with some of the questions raised by this sub-discipline, I had planned that the chapter would consider how we, as disabled subjects, reclaim the 'making' process that has had so much to say about us but, very often, without our input (see Oliver, 1993) – especially if we have been disabled since birth and were 'rehabilitated' as children. *Remaking* seemed the appropriate metaphor, at the time of planning: it seemed to describe both the medical practice of rehabilitation and, potentially, my acts of resistance too. My creative process has shown me that this overly neat parallelism – this nice little chiasmus whereby medical remaking could be balanced against the remaking of resistance – could in no way express the mess and the pain of the ideas I wanted to grapple with.

Like the physiotherapist in search of symmetry in the body of her hemiplegic patient, I was forcing the chapter into a position that was unnatural for it, and for a long time I was exasperated and I could not understand why my ideas were not flowing. I wanted the two sides of the remaking 'equation' to sit nicely on the seesaw for a photo opportunity, for the snapshot that would show a tidy, ordered final chapter exhibiting all the answers. Of course, I ultimately wanted the seesaw to tip in favour of resistance, so that I could show medical practice that it needed to see what remaking was actually *doing* to its patients. But above all, I wanted this metaphor of 'remaking' to work. And if it wasn't going to work, I would force it!

This chapter *is* about remaking, and it does deal with the issues described above. I could only write it by starting with the notion of remaking. But I had to let the metaphor of remaking go, in order to find out where and how it was applicable, and where and how it was not. It was not, in the end, a very useful metaphor for describing my experience of rehabilitative therapies, nor for exploring how to go about 'counter[ing] the offensive call' (Butler, 1997a, p. 2). But when I let it go and allowed it to surprise me, I found that it was still relevant to the work of the chapter in unexpected ways.

Why 'the wobbly body'?

This chapter is much more concerned than the other three with the phenomenology of rehabilitation and with embodied knowledge. To write it, I required a language to conjure and reflect on bodily, psychic and intersubjective confusion about what 'impairment' was, and where, or in whom, it lodged. Not only this, but I was also seeking to reconstruct pre-verbal 'experience', and draw out connections with my contemporary mode of moving through the world. In the course of the personal writing that gave the chapter its ambivalent relationship with the notion of 'remaking', I alighted on the term 'the wobbly body', which, with its deployment of a word often used by or for children, felt to me as though it captured something of the child's sense of her unsteady physicality in the world, and of her sense that her body was vulnerable in a way that others' bodies were not. As the chapter progresses, the term 'wobbly' comes into contact with the term 'doubt', as I explore the consistency of 'wobbliness' and the question of how it gets laid down in the body, and how it might be transmitted between bodies. 'Wobbliness' will acquire new layers of meaning.

While I was working on the chapter, it came to my attention that the comedian Francesca Martinez, who has cerebral palsy herself, chooses to describe herself as 'wobbly' (2014). Of this term, she notes in her memoir:

> I had spent years accepting other people's definitions of me and doing so had filled me with shame and negativity. All my life I'd hated saying 'I've got cerebral palsy.' And now I realised that I never had to say it again. I was just Francesca and Francesca was wobbly. My neighbour's kids had called me 'wobbly' years ago and I loved it. It was accurate and non-judgemental and *cool.* I hadn't realised that I could *choose* how to view myself.
>
> (Martinez, 2014, p. 224, emphasis in original)

Here, claiming 'wobbly' is associated with a rejection of internalised shame and with a refusal to use stigmatising language about herself. I very much identify with Martinez' desire to find words other than 'cerebral palsy' for describing her embodiment – a term that I too have struggled to use about myself. My own project in this book – and particularly in this chapter – is to make visible my process of finding and claiming a language of my own with which to speak about my body and my experiential knowledge of impairment. Although Martinez' memoir is very different from my book in its approach, and is perhaps more optimistic than I am about the potential for self-determination, I think we both share these goals. Nevertheless, it is important to point out that the work performed by the term 'wobbly body' in this chapter is different from the work 'being wobbly' does in Martinez' memoir. Even if both usages help us to think phenomenologically about a physical impairment called cerebral palsy, Martinez' deployment of the term 'wobbly' is about finding a language that enables her to embrace her embodied self, whereas my usage is about mining the embodied, intersubjective and cultural experience of impairment to think about how it became a site where wobbliness could reside.

Content warning: Being made to doubt

As the paragraphs above suggest, this chapter was written during a period when I was trying to make sense of the form and structure that my anxiety took. Or should I say, to give form and structure to my anxiety? Or perhaps, to dismantle that very form and structure? The chapter seeks to take its reader into the strange and disorienting place where these two questions do not seem to contradict each other – the world of the pre-verbal child and the adult who is attempting to narrativise an unspeakable (wordless) experience. Functioning partly as a testament to the strength of feeling that this process evoked in me, and to my fear that the process would break me, the chapter therefore uses language that some may regard as extreme, or incommensurate with the experience of rehabilitation. In a similar vein, I also refer to a film, Pedro Almodóvar's *The Skin I Live In* (2011), whose difficult themes (rape, surgical experimentation on a human and forced gender reassignment surgery) are made more uncomfortable by the fact that it is hard to decide what the film is 'doing' in its treatment of these issues. *The Skin I Live In* is the kind of text that prompts the questions: why does this film keep unsettling my ethical compass? With whom should I empathise? How should I read this film? What position should I take up? As we shall see, this feeling of doubt mirrors something I want to emphasise about the *(im)positioning* of the pre-verbal child undergoing rehabilitation.

The terms 'unmaking', 'remaking' and 're-unmaking', and my use of them, will be discussed in more detail as the chapter unfolds. My eventual use of the term 'unmaking' to describe the rehabilitative procedures I underwent as a child is potentially controversial given that Elaine Scarry (1985) deploys the same term exclusively in the context of structures of war and torture. This usage raises ethical issues about lexical choices and representation, but it also raises the question of what it means to have an experience as an adult, and what it means to have a similar experience as a pre-verbal child. A procedure that an adult understands as enabling, and as being in the best interests of the child, can be experienced as punishing for the pre-verbal child.

In relation to the appropriate use of language, Scarry writes that 'the words "someone is being tortured" cannot be, and are never, pronounced unless it *is* the case that someone is being tortured' (1985, pp. 9–10, emphasis in original). Torture is a term with a very specific meaning in the context of international law. It is offensive to those who have suffered torture if we deploy it outside of this context. Through language, the child learns that her own suffering is relative, she learns that there are others who suffer more than her, and she is socialised into using signifiers appropriately according to context. But what of the pre-verbal child? What if, for her, a particular bodily sensation (such as hunger) feels terrifying, since she has no control over how, or when, she will be satiated? And what if a sensation continues, or is experienced regularly, and the child is repeatedly made to feel her own impotence in relation to her body (see Klein, 1997b)? How can language be used appropriately to *take account of the child's experience*? When Scarry (1985, p. 49, emphasis in original) writes that '[t]he goal of the torturer is to make the one, the body, emphatically and crushingly *present* by destroying it, and to make the other, the voice, *absent* by destroying it', is it unethical that I identify, in some ways, with the experience of the prisoner described here? I should be clear that I did not usually experience physical pain during physiotherapy. I also, of course, know *now* that those who treated me did not intend to hurt me. But I did not know this then. This suggests to me that the structure of physiotherapy, *as I experienced it as a pre-verbal child*, could indeed be described as a 'structure of unmaking' (Scarry, 1985, p. 20). Indeed, since I *do* identify with the description of the prisoner's experience which Scarry gives, it strikes me as unethical *not* to explore how and why the term 'unmaking' can be morally appropriate in the description of pre-verbal experiences of this kind.

There is a spatial and temporal double-ness, or even a triple-ness to the experience(s) I discuss in this chapter – a triple-ness that can be aligned with the three questions I posed at the start of the chapter, about the time of rehabilitation. Time is, again, my preoccupation here. The experiences I relate are both of the past and simultaneously of the present, in the sense observed by Jacqueline Rose, of childhood's persistence (1984). To understand the past psychoanalytically, one starts with the present. To understand the present psychoanalytically, one goes to the past. At times, past and present are both there at once in my writing, compressed and confused, as they are in my experience. Yet this chapter also investigates a third temporal phase, between the past and the present, a phase of dissociation, of self-protection, of escape from the 'wobbly' body. This might seem odd in one sense, given that I have had this same 'wobbly' body all my life, but it is this very oddness (along with the multiplication of meanings that become attached to the term 'wobbly') that interests me. I contend in this chapter that odd things can happen to an adult body, when odd things (or should I say, normal, procedural things?) have happened to the pre-verbal body. Perhaps a simpler way of saying this is that the personal writing in this chapter relates not only my experience of so-called rehabilitation as I (do not) remember it, but also my experience of *not-remembering* it in psychoanalysis. Repetition functions as its own kind of remembering (Freud, 1958a). My interest here is in the specific bodily resonances of this process in my case. If psychoanalysis is experienced both in terms of its capacity to *re-member me* and yet also, simultaneously, in terms of its capacity to *take me apart*, what are the implications of this for resistance? I hope that my own ambivalent experience of psychoanalysis as the space of re-encountering the wobbly body can offer new ways to imagine the shape of resistance to an oppression that has been internalised inside the body.

In this chapter, I often refer to myself in the third person, as 'the child' or 'the pre-verbal child', finding it easier to speak theoretically in this way. I am aware that this construction might seem to universalise. Although I am speaking about an experience that is unique to me, my hope is that the theoretical work undertaken here will also speak to others. The perception of auto-ethnography as a research method without high status or established credentials (Muncey, 2010) and my own concerns about the academic legitimacy of my project in this chapter have, no doubt, led me to deploy the third person defensively, but I also use the third person angrily, in a strategically essentialist way (Spivak, 1987), as a call for (adult) children who have been 'rehabilitated' in similar ways to mobilise.

Becoming the 'wobbly' body: Towards a psychoanalytic phenomenology of physiotherapy in childhood

As the personal writing at the opening of the chapter suggests, although the body I brought into the physiotherapy studio was (according to a normative, medical model of the body) a 'wobbly' one, this is not the whole story of my body's wobbliness. In this section I seek to tell more of this story, suggesting that there is far more to it than the medical descriptor 'cerebral palsy'.

Knowing oneself to be 'wobbly'

The child knows her body to be wobbly in comparison with those bodies around her. This knowledge is obtained primarily by social interaction, via the look of the Other, which transforms the child's body into a body-for-the-Other (in this case a disabled body), to recapitulate my discussion of Sartre's (2003) work on 'The Look' in Chapter 1. This knowledge is also imparted to the child (although gradually and incrementally) through a frustrating experience of bodily being in the world, in which she begins to discover that the world was not made for people like her (everyone else is rushing around at moments when she needed to go slowly). Nor is the world made for people who use one hand, where others use two. Yet even here, we are discussing 'wobbliness' as a quality within a social context: a physical space in an inhabited world is always also a social space. When Merleau-Ponty (2002) uses the experience of the patient to illuminate intentional movement, it seems that he sometimes neglects to think about the ways in which the physical world with which we interact has been designed to match the intentions of a particular kind of 'normal' body, as Ahmed (2006) has shown. The world is not experienced in the same way by all bodies.[3] We saw this in Chapter 3, in the context of a discussion of Fanon's (1986) exploration of the disintegration of the black man's corporeal schema in the white world.

Indeed, in her famous essay, 'Throwing Like a Girl', Iris Marion Young (1980, p. 141) observes that '[t]he female person who enacts the existence of women in patriarchal society' is compromised in terms of bodily intention by the tension she experiences between subjectivity and objectivity, between existence for herself and existence as a woman in patriarchal society. Young argues that '[f]eminine bodily existence is an *inhibited intentionality*' in that it is perceived as unfeminine to comport oneself with an attitude of physical capability in relation to certain tasks (p. 146, emphasis in original). Interestingly, it is not that the feminine body is actually incapable of the task, but rather that to enact feminine existence is to perform 'hesitancy' (p. 147). Feminine existence requires the 'withholding' of 'motile energy' (p. 147). Is a similar expectation placed on the disabled body? Does the *expectation* of disabled comportment partly produce such comportment? And how does wobbly comportment translate into a specific kind of experience of being in the world? These questions preoccupy me throughout the section.

My personal writing posited a relationship between physical wobbliness and doubt. Later in the chapter I will discuss my contemporary experience of what I call 'proprioceptive doubt', using phenomenology to reflect on its qualities as a bodily ordeal in-the-now, and object relations psychoanalysis to probe further into its relationship with the wobbly body of the past in the physiotherapy studio. For now, I want to stay with the past experience of the wobbly body, but to re-introduce Brennan's (2004, p. 1) notion of the 'transmission of affect', in order to rethink 'wobbliness' as an attribute that might move between people. I also want to problematise the Cartesian dualism inherent in the construction of 'wobbliness' as a quality of body and 'doubt' as a quality of mind. To do this, I draw on Brennan's contention that 'the traffic between the biological and the social is two-way' (p. 25). The notion that 'the social or psychosocial actually gets into the flesh' underpins my argument about doubtful bodies and wobbly minds (p. 25).[4]

Three sources of doubt

The doubt that gets inside the body of the child in physiotherapy might be understood as emanating from three principle sources. I discuss these three sources in turn. In the first place, doubt springs from the physiotherapist's insistence that activities have to be performed in ways that seem counter-intuitive or even impossible to the child. Socks have to be put on with two hands when they could be managed perfectly well with one; the heel of my left foot has to be put down when my involuntary walking action does not involve putting my heel down. Via feedback from the physiotherapist, the child internalises a version of her body that gets everything wrong, that contrasts with her perception of the experience of her body in the world: *to her*, the movements of her body *feel fine*. We might seek to understand this disjuncture in phenomenological terms, via a disturbance of what Thomas Fuchs calls 'the transparency of embodied consciousness' (2005, p. 96). Fuchs (2005) explains that in its role as a perceptual tool, the body is normally experienced as being transparent: our embodied experience of the world comes to us via a lack of conscious awareness of the body itself. How might an experience of being forced to become conscious of the medium for perception alter the subject's relationship with that medium, producing an unusual awareness of the body's mediatory role? The wobbliness of cerebral palsy has been contaminated by wobbliness of another kind: a cerebral doubt about the rightness of doing things in a wobbly way. Although this doubt might indeed be 'cerebral' for an older child, where does this doubt lodge in the pre-verbal child?

The second source of the doubt experienced by the pre-verbal child in the physiotherapy room might be a personal projection on the part of the physiotherapist into the child. In the passage of personal writing, I contrast my own unsteady body with the firm, instructive, confident body of the physiotherapist. In the context of the clinical encounter, Diprose has observed that we need to be able to acknowledge that 'the clinician is a body' (2002, p. 119). Noting that it is often the invisibility of the clinician's body in the consulting room that is problematic, since this body is 'no less in play' than that of the patient (p. 117), she writes:

> [t]he clinical encounter is not just an encounter between a singular body (the patient) and the norms of medical discourse in the form of the ear and the pen of the clinician. The clinician may be an agent of medical discourse and therefore an agent of domination, as Foucault suggests, but he or she is also a body.
>
> (Diprose, 2002, p. 115)

Until recently, few have considered the role and significance of the doctor's body and subjectivity in the consulting room, although new work in the field of medical humanities has begun to address this important issue (for example Winning, 2012). The affect of doubt, whilst not originally belonging to the child, has lodged itself in her body: a convenient space, as a wobbly one, for the location of doubt (see Brennan, 2004). Brennan demonstrates that a process that is often understood as psychosocial (projection and introjection of a feeling) can be 'biological and physical in effect' (p. 3).

The relationship of medical authority to its own doubts should also be considered in terms of its potential impact on my personal experience of doubt. In his surgical memoir, *Complications*, Atul Gawande tells us that there is 'a saying about surgeons', which goes, '"Sometimes wrong; never in doubt"' (2002, p. 15). This saying offers insight into the necessity of disavowing doubt in the service of acting quickly and making decisions that will hopefully save lives. Leader and Corfield (2008) speculate that sometimes doctors enter the profession because of a particular kind of relationship with the idea of mastery. They note that 'Freud thought that the popular childhood game of playing doctor meant repeating in an active way what one had been subjected to' (p. 314). Although Leader and Corfield qualify their claims about why doctors might be drawn to the profession by suggesting that 'few doctors would consciously subscribe to the Freudian idea of all-powerfulness and mastery', they assert that these attributes are nevertheless often present in the medical environment, with the GP perhaps projecting 'omnipotence' onto the figure of the 'consultant' (p. 314).

Meanwhile Balint – who was working on these issues in the 1950s – proposes the notion of the '"doctor's apostolic function"' (2000, p. 215), by which he means that 'every doctor has a vague, but almost unshakably firm, idea of how a patient ought to behave when ill' (p. 216). Drawing on his work with GP discussion groups, Balint concludes that

[i]t was almost as if every doctor had revealed knowledge of what was right and what was wrong for patients to expect and to endure, and further, as if he had a sacred duty to convert to his faith all the ignorant and unbelieving among his patients.

(p. 216)

The language of faith and conversion here is intriguing in relation to a discussion of the self-doubt that – I argue – gets situated in the rehabilitated child. If the physiotherapist is the apostle, the child must come to be converted into a disciple, and must come to view her own understanding of her body as bad and wrong, in contrast with the 'good', 'correct' way of seeing it modelled by the medical professionals (see also Oliver, 1993). According to this paradigm, there is no room for ambiguity: the apostolic doctor maintains a monopoly on certainty, such that whatever doubt is present in the environment about a particular course of action is projected out *into* the body of the child. And doubt there will surely be, since there must inevitably be a great deal of uncertainty about how the effects of the child's impairment will unfold.

As Balint's (2000) work suggests, the medical professional is not the only one seeking to rid himself of doubt in the medical encounter. Balint (2000, p. 25, emphasis in original) posits that the patient approaches the doctor in the first place with *'the request for a name for the illness'* – the patient wants to understand 'what is his illness, the thing that has caused his pains and frightens him?' (p. 24). The doctor–patient relationship that Balint analyses is a dyadic one, structured in terms of the patient's '[o]ffers' and the doctor's '[r]esponses' (p. 21). Both parties are invested in the dispelling of doubt, which can be achieved through the process of diagnosis and, subsequently, through therapy; indeed, Balint notes that '[d]iagnosis has as reassuring an effect on the doctor as on his patient' (p. 41). Yet a different dynamic is in play in the case of the triadic medical encounter of physiotherapist, parent and pre-verbal child. Here it is not the child who is seeking either a name for the symptoms, or therapy for the symptoms. This therapeutic encounter is therapeutic then, not for the child (who had no reason to doubt in the first place), but perhaps for the parent who needs first to alleviate doubt about the child's symptoms and then to believe that the physiotherapist is indeed the apostle who will show the way. In this triad, it is likely that both physiotherapist and parent have (conscious or unconscious) doubt and fear. Some or all of the following questions are likely to be in play between them: what are these symptoms of motor impairment that the child displays? What is to be done about them? Is physiotherapy the best course of action? How will the child respond to the treatment? What will the physiological and psychological impact on the child be? None of these are the child's questions or doubts; they belong to the adults. Yet, as I argued in the previous chapter, for parents who have received a diagnosis of impairment in their child, to be in doubt about the child's future is to be in shock and discomfort.

In this section I have argued that we need to understand the wobbly body of the child in the physiotherapy room as being more than the product of an impairment called cerebral palsy. We need to take into account a process of coming-to-embody-doubt that diagnosis and rehabilitation entail. Although the body is 'made' through the birth trauma, it is also 'made' through physiotherapy: I have been asking how we know what happens when these two very different manifestations of 'making' interact with each other. If the birth trauma re-orients the developmental map in ways that remain mysterious, what kind of reading – interpretation – of the map is physiotherapy? Whilst the term 'rehabilitation' suggests 'remaking', my own reconstructed experience of the affects at play in the rehabilitation room suggests that the term 'unmaking' is actually more apt (also seen in Chapter 3). Physiotherapy is supposed to treat the unsteady body, to make it less wobbly. But what if, by introducing doubt, it makes it more so? What if it redoubles the trauma of the birth injury? In the next section, I take up the metaphor of 'remaking' to describe not the medical rehabilitation process, but the act of self-salvaging that it precipitated in my case. With reference to personal experience, and to another case study – Pedro Almodóvar's 2011 film, *The Skin I Live In* – I take up the second question of the chapter: how did I stop being a wobbly body, rescuing myself from the space of so-called 'rehabilitation'? The idea of skin plays an important role in this self-defence process, so I begin by exploring skin as a literal and metaphorical barrier.

How did I stop being a wobbly body? Self-protection, remaking and scar-resistant skin

In object relations psychoanalysis, the skin is recognised as having an important role in facilitating the infant's experience of containment, since it literally contains the organs of the body and prevents everything from spilling out (Anzieu, 1990, 1989; Bick, 1968). It functions as the boundary between the internal world and the external world. The psychoanalyst Anzieu proposed the notion of the 'Skin Ego' as a means of conceptualising the role of the skin in early object relations (Anzieu, 1989). We need our physical skin to survive, but we also require a metaphorical skin, a capacity to contain and regulate our feelings (Anzieu, 1990). For the pre-verbal child, the two functions can hardly be disentangled, since the containment of sensations (proto-feelings) is primarily performed through the touch, and the holding, of the primary caregiver (Anzieu, 1989). In her paper 'The Experience of Skin in Early Object-Relations', the psychoanalyst Esther Bick proposed the notion of '"second-skin" formation' (1968, p. 484) as a mechanism of self-containment deployed by the infant whose experience of being contained has been inadequate in certain ways. According to Bick, for the new-born infant, 'the parts of the personality are felt to have no binding force amongst themselves' (p. 484) and require an external object that will be capable of holding these parts together. For Bick, 'this containing object is experienced concretely as a skin' but when there are difficulties and the infant's sensations are not fully contained, a '"second skin"' is constructed by the infant as a means of protection (p. 484). In cases where the infant's fragmented self goes consistently uncontained and un-integrated, 'dependence on the object is replaced by a pseudo-independence, by the inappropriate use of certain mental functions, or perhaps innate talents, for the purpose of creating a substitute for this skin container function' (p. 484). This pseudo-independence can manifest itself as what she terms 'verbal muscularity' (p. 486). Later in the chapter I consider the precocious use of language in the terms of Bick's argument.

I suggest that the pre-verbal child subject of physiotherapy might deploy a metaphorical second skin to protect herself from the trauma of the 'unmaking' process. In this part of the chapter I am exploring the qualities and nature of that second skin via a discussion of *The Skin I Live In* (2011), which deploys this idea very literally. As we will see, the process of defensively 'remaking' the self is a many-faceted act, which is simultaneously helpful and problematic, creative and destructive, oppressive and emancipatory. The film helps to articulate some of the complexity of the concept of second skin.

Discomfort and *The Skin I Live In*

As previously noted, in my reading of Almodóvar's *The Skin I Live In* (2011), I will be suggesting, perhaps controversially, that the film's disorientating handling of the disturbing themes of forced gender reassignment surgery resonates with the experience of the disabled child who is forced to undergo rehabilitative physical and surgical procedures in order to remake her body in the image of the 'normal' child. The film also gives me a valuable metaphor for describing my own experience of defensively remaking myself: scar-resistant skin. I want to stress that I am not characterising physiotherapy or other rehabilitative therapies as sadistic *per se*, but rather that I hope to show what they might *feel like* for the child who has no rational understanding of what they are for. Although I am uncomfortable about juxtaposing the events of the film with my own experience, I am interested in the generative quality of this discomfort. Drawing on the insights of Wiegman (2012), I do not want to disown the comparison but rather I think it is worth staying with my investment in writing about *The Skin I Live In* and my more recent desire to distance myself from the text. The latter is related to the changing intensity and status of anxiety (that is, internalised oppression) in my life, which has become less all-consuming partly as a result of the analysis undertaken in this chapter; for this reason I am very attached to the connections made in this chapter, which have been therapeutic for me.

To briefly summarise the key themes and events of the film: it features the sinister Dr Robert Ledgard, a plastic surgeon who is intent on creating a transgenic skin that will be resistant to burns and mosquito bites. This project has come about as a result of Robert's wife's suicide: she takes her own life after being involved in a car accident that left her with horrific burns. Robert has tested the skin he has created on the mysterious Vera, a patient whom he keeps captive in his own home. It emerges towards the end of the film, in a disturbing twist, that Vera used to be a man (Vicente) and was forced to undergo vaginoplasty at the hands of Robert, and to inhabit a 'second skin': Robert has remade his male captive as a woman. This act is apparently undertaken to punish Vicente for raping Robert's psychologically vulnerable daughter Norma, who later takes her own life.

Narrative: Penetrating beneath the skin?

The Skin I Live In is a film that is obsessed with surface and depth, yet whereas we might expect it to deliver a moral message about the dangers of a 'skin-deep' engagement with the world, in fact, depth is equally deplored, associated only with sexual violence (penetration), and not with any sense of empathy or connection. Early in the film, a series of acts of penetration instigated by the character of Zeca seem to trigger the unfolding of narrative in a film which, in other scenes, appears weighted down with a sense of the impossibility and undesirability of change. It is Zeca's unsolicited arrival at Robert's gated country estate that interrupts the stasis: by masquerading as a tiger for carnival season, his menacing presence draws attention to the diegetic and extra-diegetic attempts to minimise the mask's status as mask. Apparently representing the chaos, but also the animation, which ensues from penetrating the mask, Zeca is on the run and wanted for breaking and entering a bank. He catches sight of Vera via the camera system that is rigged up to guard Robert's mysterious captive, and, mistaking her for Robert's dead wife with whom he had an affair, rampages lustily around the house in search of her, bursting into one room after another, having tied the housekeeper Marilia (his mother, and Robert's, we later learn) to a chair and gagged her with a household cloth that we see him stuff into her screaming mouth. Marilia is thus physically restrained in front of the silent surveillance screen, her jaw dropping as she watches Zeca's rape of Vera play itself out before her eyes, which she seems unable to avert. Is she an analogue for the spectator, also positioned as a complicit, yet impotent, voyeur? This image of Marilia seems to pose the question: (how) should we watch this film? As I shall argue, the film continuously refuses a clear answer to this question, or a clear point of identification: in this sense it mirrors the representation of early childhood rehabilitation as disorientation, for which I will argue in this chapter.

This scene of violent entries (culminating with Robert shooting Zeca dead as the latter climaxes on top of Vera), from which the eye of the film camera does not flinch, contrasts dramatically with the slow but pregnant pace and eerie tone of the preceding scenes, in which we see the surgeon Robert precision-engineering his scar resistant skin. There he is seen moving deliberately and carefully around his lab with test tubes of blood, petri dishes and needles; in another scene we discover that he has created a gigantic screen for watching Vera from the adjoining room; her naked, reclining body is overtly objectified for contemplation and visual pleasure (Mulvey, 1975), juxtaposed as it is with the numerous vast artworks of nudes that hang in his bedroom. It appears that Robert wants only to look, and not to touch.[5] Without Zeca to shatter this horrific, but ordered, arrangement, and Marilia to narrate the intertwined fates of Robert and Zeca leading up to the present, would we even have a narrative? Vera appears to exist in the monotonous continuous present of her captivity (see Baraitser, 2017),[6] and Robert in his laboratory, a glass capsule encased deep within a cave. There is a sense of existence as a form of preservation – literally, in the laboratory freezers containing human tissue, and inside the scar-resistant skin that Vera wears – that can persist only as long as its ghastly equilibrium is undisturbed. Zeca's desire pierces the second skin of these enclosed spaces, initiating narrative and a traumatic re-visitation of the past (as does psychoanalysis in the narrative of this chapter).

Where to look, how to be?

We are disturbed from any attempt to *become absorbed* in the film by its constant attacks on the possibility of a settled standpoint from which to view comfortably and to start to build identifications. As we shall see later in the chapter, I argue that the interruption of absorption and flow is an embodied effect of early childhood rehabilitation. Formally, then, the film creates an experience of disruption, disorientation and doubt that mimics the 'unmaking' of rehabilitation. Who is – to use Mulvey's (1975, p. 18) term – 'the spectator's surrogate'? Whereas conventionally, the gaze of the camera and that of the spectator are disavowed to create the illusion of reality (Mulvey, 1975), here the spectator is shamed into self-consciousness as s/he seeks to find a comfortable place from which to observe. The viewer's gaze is constantly staged as complicit, either with the internalised misogyny of the inert Marilia, who frames her own maternal body as an accomplice by invoking the 'insanity' she must be carrying in her 'entrails', or with a (rehabilitative) misogynist male gaze of Robert, marvelling at the flawless female body it has forcibly created. The rehabilitative gaze, like the medical gaze, is usually placed on the side of moral rectitude, of social good, of enablement. What has happened to it here?

The gaze of the spectator who desires Vera's body, as demanded by the aestheticising, scopophilic camera work that luxuriates in her curves and her deep brown, melancholy eyes, soon finds itself disgusted by its identification (however brief) with Robert's perverted gaze, and by implication with his project to 'rehabilitate' the young man who raped his daughter by turning him into an attractive young woman. The film can be read as mocking the straight male desiring gaze, by confronting it with the knowledge that, not only is it desiring a body that has been forcibly subject to illegal and violent scientific experimentation (the transgenic skin), but also that it is desiring a body that has been male. The straight male gaze, goaded to take pleasure in looking upon Vera, finds itself shamed as perverted and homophobic/transphobic.

Yet it is not as if there is an alternative, emancipatory, female or queer gaze with which we are invited to identify. Insofar as we could feel a sense of identification with Vera-as-victim, this is frustrated by her apparent lack of a story. Whereas the lives, fortunes and motivations of the other characters are soon elaborated in flashback, Vera's history remains an empty space – that is, until we begin to understand her connection with Vicente. This understanding theoretically should give depth to her story. Yet whilst this revelation may lead to feelings of revulsion when we find out that Vicente too is guilty of sexual violence, more fundamentally, the device that most disrupts the possibility of historicity in relation to Vicente/Vera is the decision to cast two actors – one male, one female – in the role. We meet Vera long before we meet her male counterpart, and as per the conventions of narrative, we expect to gain insight into who she is. To find out that she is actually *another body* creates a radical disjuncture in the film text, like a piercing of the skin-we-live-in for the duration of our spectatorship. This extra-diegetic switch-of-bodies mimics the irreversibility of the surgery that has transformed Vicente beyond recognition, whilst also rendering invisible the physical suffering – the marks of trauma – associated with the forced transition. The marks s/he makes on the wall of the room where s/he is kept in captivity externalise that which has been erased from the skin, but whilst they measure and represent the passage of time, these inscriptions only allow time to be endured, but not for it to be lived (see Baraitser, 2017). Even when we understand that s/he *is* Vicente, the lack of a visual connection between Vera and Vicente onscreen serves to overwrite the connection that we 'know' rationally via the narrative; it allows the male character of Vicente to be-a-person with a history while Vera remains an object – the plaything of Robert, and of the camera. To use the terms I developed in Chapter 1, we could say that as Vera is subject to the over-looking/overlooking gaze: s/he is simultaneously seen too much by the camera that is intoxicated by her femininity, and yet wholly unseen; the intensity of the sight of her body (like the intensity of the sight of a disabled body) somehow interrupts rational knowledge of her personhood and agency. Even if the twist in the story resolves the sadistic-voyeuristic desire to demystify Vera (Mulvey, 1975), what has been uncovered is literally the thing that, for Mulvey, the controlling male gaze of the camera is structured to disavow: woman-as-castrated-man. Thus it is as if the decision to cast two actors in the Vera/Vicente role is the only way to erase this trauma, this arrival of the event that must not happen (castration). By keeping the two versions of the character visually distinct, the camera denies the very thing that the narrative is asserting. Vicente's male agency remains intact (if threatened) as long as Vera remains without a story. Just as we begin to think she is gaining a history, this turn of events returns her to objectification and the sphere of 'fetishistic scopophilia' that 'can exist outside linear time' (Mulvey, 1975, p. 14). This reminds us of some of the fundamental questions of Chapter 2: who is allowed to develop, and what gets named as development? We might add, drawing on the argument from Chapter 3: how does the discourse of rehabilitation legitimise itself by associating itself with certain subjects and allowing them to be claimed for development and "'rehabilitative futurism'" (Mollow, 2012, p. 288; see also Puar, 2017a)? In this chapter, as elsewhere in the book, I am interrogating the entitlement of rehabilitation to sit comfortably on the side of a future that unfolds smoothly.

By drawing attention to the film's disorientating attacks on absorption and on narrative, I am suggesting a parallel with a pre-verbal experience of rehabilitation, which, as we shall see, cuts through the flow of time, constantly demanding the impossible. The film shames us for looking, it shames us for wanting to take up a position, and it also prevents us from identifying with the only character who begins to command our sympathy (Vera), by interrupting the possibility of narrative in relation to this character. The shame of taking up a position is also part of the early experience of rehabilitation, I am suggesting: the position (both postural and perspectival) of the child is shown to be 'wrong' in ways that are incomprehensible to her.

In representing Vera as outside of linear time and history, the film also reminds us of the psychoanalytic notion of the defence mechanism: that mode of preserving a fragile equilibrium inside the self, in the face of trauma. In this space of self-defence, change-over-time must be avoided. The film's use of skin to symbolise both (defensive) containment and the attempt to *erase* trauma helped me to analyse my own experience of being, in a certain sense, outside (or perhaps buried inside the skin) of the latent knowledge of my trauma. Before turning to my own 'scar-resistant skin', I will reflect further on how the representation of skin and its proxies in the film probes the boundaries of identity and self-knowledge. This leads me into a discussion of the film's problematic use of the gendered body as a site of 'rehabilitative' erasure.

Layers of protection; layers of identity

It is in the context of fraught relationships between surface and depth, as well as between seeing, knowing and complicity, that clothes, fabric and skin take on enormous significance in the film. In a scene preceding that of his kidnap, we see Vicente dressing a faceless, asymmetrical, uncanny straw mannequin in the window of his mother's clothes shop. It is hard to avoid seeing a visual parallel between the mannequin and the burnt, bandaged body of Robert's wife, which we have just witnessed in a flashback to her suicide, the latter – according to Marilia's account – being itself triggered by catching sight of her disfigured appearance for the first time. In the accumulation of idealised, stylised and disfigured representations of the female body (nudes, mannequins, seamed fabric and clay sculptures inspired by Louise Bourgeois' art – another overt intertext in the film, which references the scar-resistant skin), it seems that the film is playing very deliberately and interrogatively with age-old ideas of femininity as a beautiful display that masks unspeakable horror – a horror that must be controlled by (rehabilitative) male acts of looking and intervention (see Mulvey, 1975). Fear of women seems to line up with the fear of disfigurement and disability here. The burn-resistant transgenic skin that Robert develops, in which he encases Vera, thus appears to be associated with the attempt to erase not only pain and scarring, but also the horror of what might lie beneath the skin (a separate identity, a separate agency). This is rehabilitation as aesthetic control, it is rehabilitation as the disavowal of difference – and, as we saw in Chapter 2, the ethical status of rehabilitation is only guaranteed when it is understood as a practice of substantial rather than superficial (aesthetic) change. In an early scene, Robert uses a blow torch on Vera's skin and she is (mostly) unable to feel it: the skin is thus much more than a container, here, it is supposed to prevent the very sensations of liveliness that remind us of our existence.

Clothing, as a proxy for skin, is referenced frequently in the film, connoting both the potential for entrapment and the cultivation of a recognisable identity. As we shall see in my discussion of my own experience of being 'unmade' by rehabilitation, the concept of second-skin-as-defence also carries a valence that pulls in two directions at once. Robert's daughter Norma, confined to a psychiatric hospital in the latter part of the film, refuses to wear tight, feminine clothing, apparently tearing it off: we might read this as a bid for sanity and life. Robert wants her to wear feminine clothing so as minimise her appearance as a psychiatric patient. This detail echoes and foreshadows other scenes in which fabric is ripped up by Vera, either in an angry rejection of feminine attire (identity), or to use strips of fabric for clothing her sculptures, whose patchwork seamed bodies resemble her healing second skin. The recuperation of the torn fabric perhaps gestures towards the entanglement of making and unmaking (Scarry, 1985; see also Butler, 1997a), and to the role of re-unmaking in the process of coming to resist oppression. What I mean by 're-unmaking' will become clearer as the chapter progresses, but essentially I am arguing that the traumatic repetition of 'rehabilitative' undoing is integral to the process of becoming a subject-that-can-resist – that is, to going beyond existence as a resistant subject.[7] The act of stitching together figurative sculptures places Vera in the role of the rogue doctor enacting surgery, and yet the dolls' visible seams also bear witness to the suffering that cannot be seen on Vera's body. At the end of the film, when Vera finally escapes and returns to her mother's clothes shop, she wears a dress that s/he (as Vicente) had taken with him on the day of the kidnap, in the hope that her mother and former colleague will believe that she really is Vicente. The film ends before we find out their response, although the pregnant pause before the film fades to black seems weighed down by their bewilderment. The film seems to ask: is it possible for Vicente-as-Vera to re-enter the diachronic space of narrative, to have a history that can be affirmed in the intersubjective encounter, or has the total transformation of the skin he lives in (and the erasure, thereby, of agentic masculinity) deprived him of this? In keeping with its commitment to unsettling identifications, the film refuses to tell us whether Vicente can be 'identified'. Can the trauma of unmaking ever be fully comprehended, worked through and repaired?

As we have seen, the decision to cast two actors in the role of Vera/Vicente could be read as colluding with Robert's desire to remove Vera's bodily history as Vicente (see Lemma, 2013). Furthermore, it could be read as being complicit with discourses that promote normative notions of binary gender.[8] What does it mean that a character who has forcibly undergone gender reassignment surgery is played by a non-transsexual actress? How does such a casting decision – and in particular of a very beautiful cis-gendered female actress – affect our ability to perceive firstly Vicente's physical trauma but secondly the plight of trans people, who remain extremely marginalised in contemporary Euro-American culture, and who may struggle to obtain recognition to live as their desired gender? Given the intersection here between contemporary disability politics and trans politics – in the sense of the body as a site of interpretive struggle – it seems important to briefly address the film's gendering of the body, which is inextricable from its fascination with erasure.

Trans and *The Skin I Live In*

It should be said that this is no more a film about trans experience than one about disability and rehabilitation: its topics are rape and forced surgery. Yet it raises questions about embodied memory and the relationship between the body one feels oneself to have, and the body that one may be seen or required to have, issues which Lemma (2013) identifies as pertinent to her psychotherapeutic work with a transwoman, and which resonate for me as I seek to articulate 'remaking' in my own lived experience of rehabilitation. Moreover, it seems to me that the film's (non-)representation of trans experience does make an uncomfortable intervention in the politics of embodiment; to avoid discussing the film at all in terms of trans could be to reinforce some of the erasures that the casting decisions seem to enact.[9] On the subject of embodiment, Lemma writes:

> Winnicott grasped the challenge imposed by our embodied nature when he reminded us that it is easy 'to take for granted the lodgment of the psyche in the body and to forget that this again is an achievement' (1988, p. 122). This 'lodgment' – Winnicott (1970) elsewhere referred to it through the somewhat poetic image of the 'psyche in-dwelling in the soma' – brings home the rootedness of mental structures in early sensory and affective experience (Freud, 1923).
>
> (Lemma, 2013, p. 278)[10]

Lemma draws on this concept of 'lodgment' to suggest that we are all caught up in the difficult work of attempting to 'transform the body one *has* into the body one *is*' (p. 279). Although Lemma's inclusive language here is intended, I think, to de-pathologise trans experience by invoking a spectrum of experience, I am troubled by the certainty of the delineation between the 'has' and the 'is'. I think it carries a risk of reifying embodiment – and binary gender – even if this is not the intention. The body, in this Winnicottian formulation, is the immutable 'home' that houses the mutable 'psyche'. The assumptions upon which Lemma's (and Winnicott's) distinctions are founded are widespread not just in object relations psychoanalysis, but in disability studies too. We need only think of the way impairment is mobilised as an 'is' – and I too make this move; there is an inevitability to it when we are operating within a particular cultural frame, just as there is an inevitability to the commodification discussed in Chapter 3 (see Lesnik-Oberstein, 2008). The challenge is to recognise the work being done by the 'is' and not to take it for granted as universal.[11]

Trans identity could be said to problematise received ideas about the location of the 'is', and yet, as Gherovici points out, the hardening of these received ideas can also be traced in the recent history of psychoanalysis, which has historically been much more open to gender fluidity:

> What makes a man a man and a woman a woman is a question that has come to psychoanalysis from hysteric patients. The position on bisexuality held by Steinach and Benjamin [early psychoanalytic theorists of gender] seems closer to a queer notion of sexuality in which genders are placed in a continuum beyond a strict binary. Paradoxically, the liberal discourses of gender identity support a sort of essentialism about gender identification. A collaboration

between psychoanalysis and transgender discourse would thus open the way for an alternative.

(Gherovici, 2011, p. 15)

Interestingly, Gherovici draws out a connection between 'liberal discourses of gender identity' and essentialism; this chimes with the debates around maternal bodily autonomy that I charted in Chapter 3, where the body as 'possession' – as a thing that we 'have' – was identified as a product of liberal individualism. As noted there, the dominance of such discourses (and bodily practices informed by them) makes it difficult to think or operate outside of them. In this chapter, I seek to reflect on the relationship between the impairment I 'have' and the impairment that I enact, suggesting that there is a fluidity between these that is difficult to unpick at the level of experience, especially where impairment is a feature of childhood. The reification of impairment within the dominant discourses of medicine and health, alongside the desire to minimise its presence, has in my case led to a sense that I am not being encouraged to become the body I 'have' (since this is what we are to call my impairment within the confines of liberal individualist discourse), but rather, that I am being encouraged to 'become' an altogether different sort of body, one that I can never enact successfully – an able body. Where, in amongst all of these different layers, is the body I 'have', and where is the body I 'am'? How can we be sure of where the distinction lies when what is in question is pre-verbal 'experience' – something that can only be retroactively governed by notions of 'has' and 'is' anyway? Whilst I would want to retain the sense of the *plurality* of disability experiences and, indeed, trans experiences – which, it should be noted, Lemma (2013) also emphasises – I hope that this critical interrogation of the idea that, for all of us, *there is a body that is 'there' for the having* has resonance both in disability studies and in trans studies. I would want to ask: which bodies make the apparent alignment between the 'has' and the 'is' seem self-evident? What can we learn about the instability of this self-evidence from those bodies that prise apart the 'has' and the 'is'? How does rehabilitation in early childhood maintain or disrupt the continuity between the 'has' and the 'is'? To probe these questions further, I now turn to the theme of 'scar-resistant skin' in my own experience, as an example of a multivalent phenomenon that both protects and erases the self.

Scar-resistant skin

The Skin I Live In raises the question: where in the body's 'memory' will the trauma of the forced vaginoplasty be held, if not on the skin? What is the location of trauma in the psyche-soma, when the physical traces of suffering are removed from the body's surface? These are questions that will resurface in my personal writing, when it comes to discussing my own, self-made, defensive second skin. The body that is prevented from bearing the traces of its own psychic and somatic suffering is, I would argue, a profoundly oppressed and abject body (although the phenomenon of 'passing' certainly complicates this statement). How does such a body authenticate itself and prove the physical ordeal it has undergone to the Other? When I watched *The Skin I Live In*, the concept of a skin that would be capable of resisting burns and scarring captured my imagination. The film literalises something that, for me, had significance at a psychic level. The notion of a scar-resistant skin, which renders the signs of trauma invisible, resonated with my own experience of passing as non-disabled and, more profoundly, with presenting a self to the world that would seem undamaged by the pain of having been reshaped by physiotherapy. In the next subsection I ask: can we draw parallels between the violence done to Vicente, and that to which the disabled child is subjected, through regimes of remaking? How is it different when a young child, rather than an adult, is the subject of medical remaking?

***

If I am to want a body that is more like yours, I must firstly no longer want to inhabit my own body. But be under no illusions, I am doing this 'wanting' for you, not for me. I am exiling myself from myself, in order to climb inside you – or are you climbing inside me? I am climbing inside a skin that you have fashioned for me, a skin that is grafted on top of my own, designed to suffocate the self that's inside. I am becoming Vera in her scar-resistant skin, so beautiful in appearance, her body unmarked by any visible traces of trauma.

Yet even Vera can remember the Vicente she once was; her resistance is in her conscious memory of a self that had agency. How can I remember how to resist when I cannot remember my former self? Be very wary of my agreement to the procedures that remake me. I am agreeing only because the second skin has no provision for my disagreement: it disallows the signs of my suffering. In the second skin's quality of 'resistance to scarring', there lies my own resistance, my own power to resist your oppression of me. When we say that my skin is scar-resistant, we do not realise it, but that is EXACTLY where I have placed my power of resistance: in the very fabric of my oppression. My resistance, which could otherwise be used to struggle free of my second skin, is actually bound up in a process of making that very skin appear flawless, appear resistant to burns, to scars, to pain. I cannot, in fact, resist because the psychic labour of resistance has been exhausted in the very creation of my scar-resistant skin. I have used up my resistance in becoming resistant. How very clever of my oppressors (and me!) to think of a way of using up all my potency in the service of my own oppression. I am itching to get out of my second skin! I shall scratch and tear it off. I shall scratch as a means of resistance, rather than resisting scratching.

My anger, my outward-facing resistance – the force that might lash out – has been transformed into a skin that is apparently resistant to your attempts to invade. The trauma you attempt to inscribe on my second skin will not mark it because I know you cannot bear to see those marks. It runs down it in rivulets, like water running down a raincoat. Where does the trauma go? I am left with a second skin that appears flawless, a skin upon which trauma is invisible: that is my nightmare. Don't be fooled by the invisibility of the trauma. Though I appear not to suffer through any of your invasive procedures of remaking, the trauma is held in the very work of wearing the flawless mask, in the act of passing as non-disabled. To resist would mean no longer being 'resistant'. No longer holding myself captive inside the resistant membrane of my second skin. To resist would be to remove the mask, to show you the deep scars on the skin beneath, to walk with a limp because that is how I walk, to manifest my permeable, permeated self. Can you bear to see it?

The process of remaking me was about trying to minimise or even remove the signs of the birth trauma from my body. In this sense it was about making my body appear unmarked by trauma. But in remaking me you redoubled the trauma; seeking both to deprive me of the signs of a trauma that was mine and to re-traumatise my body by asking it to be something other than what it was, by asking it to be a body without a disability. A flawless body. Where was it safe for me to put my trauma? Where could I keep hold of my flawed me?

Scar-resistant skin is not a form of resistance. It is a way of hiding my suffering, in order to oppress myself and to let you go free.

***

I propose in this personal writing that the child-subject of physiotherapy assumes a 'scar-resistant second skin' as a way of protecting those adults around her from knowing how traumatic these 'rehabilitative' procedures actually are. The scar-resistant skin also makes it possible for the child to undergo a range of procedures in a relatively dissociated state, since it protects her from knowing the feelings these procedures provoke in her. In the next subsection, I will draw on and develop Winnicott's (1990b) concept of the 'False Self' to explore these ideas.

False selves or false bodies?

In *The Skin I Live In*, Vicente (as Vera) deploys a range of resistance techniques to maintain a connection with his male self (Lemma, 2012). In her reading of the film, Lemma (2012) suggests that the walls of the cell in which Vicente is imprisoned take on a containing quality, standing in for the lost physical body. The inscription of markers of the passage of time on the cell walls substitutes for the body's ability to show the scars bequeathed to it over time. Vicente's mind, too, is seen as a resource for containment in the absence of the body: in using yoga to 'create a safe place within', the 'true masculine self' of Vicente 'is protected in his mind even if his actual body now *looks like* that of a woman' (Lemma, 2012, p. 1298, emphasis in original). But how does a pre-verbal child maintain a connection with a prior self if, prior to remaking, there was not yet a secure sense of self? How is resistance possible for one that is not yet even a subject?

The double meaning of the verb 'to resist' is the centrepiece of the writing; it highlights the way in which an angry energy in the self comes to be used to oppress the self. To resist can mean to channel one's energy into overthrowing an oppressor, but it can also mean to channel one's energy into holding back from acting. Both 'active' resisting and 'passive' resisting require energy, and, in making this linguistic link I am proposing that the compliant child exhausts her (potentially angry) energy in holding back from knowing herself. The making of her scar-resistant second skin has exhausted her energies. This skin repels, and is impermeable, even to her own feelings, since these might be feelings of wanting to resist being unmade. Instead of being directed *outward* at the forces that seek to remake the child, resistance is effectively turned against the forming self in a process of becoming 'resistant'.

Winnicott regards this protection of the self from the self as 'False Self' functioning (1990b). False Self functioning takes place when the child's need for 'omnipotence' is not nurtured by his or her carers but is immediately replaced by their own needs (p. 146). Winnicott observes that:

> [W]here the mother cannot adapt well enough, the infant gets seduced into a compliance, and a compliant False Self reacts to environmental demands and the infant seems to accept them. Through this False Self the infant builds up a false set of relationships, and by means of introjections even attains a show of being real.
>
> (Winnicott, 1990b, p. 146)

Whereas in the film, we could argue that the adult Vicente remains connected with reality (the challenge is intersubjective: to convince those who knew Vicente that Vera is indeed he), the child who functions as a 'False Self' only 'attains a show of being real'; realness is display, even for herself. Her challenge is intra-subjective.

I draw a distinction between the pre-conceptual child's experience of being 'unmade' and that depicted in *The Skin I Live In*, not to undermine the enormity of the crimes committed upon Vicente's body in the film, but rather to highlight the gulf between experiences that can be understood by an adult mind and those that happen to the subject prior to the formation of a mental apparatus for digesting and making sense of them. This distinction enables us to think differently about medical procedures that appear to be helpful, or, at the very least, as neutral, to the adult mind. But perhaps we need to abandon a rational adult perspective that seeks to draw sharp distinctions between inside and outside, literal and metaphorical, concrete and symbolic, body and mind, since the child that I was had none of these distinctions. In this chapter I use creative writing to try to reconnect with a mode of existence that was not governed by such distinctions (even though using language entails distinguishing, of course).

I contend that the 'False Self' can be experienced at a bodily level, by proposing the notion of the 'False Body'. I am aware that in developing this concept, I am positing the idea of a true, authentic body, which I have recently been problematising with my questioning of the essentialism entailed in a distinction between the 'body one is' and 'the body one has' (Lemma, 2013).

Winnicott's concept, too, reifies a notional true self. I am conscious that the model of the False Body has its flaws but I want to work with it, to see how far it goes in helping to build a *phenomenology* of inauthenticity – that is, I am interested in how it helps to reconstruct the (non)feeling of disconnected bodily being in the world.

The 'False Body' is another construct (like the scar-resistant skin) that the child uses to remake herself in the face of procedures of unmaking. Physiotherapy manipulated my body so that I gradually grew into my very own second skin: I was encouraged to assume a False Body, to move my limbs in ways that were not my ways of moving, to leave behind the embodied ways of being and doing that I had developed and established for myself. I was instructed to abandon the embodiment I had been coming to know as myself and to embrace ways of being in the world that involved conscious effort and attention. I now know that these embodied ways of doing and being sought to minimise the signs of the birth trauma on my body, to normalise my body. They could therefore be understood as a means of removing the *signs* of the first trauma whilst – as I felt it – simultaneously inflicting a further trauma whose name was 'the imperative to pass', whose name was 'second skin',[12] whose name was 'False Body'. For the pre-verbal child, the thing that is destroyed by a regime of physiotherapy is not an identity but a bodily self. My embodied being was no longer mine; I could not be spontaneous with it.[13] The False Body I inhabited, was, moreover, *not* a wobbly body. Yes, it was still a body with cerebral palsy – it could not stop being *that* – but it was a body that could move freely, without proprioceptive doubt. I now think that I was very dissociated from this body.

The notion of the False Body has presented itself to me because, in the process of becoming aware of my own False Self through psychoanalysis, I started to experience a profound and terrifying distrust of the body I have. I came to interpret this apparently 'new' feeling of bodily doubt and distrust as a repetition of my early experience of being unmade by physiotherapy: an experience from which I defended myself by developing a False Body and a scar-resistant skin. The 'new', terrifying experience of my body played itself out in terms of massive proprioceptive doubt, accompanied by intense anxiety. Doubt about the positioning of my body in space, in relation to other objects; doubt about whether I could trust my voluntary bodily acts to turn out as I intended; doubt after the event about whether my body had performed a particular act or not. Although the intensity of this experience has decreased over time, its residue remains in my day-to-day life. In Merleau-Ponty's terms, it might be understood as a disruption of the 'habit-body' (2002, p. 95). It is hard to explain what this feels like, not least because I carry with me a deep shame about what I fear that others may perceive as a 'mad' embodied experience of the world. The process of unbecoming the body I have learnt to be, or of shedding my second skin, has involved excruciating doubt about the positioning of my body in the world, and the capacity of this body to move through the world without causing harm. The 'true' body seems to be a 'bad' body – one I cannot trust. How am I to understand the doubt, and the sense of being bad, associated with the 'true' body?

What happened when I returned to the 'wobbly body' of my childhood? Suffering, re-unmaking and resistance

Day after day, this doubt I carry inside me cuts through my thoughts. Cuts through me like a knife intent on severing skin, on severing bone, on severing muscle. But mainly just intent on severing a train of thought.

Doubt is the surgeon who severs continuity.

I am trying to do, trying to make, trying to construct, and in comes the knife. When I had my second skin, I could resist the knife, I could repel it. I grew the second skin so that I could close myself off from those voices which told me over and over to try again, those interrupting voices which came in and disintegrated me, cut through me and sought to doctor me. I couldn't feel much when I had my second skin, my false body, but at least I could think. There was no pain but there were words. Cut through my second skin with your knife of feeling and yes, you bring me alive but you also deprive me of the only continuity I had, this shell of thoughts that now is always interrupted by doubt as my body moves hesitantly through the world.

I do not know how to tell you about how the doubt feels now I am here, seated at this desk. I only know when I am outside, in amongst the bodies, trying to move, and yet paralysed by wordless doubt, panic and confusion. Out there, only feeling.

As the thoughts attempt to construct themselves, so the knife cuts through them and unmakes my sense.

Here, now, seated, secure, supported by the chair, I have a mind.

There, out amongst the bodies, in the street, where I too am a body, I am taken back into that place where I was only a body, so long ago. There is so much doubt – no, terror – as I walk along. Here, now, at this desk, I shut out that bodily unknowledge, that spatial uncertainty, that sense of being out of balance, off kilter, wrong, wrong, wrong. Here I have words. Here I have thoughts. You see me type, you know I am coherent. Out there, the thoughts peel off me, the words bounce off me. The words are afraid of me. There are no words out there, out there, out there in the wordless confusion.

Body. Space. People. Panic. Self. Other. Collapse into.

I am trying to use thought to make something cohere which will not cohere. It feels very post-hoc. It feels very forced. You tell me that I have always had language to make sense of these things. Language has always been my thing. How can it be that this other thing, this experience of being terrified while out in the street, exceeds my grasp? But here's the thing.

Language has been my second skin.

Language has protected me from knowing.

Language is my way round, my way out, but not my way THROUGH.

I cannot write of these things because I do not know how to use language to take you inside them. I long to gather you up and take you inside my body, inside my body when it stands on a busy street.

When I shed my second skin, when I step out of my false body, I do not yet know what will be left to me. The first skin I have is very thin, very young, very permeable. As for the 'true' body ... it exists mainly in the doubt as I walk along, in the stopping to check, in the humiliation, in the uncertainty, in the panic and the confusion that haunt my movement. That is the true body exerting its presence, speaking about its subjection all those years ago.

***

Here, language comes to be understood as a defensive structure that maintains existence inside the second skin, as Bick (1968) suggested. I found this final chapter extraordinarily difficult to write, perhaps because, in writing it, I am seeking to enter a place that for me has no words. This wordless 'place' is, in the present, the panicky feeling in the street about a body that is perceived to have moved 'wrongly' and caused harm. When it was experienced originally, pre-verbally, this wordless place was the 'rehabilitative' interruption to the continuity of bodily sensation: the demand, in physiotherapy, for the body to do something or move in a way that felt wrong to it. In the time in between the early experience *in feeling* and the contemporary experience of coming back *into feeling*, I created a second skin that was, effectively, made of language. Language was a means of barricading myself in, and even, strangely, a means of getting out, as I write in the passage above. I think here of my use of reading as a means of escapism as a child and as a teenager; I think of the very childhood archive on which I have drawn to write this book – of *The Secret Garden* (Hodgson Burnett, 1987 [1911]), and of the hinterland of other classics that feature disabled children, which led me into the territory of this book, even though they are not, ultimately, its direct object.[14] I think also of the walls of Vera's cell in *The Skin I Live In* (2011), over-written with words and marks from floor to ceiling – the date, and the word 'respiro' ('I breathe') repeated over and over. Language here is literally inscribed on the containing shell, but is unable to pierce it; it seems to record a continuous present rather than to make history. For me, language was a resource – and a very expansive and flexible one too, through which I deceived even myself – but it was a resource for gliding across, around the edge, for getting from A to B in a relatively dissociated state. If the question, however, is about finding my way THROUGH, language is nowhere to be found.

What I feel I have lost in the psychotherapeutic journey *through* or *into* my pain is the continuity of thought – the unmarked, unpierced, scar-resistant shell of thought – that I was able to create.[15] I conjecture that I originally retreated into this shell during a rehabilitative process that must have felt as though it was disintegrating me. The idea of the 'protective shell' (Tustin, 1990) captures the experience of the hollow continuity that I was able to produce for myself using my linguistic second skin, an integrity that could repel feelings that sought to cut *through* or cut *into* me. In the personal writing, I note that language did not, in its defensive incarnation, allow me *a way through* – it simply maintained the shell. However, the doubt I have experienced in the shedding of my defences has been experienced as something that cuts *through* continuity, which *interrupts* my train of thoughts with the constant need to check. I am thus using a surgical metaphor of 'unmaking', or unwanted cutting through, to describe both the original process of physiotherapy (which was experienced as a spatial and temporal interruption) *and* the later psychotherapeutic process of shedding the protective shell.

Automatic pilot

Earlier in the chapter I drew on an essay by Fuchs (2005) in which it is argued that when it functions normally, the body is felt to be transparent. It is the medium through which we come to know the world, but in order to perform this perceptual function, the body itself must fade into the background. Fuchs examines a disturbance of the bodily schema in which the body's transparency – its so-called '"as" structure' (p. 101) – has been lost. Rather than being the instrument of perception, the body becomes an object to be perceived. The alteration is associated with an activity that Fuchs names the '[e]xplication of the implicit': this is what happens when, by repeating a word over and over, it is possible to make that word sound alien, or incorrect (p. 101). Fuchs also gives the example of a musician who must allow his body to play the instrument in an automatic way: the musician 'stumbles in his run' if he 'concentrates on his single fingers' (p. 101). To the extent that it disturbs 'former familiarity', the activity of explication results in 'alienation or disintegration' (p. 101).

Fuchs associates this disturbance of perception with the psychiatric label 'schizophrenia', and provides an example from case material, from which I quote here:

> A 32-year old patient reports that at the age of 16, he had become more and more uncertain whether his personal things really belonged to him or had somehow been exchanged for others. [...] When leaving things on his school-desk inattentively, he later began to doubt whether they were still the same, and had to throw them away. [...] Now he could not trust his own hands any more, and doubted the simplest actions. [...] Every movement was like an arithmetical problem that had to be pondered over with extreme concentration.
>
> (Fuchs, 2005, p. 101)

Here we see a deep distrust of both the body's automatic capacities and of the safety and amicability of the environment. When I first read the vignette, I immediately identified with some of the characteristics – in particular, the distrust of the body that leaves things on a desk 'inattentively' and the idea of needing to bring 'concentration' to the slightest bodily movement, to ensure that it is undertaken correctly.

My own arrival in the wobbly body that I feel myself to have inherited out of nowhere, but which I in fact understand as a 'return of a repressed body',[16] has all the qualities of a loss of bodily transparency as described by Fuchs. Yet if I am aligning bodily transparency with the protective shell of psychic defence, is there a sense in which the healthy, automatic use of the body as a transparent tool might be associated with a desire to eschew what has been repressed – not just in my case, but for everyone, or even at a cultural level? Why should we valorise the automatic over the 'explication of the implicit'? Indeed, might we not regard the labour of critical theory (or indeed psychoanalysis) as an example of the latter, and value it for its potential to bring the 'implicit' into our field of vision?[17] Whilst I find Fuchs' (2005) model illuminating, for me it fails to trouble the binary of health and pathology sufficiently. The medicalised framing of Fuch's phenomenological insights troubles me, as does his use of the psychiatric label 'schizophrenia' (which I am fortunate never to have had the experience of being given myself). My psychoanalytic return to the 'wobbly body' – by which I mean a body that doubts itself – has been maddening: it has taken me to the brink of an experience that could be called 'madness'. I use scare quotes here for the term 'madness' as a way of querying the pathologising attachment of such a label to an individual: I would instead like to draw attention to the socio-cultural madness of expecting that a child with an impairment might miraculously become able-bodied, if she would only perform the physiotherapy exercises correctly.

I now want to think further about the changing place of language in my lived experience of a body that was once transparent, and which has become opaque and wobbly. If language is capable of helping us with the process of releasing affects (Brennan, 2004), how is it that we can also grow up using language as a defence, as a protective shell, as a thing that actually *prevents* us from going into feeling, sensation and the body? In the next section I want to show how and why I think that happened for me.

Language that stays on the surface, language that (re)connects with the body

I've been told I was quick to master language. I mastered it to ask for what I needed, instead of moving to get the thing, because moving was hard for me. Talking instead of doing. It worked. I got what I needed. The miracle of speech, in contrast with a singularly, relentlessly un-miraculous body.

Try again!

Concentrate ...

You can do it!

Moving was hard for me, but it became impossible. Not because of motor difficulties (though those were there too) but because of the impossibility of getting it right. I left that body – MY body – behind at that point. It became a small kernel inside a much more prominent false body, which I had protected with a thick, scar-resistant second skin. That false body could not be hurt, because the repetitive words of the physiotherapist just bounced off its hard, linguistic exterior. Her words could not harm me because I was already in a flight of fancy, I was inside the world of the latest book I was reading, I was not really there. I countered her offensive call by disappearing, leaving just a false body and a thick skin as signs that I had once been there. I remade myself as a disembodied story-self.

*You want a miracle? Here's your miracle, though it's not the one you want: I
survived your offensive call, by remaking myself elsewhere.*

***

For me as a child, the process of rehabilitation offered itself as a process in
which words came unmoored from their referents. Picture the scene: I am told, as
I place my foot on the ground, 'no, that's wrong, you've got it wrong'. I have to
repeat the action. Yet in my body, I felt nothing to be wrong in the action I
performed. Today, when I walk, I worry that it would be possible to do harm to
another without feeling anything at all in my body. Back then, I internalised a
sense that my movement was 'wrong' (a 'wrongness' that translated, at an un-
metabolised level, into a strong sense of having done harm). The message I
internalised was at odds with my bodily perception: it simply did not *fit* with
what I had experienced in the external world. My foot, as I placed it on the floor,
felt fine. Yet I was told that I'd 'got it wrong'. How could I in*corporate* – bring
inside my body – this radical dissonance of word and sensation, this massive
disjuncture between linguistic description and physical, spatial experience, whilst
maintaining my sanity?[18] How confusing would such a disjuncture be for the
child who is pre-verbal, or just at the point of entry into language? This
mismatch, I now know, could *not* be incorporated without my going mad. I only
know this now because of how close I have come to madness as I have sought,
in my repetition of the trauma, to knit offensive word ('wrong') and bodily
sensation ('fine') together in a manner that simply *does not go*.

In my narrative of events, I read this experience of an impossibly painful
dissonance as the site of the splitting off of a linguistic self from the bodily one.
I allowed body (and with it, sensation and feeling) to go its separate way from
mind, from thought, from language. Unable to perform an impossible integration,
I maintained identification with a linguistic self. I remade my unmade self in
language. This appears to be a strange reversal of Scarry's (1985) image of the
present body and the absent voice, yet I am arguing that this is a voice without
the strength to speak its own truth. For a very long time I was able to make a
good show of being a self with agency because I was always able to do things
with words – to borrow from Austin (1975) – as long as they were just words,
and did not need to be 'incorporated', did not need to be made meaningful,
feelingful, alive. Psychoanalyst Joyce McDougall explores a similar scenario
when describing the type of patient who conducts a kind of 'pseudonormal
communication with the rest of the world [...], in which words [...] tend to be
divested of their emotional counterpart' (1989, p. 30).

Coming to recognise the 'offensive call' as such

Where does this leave me in relation to the question of resistance? I began the
chapter by explaining that I had initially thought that the metaphor of 'remaking'
would permit me to discuss both what was done to me and what I need to do to

resist that unwanted interference. I had thought that 'remaking' would, as a term, provide a neat symmetry whereby the offensive call that remade me could be answered with the riposte, 'no, I shall remake myself, I shall claim the identity I choose!' The process of writing this chapter revealed to me a far messier state of affairs. Indeed, I discovered that the term 'remaking' applied not so much to the clinical procedures enacted upon my body as to an act of self-made self-protection from those procedures. Remaking was associated with the defensive practices of the pre-self. It was a response to the physiotherapy that had unmade me. It took the form of constructing a scar-resistant skin (language), and a False Body that was capable of doing exercises in a mindless, robotic way. Meanwhile, the physiotherapy and other medical procedures that I endured would more accurately be described as having *unmade* me, in the sense of having interrupted the continuity of my experience, introducing doubt and fear. Remaking myself in the midst of these constant and unrelenting interruptions that pierced through my developing sense of self, I fled the scene of unmaking to a world of language. Though I was unable to perform the miracle demanded by the Other, that of remaking myself in the image of a normal child, I could always rely on language. I have argued in this chapter that in spite of this, there was one verbal miracle I could not perform, and that was the one of – to use Butler's (1997a, p. 2) term – 'counter[ing] the offensive call'. To do this would have entailed a simultaneously liberating and paradoxically re-enslaving engagement with 're-unmaking', which I was only later enabled to do, via psychoanalysis.

Why do I maintain that even as a very capable linguistic self, I could not 'counter the offensive call' that first brought me into being as a linguistic subject? I suggest that, in the process of coming to inhabit the linguistic false self that dissociated from body and feeling, I lost all conscious knowledge of the 'offensive call' as such. Occupying the space of the linguistic self must have entailed an identification with the offensive call itself, with the 'you are wrong' of language. Yet, in a process of 'introjection of the aggressor' (Ferenczi, 1999), it also became impossible to see that the 'you are wrong' of the Other's language was harmful to me. It became, simply, my own experience of myself, in a terrifyingly toxic but sanity-preserving move on the part of the ego.[19] Whilst poisonous, it was also simple, in contrast with the self-destroying conundrum of the wrong-fine disjuncture I described. When one's own speech itself enacts the offensive call as though it were one's own (in a reproduction that I have discussed in terms of internalised oppression in other parts of the book), the offensive call, chameleon-like, has already insinuated itself into the self, appearing as a very quality of the self rather than as a contaminant. I use the language of disease here in a conscious attempt to draw out the connections with my earlier discussion of the protective second skin which has been – somewhat paradoxically – penetrated and unpeeled in the process of recovery. In the personal writing on scar-resistant skin, I wrote that '*to resist would mean no longer being resistant*'. To resist would entail vulnerability.

What I am suggesting is that I can only come to resist the offensive call by first being penetrated by it, by first being wounded by it, by first allowing myself to be permeable to, and permeated by, affect. Specifically, I must be permeated by offence: I must be offended by the call. As an impermeable subject, I am unable to take up a counter-position in response to the offensive call. This is due to my identification with the very one who hails me. My very inseparability from my interpellator – my Other within – is what makes it impossible to feel the offensive call as such. My disentanglement from the Other within is the founding of my capacity to be wounded by the Other from without, for the first time.

In *Excitable Speech*, Butler argues that the experience of being interpellated into language is simultaneously disabling and enabling (1997a, p. 2).[20] So, although entry into language is 'the condition of possibility for the speaking subject' (p. 28), it is also to be brought into a system that pre-exists us and that is, inevitably, on the terms of the Other, and in the time of the Other. Thus '"injury" is performed by the very act of interpellation' and not only by hate speech: we cannot 'regulate fully the potentially injurious effect of language without destroying something fundamental about language and, more specifically, about the subject's constitution in language' (p. 27). I have been suggesting in this chapter that the process of interpellation does not, however, cause injury in equal measure to all, and that there are ways of being closed off to (that is, defending oneself from) its injuring force. In my own case, since the linguistic self with which I later came to identify was also the one that had internalised a message of being 'wrong', it was not possible to recognise the offensive call as such. If interpellation always has the dual nature that Butler ascribes to it, then perhaps the call did not penetrate my protective shell, or wound me in its enabling way. This is somewhat paradoxical given that the protective shell was, in my case, a defence made of language. Butler argues that when one is hailed by a misnomer, one protests against this, and is, as a result, 'still constituted by discourse, but at a distance from oneself' (p. 33). Yet to be at a distance from oneself, to protest against a mistaken interpellation, it is necessary that there is first a 'oneself' to do the protesting. My defended self, whilst being very adept with language, was in some sense not fully constituted as a self, until it later was able to perceive the toxic properties of the offensive call as such.

How, then, do (pre-)subjects that have been unmade by trauma begin to be able to 'counter the offensive call'? The first stage, I would contend, is to become conscious of the call as offensive. But this knowledge is not something we can simply *come upon*, should we wish to know it, as this chapter has suggested. Indeed, it is my hope that this chapter, with its peculiarly laborious and long-winded way of saying something apparently – deceptively – simple, has sought to enact something of the strange 'to-and-fro' negotiation with my unconscious that the process of *speaking* has entailed for me. Psychoanalysis works by making a trauma available to thought, but to do this the trauma must first be repeated, and repetition *means* repetition – it should not be romanticised. Taylor (2014, p. xiv) observes that the psychoanalytic process 'can be hazardous', pointing out that the tool of transference, upon which the process relies, 'is a cool label for a very heated, sometimes incendiary, process'. In order to understand that I was, once upon a time, unmade by medical procedures enacted upon my body against my will, I have first had to be unmade again in psychoanalysis. This means enduring the terror, the panic, the confusion of the child, and not knowing what on earth is going on. This means not being able to know these feelings as a repetition, but instead simply hating the 'therapeutic' process for the way it is *undoing* me. It did not feel as though my analysis was about the past; it never did, and indeed I have no proof that it *was* about that, only my interpretation, my speculation, the narrative I (co-)created. Taylor writes that '[f]or many people, experiencing the past *as* past, allowing it to become truly historical, is very difficult' (p. xii): this is certainly my experience. How can the past become the past when it could not be witnessed as the present, when it was being experienced? How can we unsettle oppression from the space in which it has embedded itself inside ourselves, when we could not observe it making its impression in the beginning?

I am suggesting that, paradoxically, the healing process of psychoanalysis *repeats* the offensive call. It repeats the offensive call, but this time, the subject can – perhaps only fleetingly – hear that call as such, as if for the first time, and can be wounded by that call and can begin to find ways counter it. The repetition of the injury in this way has the potential to inaugurate a different kind of relationship between psyche, body and language; a more reciprocal one in which the subject is, in Butler's terms, truly 'animated' by the very thing that has also injured her (1997a, p. 46). This is where it starts to become possible to resist internalised oppression. This is the starting point for the flourishing of a political consciousness.

Notes

1 Francesca Martinez (2014) chooses to describe herself as 'wobbly' to avoid the stigma associated with the term 'cerebral palsy'. I shall briefly discuss her use of the term, and my own, in the early part of the chapter.
2 On 'stickiness', see Ahmed (2010) – for example p. 69.
3 Ahmed (2006) provides an excellent defamiliarisation of the concept of comfortably inhabiting space through her discussion of the factors that make it possible for Husserl to inhabit the world of the philosopher.
4 However, as I note throughout the chapter, where the experience of the pre-verbal child is concerned, it is, in any case, false to posit a distinction between body and mind.
5 Of Robert, Harrang (2012, p. 1305) observes that he 'represents a person for whom the outer appearance of the body – skin, at a concrete level – is synonymous with personal identity'.
6 In the context of a discussion of time and incarceration, Baraitser writes that 'there are conditions under which attachment to "the present tense" is neither choice, nor simply a matter of remèmoration, but a structural condition of the present' (2017, p. 116).
7 Later in the chapter, I shall be exploring the multivalence of 'resistant' subjectivity.
8 For a nuanced discussion of gender as non-binary, see Aizura (2006).
9 It is beyond the scope of this chapter to discuss the film's treatment of trans issues at length. Whilst I do not self-define as trans, I consider it important for disability studies to nurture and build alliances with trans studies (see Slater and Liddiard, 2018).
10 Details of the literature cited by Lemma (2013) are: Freud, S. (1961) 'The ego and the id', in Strachey, J. (ed) *The Standard Edition of the Complete Psychological Works of Sigmund Freud, Volume XIX (1923–1925): The Ego and the Id and Other Works* (trans. J. Strachey), London, The Hogarth Press, pp. 1–66; Winnicott, D. (2010) 'On the basis for self in body', in Winnicott, C., Shepherd, R. and Davis, M. (eds) *Psycho-analytic Explorations*, London, Karnac, pp. 261–283; Winnicott D. (1988) *Human Nature*, London, Karnac.

11 On the subject of mutability and the location of the 'is', it is interesting to note that the term 'second skins' – which Bick (1968) uses to denote a psychic defence – is also used by Jay Prosser (1998) as a metaphor for the embodied experience of the post-operative transsexual. For Prosser, the concept is usually associated with bodily fulfilment in that it represents the much-yearned-for endpoint of a journey to actualise the internal lived experience of the self. This contrasts with Bick's use of the term, since, for Prosser, it is the transsexual's first skin that masks the authentic self. In both cases, a notion of authenticity is mobilised.

12 Winnicott's concept of the 'False Self' might be regarded as compatible with – perhaps even analogous with – Bick's (1968, p. 484) aforementioned notion of '"second-skin" formation'.

13 On the association of spontaneity with the True Self, see Winnicott (1990b, p. 146).

14 This includes, among others, Johanna Spyri's (2009 [1880]) *Heidi* and Susan Coolidge's (2012 [1872]) *What Katy Did*.

15 Tustin (1990) uses the term 'protective shell' to describe a psychic defence deployed by children who have been 'abruptly wrenched away from' their mothers (p. xii); these children seek to 'protect their soft vulnerability by engendering the delusion of having an outer covering to their body, like a shell' (p. xi). Whilst I would want to critically examine the way in which Tustin connects this defence with the label of 'autism', which I see as a controversial move, I do find the metaphor of the protective shell – like the figure of the second skin – suggestive for thinking about how the infant maintains a sense of the integrity of the body during experiences that feel disintegrative.

16 In relation to this idea, see Soth (2010/11). N.B. Soth is discussing the return of the body at the level of psychoanalytic culture and practice – my use of the notion of the 'return of the repressed body' is thus somewhat different in that I am talking about individual experience.

17 I am grateful to Nick Hocking for suggesting this idea, which also chimes with Ahmed's (2006) concept of '(dis)orientation'.

18 This is also the dissonance of seeing the actress playing Vera and being told 'Vicente' – we are brought out of our absorption in the film by an awareness that the one does not simply 'translate' into the other.

19 This defence is also discussed by Wright (1991, p. 45) in terms of 'seeing what the mother sees' (see my discussion in Chapter 1).

20 As I discussed in Chapter 3, metaphors of disability proliferate in Butler's discussion.

Conclusion

As I sat down to write the conclusion to the doctoral thesis on which my book is based, a question popped into my head. The thesis was titled *Making the Disabled Child: Critical Disability Studies at the Intersection of Cultural Representation and Lived Experience*. Why, when I chose my title, did I select the phrase, 'Making the Disabled Child', rather than an alternative, but similar, formulation, 'The Making of the Disabled Child'? I knew I preferred the former, but I hadn't analysed why. It seemed to me that an analysis of the differences between these two phrases would provide an illuminating starting point for a discussion of the project as a whole. In this discussion, I seek to elucidate the argument of the book, as well as exploring areas of unresolved tension and paradox, and reflecting on the goals of my project and its broader political implications.

The term 'The Making of the Disabled Child' implies that the project of forming is singular and universal: the use of the definite article has this effect. There is also a suggestion of the completeness and finished nature of the process in the construct, 'the making of', which conjures up a documentary about the filming of a classic TV series. By contrast, the term 'Making the Disabled Child', in which 'making' acts as a verb rather than a noun, emphasises process and open-endedness. The lack of a definite article circumscribing 'making' allows it to resonate as multivalent. In the book I have explored subject formation and cultural representation as mobile, shifting, unfinished processes, which are mutually constitutive. I have sought to think about the intersecting discursive, psychosocial and ideological factors that 'make' a subject, and the particular inflections they take on when impairment is present. At first glance, then, the term 'Making the Disabled Child' seems to be doing what I need it to do for the (figure of the) disabled child, whose (non)formation as a subject is the subject matter of the book. And yet the phrase is problematic in its erasure of the disabled child as agent of her own making.[1] Even as she was the subject matter of this title, she was not its subject: she was its object. Does she have more 'animacy' – to use Chen's (2012) term – in the alternative formulation, 'The Making of the Disabled Child'? Perhaps there is, indeed, more ambiguity about her role in this version; the genitive 'of' at least transforms it into *her* making – a process that she may or may not be involved in. However, the phrase that withholds agency is actually a more accurate description of the majority of my project, which has been focussed on the child as the object of gazes, discourses and practices. It is only towards the end of the book, in the latter stages of Chapter 3, and in Chapter 4, that the disabled child (or, by this time, adult) is animated as an agent. I do not apologise for this focus; indeed, there was a need and a reason for it. I have argued in the book that the disabled child is 'made' by cultural forces outside of herself, which come to be internalised and lived – they become part of how she proceeds to make her world. The purpose of the book was to acknowledge and unpack these forces, with a view to exploring how they might eventually be resisted. One way of reading the narrative progression of the book's chapters, then, is as a protracted and difficult movement towards agency, which has been mirrored by my own protracted and difficult movement towards agency in psychoanalysis. Yet, as per the subtitle of the book, *Unsettling Distinctions*, my purpose has also been to problematise the distinction between agency and its obverse, for, in Chapter 4, the finding of agency is inextricable from a process of becoming aware of how one has been undone by power. I shall now briefly recap the work of each chapter in terms of its contribution to a discussion of agency.

In Chapter 1, I was interested in the formative qualities of the gaze. How might 'disability' be mediated via the gaze: how does it arrive, or fail to arrive, as part of an experience of self? How does a doubting look get incorporated as an anxious mode of looking upon the world? Is agency paralysed by the look, or can it be re-found? To explore these questions, I used a theoretical framework inspired by object relations psychoanalysis, a branch of theory which, at certain moments, projects an epistemological confidence that risks being undermined by one of its own central tenets – the existence of an unconscious, that 'core of experience that defies certain knowledge' (Cohen, 2013, p. 3). My approach in this chapter was thus marked by attention to the 'speculative' nature of my knowledge, a term that also references looking, and mirrors. Who *knows* disability, and how? How does uncertainty about what is carried in the gaze get enacted in the body of the child? How does (the lack of) diagnostic certainty translate into the gazing relationship, and into agency? How does the look communicate 'rehabilitative' desire? These were questions that I explored both in relation to my own lived experience and in my discussion of Hodgson Burnett's (1987 [1911]) *The Secret Garden* and Lessing's (2007 [1988]) *The Fifth Child*, in the context of which I grew interested in my acts of reading as acts of looking with particular consequences for the texts. Could I escape the rehabilitative paradigm in my reading and find a way of 'playing' with the text of *The Secret Garden*, which had meant so much to me as a child? By framing my own present-day gaze in terms of the reproduction of an over-looking/overlooking gaze from childhood, which both over-scrutinised me and simultaneously failed to see me – and by drawing attention to my own propensity to rehabilitate – my discussion troubled the representation of the disabled child as a simple recipient of the gaze.

The disabled child of Chapters 2 and 3 remained, for the most part, the object of discourses of 'making', yet, by introducing new strands of theory to the conceptual framework, and by developing existing strands, the seeds of resistance could begin to be sown. In Chapter 2 the hegemonic concept of 'development' was denaturalised and understood as a defining feature in the narrative of the disabled child. Central to my conceptual framework here was the work of Burman (2008a, 2008b) on the interconnections between discourses of developmental psychology (which universalises a highly specific version of childhood) on the one hand, and an imperialist model of economic development on the other. I examined a narrative saturated with the parental desire to see a child develop: Nichols' 1967 play, *A Day in the Death of Joe Egg*. Turning to the case study of Ashley X, I focussed on the way in which bioethical controversy emerges when a treatment cannot easily be defined as 'rehabilitative'. Yet as a consequence of the binary approach that bioethical discourse facilitates (Tremain, 2006), the norms of rehabilitative discourse go unchallenged. I retained an ambivalent attachment to the concept of development throughout the chapter, committed to analysing how it operates in a guise of neutrality, but also aware of my own argument's reliance on a version of developmentalism in my commitment to object relations psychoanalysis. In the final part of the chapter, as I teased out some aspects of this ambivalence through my discussion of the 'pathological' symptom as a mode of resistance, I began to find a stronger critical-theoretical voice of my own, which was capable of mediating between theories, with the goal of exploring less oppressive ways of thinking about development. Even if the disabled child of this chapter was still 'made' in relation to the developing child, I sought to make it easier for her to move in the way she wanted to move, through my attempt to re-evaluate her present-day Obsessive Compulsive Disorder symptom as a reaction to the toxic legacy of the figure of the developing child.

In Chapter 3, I turned my attention to the apparent agency – or choice – we feel ourselves to have as subjects of liberal individualist ideology (Salecl, 2010). The process of making that interested me here was that of reification: I explored the way in which the commodification of the child 'makes' or 'makes for' a particular type of experience for the disabled child. I argued, drawing on the work of Edelman (2004), Ahmed (2010) and Mollow (2012), that the child is perceived as an 'investment for the future' and that the arrival of the disabled child both disrupts the connection with futurity and gives rise to a need for this child's future to be manically reclaimed. I explored the role of the rhetoric of the child-as-gift (used in particular in relation to disabled children) in masking the commodification of all children. As Derrida's (1992) writing on the gift reveals, the desire to expel the idea of exchange does not produce its expulsion; indeed, the waiting time of middle-class motherhood is experienced as a loss precisely because it represents the deferral of productivity onto the next generation (Baraitser, 2012a). The time-consuming labour of child-rearing only intensifies the effects of reification, which play themselves out within the dynamics of the family: what place is there here for the disabled child, whose care takes yet more time? In my chapter, this discussion provided a backdrop for a consideration of the traumatic effects of the diagnosis of impairment in early childhood, with a particular focus on questions of time, futurity and promise. I examined the performativity of what I termed 'the diagnostic speech act', drawing on Butler's (1997a) work on injurious speech. In my reflections on the effects of the diagnostic speech act on the future-oriented body of the pre-verbal child, I worked towards a phenomenology of "'rehabilitative futurism'" (Mollow, 2012, p. 288), highlighting the experience of paralysis and the impossibility of resistance for a subject caught in identification with the aggressor (Ferenczi, 1999). Butler's work in *Excitable Speech* (1997a) complicates the concept of agency in language for any subject, yet I argued that for the individual who has been subject to diagnosis as a pre-verbal infant, the problems associated with 'counter[ing] the offensive call' (p. 2) are magnified.

These problems became the focus of my work in Chapter 4, where I finally sought to address the question of agency more directly, seeking to understand precisely why, for so long in my life, I had been unable to take up a position of resistance and to move beyond the internalised oppression that had prevented me from proudly taking up an identity as 'disabled'. The 'wobbly body' – a term that denotes at once the physical experience of impairment and the pre-verbal body as the site of affect's introjection – was the subject of my phenomenological and psychoanalytic investigation. I theorised the role of rehabilitation in the creation of this wobbly body in early childhood, developing an analysis of Pedro Almodóvar's *The Skin I Live In* (2011) as a film text whose attacks on the potential to become absorbed in narrative mirrored my own experience of rehabilitation as an *interruption*. What I tried to show in this chapter was that in order to resist internalised oppression, what is first required is a subject that can be pierced by the arrow of the offensive call; that the capacity to be wounded is a prerequisite in the making of a subject of resistance. The subject that has dissociated from a wobbly body has protected itself from insult but has also, in losing its vulnerability to the wound of interpellation, lost its potential to reverse the insult – has lost its agency.

In questions about attribution of agency, critical disability studies and psychoanalysis are uncomfortable bedfellows, and indeed the tension between these two fields has been a focal point in this book. Where do I ultimately stand on this debate, and what are the political implications of a book that remains committed to both approaches, in spite of their sometimes antagonistic relationship? As I draw this book to a close, and highlight some of the political and social implications of my work, I will briefly discuss Nikolas Rose's (1999) work on the 'psy' disciplines in order to ask, can psychoanalysis be radical? I will then engage more directly with the animosity between critical disability studies and psychoanalysis, in a bid to show what I think psychoanalysis can add to a politics of disability. I will conclude by returning to the figure that has preoccupied me throughout the book – the disabled child – as I seek to imagine what a different world might offer her.

In *Governing the Soul* (1999), Nikolas Rose casts contemporary psychological therapies in opposition to the anti-psychiatry movement of the 1960s, which he depicts as their forebear. Associating psychological therapies with liberalism and the anti-psychiatry movement (with which disability activism is broadly in sympathy) with radicalism, he writes that the former

promise [...] not liberation from social constraints but rendering psycho-logical constraints on autonomy conscious, and hence amenable to rational transformation. Achieving freedom becomes a matter not of slogans nor of political revolution, but of slow, painstaking, and detailed work on our own subjective and personal realities, guided by an expert knowledge of the psyche.

(N. Rose, 1999, pp. 257–258)

From my perspective, this dichotomy is a little too neat. I think that it problematically conflates psychoanalysis and other psychotherapies. Rose's (1999) thesis in this section of the book is that psychotherapy – which, along with psychological discourse more generally, has become embedded as a feature of British cultural life during the twentieth century – can be understood as a Foucauldian technology for governing the self. In Rose's (1999) analysis, the goals of psychotherapy intersect with the goals of liberalism and the biopolitical strategies upon which it depends, because both require an individual who exercises choice (or who can be enabled to choose via the psychotherapeutic process) in order to govern the self, and both characterise a lack of 'freedom' as resulting from a pathology of the individual.

Nikolas Rose's argument is persuasive, and of course he is not alone in connecting psychoanalysis with liberal thought (see Samuels, 2009). I find the argument especially difficult to refute precisely because it engages the part of me that experiences psychoanalysis as physiotherapy, as a rehabilitative training and a means of control. Whilst I agree with Rose on the one hand that, in the contemporary period, the cultural embedment of psychological thinking has brought about a paradigm shift whereby our truth is based on 'the relations between inner reality and external appearances' (1999, p. 263), I believe that psychoanalysis, by addressing itself to the unconscious, can mobilise forces that are beyond its own knowing and hence beyond its own control (Cohen, 2013). In my celebration of the symptom of anxiety-resistance at the end of Chapter 2, I suggested that in 'creating' this symptom, psychoanalysis had outdone itself, allowing something to be released that might work against the developmentalism invoked by the idea of 'getting better', or cure. This Frankenstein's monster of a symptom could potentially turn against psychoanalysis in a rejection of its 'creator'.[2] But what if its 'creator' (the therapist) was not actually interested in curing it, but only in understanding it on its own terms? My discovery prompted anger: how could the 'creator' walk away from the mess it had made so readily? In this moment I understood that I was only able to value myself according to a paradigm of normalisation, and that I believed that I could only be of interest to anyone insofar as they wanted to 'fix' me.

The revelation that analysis could be about comprehension, as opposed to cure, was a major breakthrough for me, given that I had been projecting the desire to be 'fixed' onto the psychoanalytic process from the beginning, without even realising it. Nor can I be alone in such a projection: in a culture saturated with the influence of the 'psy' disciplines, we expect therapy – especially a therapy that is part of the edifice of liberalism in its participation in a 'market of expertise' (N. Rose, 1999, p. 231) – to make us better. Yet most versions of psychoanalysis reject a narrative of straightforward 'making better', valuing insight first and foremost, and therefore sidestep the liberal imperative to prepare the subject to return to work. Moreover,

I would say, following Barbara Taylor (2014), that it is not through the experience of getting better, exactly, that one finds oneself feeling more able to live, but rather through the strength one draws out of being able to think one's own unthinkable and feel the things that feel unbearable.[3] Such a strengthening of the self is at the cost of a lengthy period of feeling worse, and of being potentially unproductive, or less productive, in the terms of neoliberalism. As Baraitser (2012b) notes, psychoanalysis disrupts neoliberal temporality by taking so long. Its outcomes are not easily commodifiable. It hardly seems like a good investment for a cash-strapped neoliberal government, post-financial crisis, and this is deeply problematic in that it makes psychoanalysis inaccessible to most people, because it is unaffordable. As a result, its status as a bourgeois luxury is reinforced and its radicalism is overlooked. Yet psychoanalysis is radical in yet another way. This is the danger of the political emancipation of the analysand. Although it would be true to say that my breakthrough made the 'psychological constraints on autonomy conscious', it *also* gave birth to a political consciousness, which could indeed become a 'matter [...] of slogans' and 'political revolution' (N. Rose, 1999, p. 257, emphasis in original). If psychoanalysis leads subjects into becoming 'attached to the version of themselves they have been led to produce' as Rose (p. 251) argues, it also has the potential to give rise to a political subjectivity that is capable of rejecting the very norms that its theories inscribe.

Disability studies has long been suspicious of psychoanalysis (Watermeyer, 2013; Goodley, 2011). Goodley's (2011, p. 94, emphasis in original) defence of a '*social* psychoanalytic perspective' seeks to bring a certain kind of psychoanalysis into the fold, but it is marked by ambivalence. He observes that psychoanalysis has been understood as having 'normalising aims' and links it with a view of disability as personal tragedy (Goodley, 2011, p. 94). It is interesting to note, though, that even Foucault's description of discourses, which aspires to avoid making normative judgments about different regimes of knowledge, has been criticised by Jürgen Habermas for its 'cryptonormativism' (1994, p. 96). Thus we might question whether it is feasible for *any* discourse to remain value-free and non-normative. Until recently, the discipline of critical disability studies has often read psychoanalysis as either depriving the disabled subject of agency in order to impose its own agenda, or as psychologising disability such that it becomes an individual problem, requiring individual agency to solve (Goodley, 2011).[4] Without wanting to refute these criticisms outright, I would distinguish here between psychoanalysis as a theoretical discourse and psychoanalysis as a clinical practice, as well as between different schools of psychoanalytic thought. As we have seen, object relations psychoanalytic discourse retains an attachment to developmentalism that often contains a normalising element, drawing as it does on medicalised notions of health and pathology. Notions of the normal and the pathological may also inhere within therapeutic practices, yet these practices also, in my opinion, have the potential to bring 'normalcy' into the consulting room in such a way as to understand and even defuse its power. Psychoanalytic therapy achieves this in an extremely paradoxical way, via a re-experiencing of the trauma of being normalised, as I argued in Chapter 4. As previously stated, what this has meant for me is that psychotherapy feels like physiotherapy. It feels like a space in which there is a rehabilitative imperative; it has seemed to me continually that the goal is to cure me. At its worst it has felt as though it is *unmaking* me, that it has produced the very flood of anxieties that constantly interrupt any sense of psychic continuity.

This might not seem to be much of a defence of psychoanalysis, and especially not for a society obsessed with pursuing happiness as its chief goal, to paraphrase Sara Ahmed (2010). What strange kind of therapy makes one feel worse? In fact, it would be incorrect to say that psychoanalysis has made me feel worse, and more accurate to say that it has made me feel *more*. But I do not want to elide the fact that in animating me – in making me vulnerable to the wound of interpellation – my psychoanalysis *has* led to great suffering, I think because I had so much suffering that had been left undone, or repressed.

Critical disability studies might well be suspicious of this suffering and of the therapeutic intervention that has (re)evoked it, asking why I should have to suffer or why I should undergo an analysis that seems to be about helping me, a disabled person, '"adjust" to disability' (Reeve, 2001, p. 626). I am sympathetic to this critique; all my life I have been seeking to adjust to the world. This book represents a step *away* from such compliance. I would in no way want to advocate a therapy that constructs my role as one of adjustment. Moreover, there are clear grounds for suspicion of psychoanalysis in this context, given its history of pathologising disabled people (Watermeyer, 2013), which I discussed in Chapter 1. Critical disability studies is right to remain on its guard. And yet, the difference between psychoanalysis and any other kind of therapy, as I see it, is precisely its capacity to facilitate the repetition of the Other's desire for me to 'adjust'. Psychoanalysis permits me to reflect on this repetition as something I transfer to the process from my past, and hence as something I invite from the world. This is not to downplay the fact that the world still has a problem with disability, but rather that psychoanalysis helps me to think about and clarify my own role and the world's role in this.

Furthermore, the conscious re-experiencing of the trauma of being normalised has made it possible for me to resist compliance, to resist normalisation, to resist the imperative to 'adjust' and *even to resist psychoanalysis itself*. But this has entailed going *into* disabling experience rather than moving away from it, in a terrifying ordeal akin to Taylor's journey of 'entering into [madness] and travelling to its roots' (2014, p. xix). It involves suffering. It seems to me that the narratives produced by critical disability studies sometimes seek to shy away from a focus on suffering, shifting very quickly into a register of resistance. Suffering is not what we as disabled people should have to go through; we are not the ones needing therapy. Suffering has become associated with the model of disability as individual tragedy and it is assumed that it cannot tell us anything we do not already know: instead, it is argued, our key themes should be the marginalisation and oppression of disabled people in a social context. I would not want to de-prioritise these themes, but rather to reach them via a different route. How can we separate out our suffering and our oppression? What if we need our suffering, as disabled people? What if our suffering needs us to attend to it? Sara Ahmed reminds us that '[t]o suffer can mean to feel your disagreement with what has been judged as good', suggesting that '[a]cts of revolution' are *'protests against the costs of agreement'* (2010, pp. 210, 213, emphasis in original). An attentiveness to the specifics of the symptom of the individual – specifics that are associated with the anguish of disability as a psychosocial experience – can, I argue, lead to a 'disagreeable' politics of disability. This would be an uncomfortable, unsettling politics that understands the 'making' of the disabled subject as something that takes place at the intersection of the inner and the outer, psyche and culture, somatic experience and discourse. It would be an 'implicated' politics (McRuer, 1998, p. 136),[5] which sees us all, disabled and non-disabled alike, as playing a role in the reproduction of a disabling society, but which simultaneously recognises the structural inequalities that give some of us more power than others.

The politics of disability that I am advocating is one in which we inhabit the suffering of disablement in order to know it intimately and thereby to unmake *it* this time around, rather than being unmade *by* it. This is a politics of disability that knows how to get angry with what's 'out-there', but whose rage is all the more politically powerful and precise because it is also fully able to take account of what's 'in-here' (Frosh and Baraitser, 2008, p. 347). Such a politics of disability appears to dichotomise the 'in-here' and the 'out-there' as though they could be neatly distinguished: my book has argued that this neatness is a fallacy of liberal individualism, and yet I would ultimately want to retain a distinction, albeit an unsettled one, between the 'in-here' and the 'out-there'. Psychoanalysis renders the 'in-here' of the unconscious more visible. Through it, it *does* become possible to see one's own contribution for what it is, and in this way to get even *more* angry with the 'out-there', for being – very often, it seems to me – so destructive and yet so unreflexive; so unattentive to either the lessons of history or the damage caused by practices of unmaking. By unmaking, I mean both the 'rehabilitative' procedures that have come under scrutiny in this book and the structures of war and torture that Scarry (1985) highlights, to say nothing of the global suffering that continues due to the legacies of colonialism and ongoing neo-colonial inequality.

Indeed, Scarry's work is relevant here, in that, in *The Body in Pain* she demands to know why, given that war and torture are held by many to be immoral, structures of 'making' are not themselves infused with a moral element (p. 22). She asks:

> [I]s it not peculiar that [...] the action of creating is not [...] held to be bound up with justice in the way those other events are bound up with injustice, that it (the mental, verbal, or material process of making the world) is not held to be centrally entailed in the elimination of pain as the unmaking of the world is held to be entailed in pain's infliction?
>
> (Scarry, 1985, p. 22)

Scarry's rhetorical question could be read as a rallying cry for those of us in critical disability studies who want to see something different happening in place of those acts of so-called 'therapy' that interrupt, disrupt, interfere with, *unmake* the disabled baby's experience of herself. By focussing on the making of the disabled child, this book has sought to demand that we consider the ethics of the acts of making in which we are engaged. It asks us to be reflexive about what is therapeutic and what is not, whilst wanting to complicate a conceptualisation of therapy as inherently liberal, normalising and unhelpful. It asks us to think what it would mean to see acts of making from the standpoint of the child who is being made, rather than from that of the rational adult, although it has also queried our capacity to know the child's perspective other than through our own adult eyes, whose vision may be clouded by our own projections and by the persistence of our own childhood in the present (Lesnik-Oberstein, 2011; Rose, 1984).

In Chapter 4 I explored the history of a child who was unmade by medical intervention and who acted creatively to remake herself, as a way of defending herself from what she experienced as an attack. Yet in so doing, the child lost herself. Could we imagine a world in which that child did not have to act in such a way, did not have to remake herself? Could we imagine a world in which she did not have to learn to mimic the 'normal child' or the 'developing child', or one in which the diagnosis of impairment would not necessarily lead to a pre-given routine of rehabilitation? Could we imagine a world that was interested in trying to understand what the child's embodiment meant to *her*, and not just what it meant to those with the power to diagnose? For it seems to me that in the scenarios analysed in this book, the responsibility to remake has, until now, been placed disproportionately on the shoulders of the disabled child. I dream of a world that could remake itself in such a way as to understand the ethics and the implications of its own acts of making.

Notes

1 In relation to this point, it should be noted that the question of the child's agency has been a major topic of debate in childhood studies – see Lesnik-Oberstein (2011).
2 I place the term 'creator' inside inverted commas to indicate the way in which the analyst – and the analysis itself – feels like the source of the symptom (and to some extent, it is, in that the process awakens the symptom), and yet the real creator is, in my case, the diagnostic speech act and the physiotherapy.
3 I am referring to Taylor's (2014) observation in *The Last Asylum* that the concept of recovery 'implies a return to a previously healthy state' (p. xix). She contrasts this portrayal with the metaphor of 'entering into [madness] and travelling to its roots' (p. xix), which she sees as a more congenial description of her own experience.
4 Goodley (2011, p. 94) contends that 'a turn to social psychoanalysis must embrace theories that do not put the problems of disablism back onto disabled people'.
5 See my discussion of the 'immune/implicated' binary (McRuer, 1998, p. 136) in Chapter 2.

References

A Day in the Death of Joe Egg, by Nichols, P. (2001) Directed by Boswell, L. [New Ambassadors Theatre/Comedy Theatre, London, from October 2001].

A Day in the Death of Joe Egg, by Nichols, P. (2011) Directed by Breen, P. [Citizens Theatre, Glasgow, 19 October–12 November 2011].

A Day in the Death of Joe Egg, by Nichols, P. (2013) Directed by Unwin, S. [Rose Theatre, Kingston, 30 April–18 May 2013].

A Day in the Death of Joe Egg, by Nichols, P. (2019) Directed by Evans, S. [Trafalgar Studios, London, 21 September 2019–30 November 2019].

A World without Down's Syndrome? (2016) BBC Two (UK), 5 October 2016, 9pm.

Abberley, P. (1995) 'Disabling ideology in health and welfare – The case of occupational therapy', *Disability and Society*, vol. 10, no. 2, pp. 221–232 [Online]. Available at https://doi.org/10.1080/09687599550023660 (Accessed 21 September 2019).

Abi-Rached, J. and Rose, N. (2013) *Neuro: The New Brain Sciences and the Management of the Mind*, Princeton, NJ, Princeton University Press.

Ahmed, S. (2006) *Queer Phenomenology: Orientations, Objects, Others*, Durham, NC, Duke University Press.

Ahmed, S. (2010) *The Promise of Happiness*, Durham, NC, Duke University Press.

Ahmed, S. (2012) *On Being Included: Racism and Diversity in Institutional Life*, Durham, NC, Duke University Press.

Aizura, A. (2006) 'Of borders and homes: The imaginary community of (trans)sexual citizenship', *Inter-Asia Cultural Studies*, vol. 7, no. 2, pp. 289–309 [Online]. Available at https://doi.org/10.1080/14649370600673953 (Accessed 21 September 2019).

Althusser, L. (1971) 'Ideology and ideological state apparatuses (notes towards an investigation)', in *Lenin and Philosophy and Other Essays* (trans. B. Brewster), London, NLB, pp. 121–173.

Anzieu, D. (1989) 'The notion of a skin ego', in Anzieu, D. (ed) *The Skin Ego* (trans. C. Turner), New Haven, CT, Yale University Press, pp. 36–45.

Anzieu, D. (1990) 'The body', in Anzieu, D. and Tarrab, G. (eds) *A Skin for Thought: Interviews with Gilbert Tarrab on Psychology and Psychoanalysis* (trans. D. Nash Briggs), London, Karnac, pp. 61–79.

Armstrong, D. (1995) 'The rise of surveillance medicine', *Sociology of Health and Illness*, vol. 17, no. 3, pp. 393–404 [Online]. Available at https://doi.org/10.1111/1467-9566. ep10933329.

Ashley's parents. (2012) '"The Ashley treatment", towards a better quality of life for "pillow angels"' [Online]. Available at http://pillowangel.org/Ashley%20Treatment.pdf (Accessed 7 September 2019).

Ashley's parents. (2018) *Ashley's Blog* [Online]. Available at http://pillowangel.org (Accessed 26 August 2019).

Austin, J. (1975) *How to Do Things with Words*, 2nd edn, Oxford, Clarendon Press.

Babycentre UK. (2019) *Babycentre* [Online]. Available at www.babycentre.co.uk (Accessed 27 August 2019).

Bakhtin, M. (1981) 'Forms of time and of the chronotope in the novel', in Holquist, M. (ed) *The Dialogic Imagination: Four Essays* (trans. C. Emerson and M. Holquist), Austin, TX, University of Texas Press, pp. 84–258.

Balint, M. (2000) *The Doctor, His Patient and the Illness*, Millennium reprint of 2nd edn, Edinburgh, Churchill Livingstone.

Bamford, E. (2010) 'The great Gina Ford debate', *Independent*, 12 January [Online]. Available at www.independent.co.uk/life-style/health-and-families/features/the-great-gina-ford-debate-1864825.html (Accessed 9 September 2019).

Baraitser, L. (2008) *Maternal Encounters: The Ethics of Interruption* [ebook reader], Hove, East Sussex, Routledge.

Baraitser, L. (2012a) 'Maternal publics: Time, relationality and the public sphere', in Gülerce, A. (ed) *Re(con)figuring Psychoanalysis: Critical Juxtapositions of the Philosophical, the Sociohistorical and the Political*, Basingstoke, Palgrave Macmillan, pp. 221–240.

Baraitser, L. (2012b) 'Communality across time: Responding to encounters with *Maternal encounters: The ethics of interruption*', *Studies in Gender and Sexuality*, vol. 13, no. 2, pp. 117–122 [Online]. Available at https://doi.org/10.1080/15240657.2012.682932 (Accessed 21 September 2019).

Baraitser, L. (2017) *Enduring Time*, London, Bloomsbury.

Bateman, C. (2012) *The Mythology of Evolution*, Winchester, Zero Books.

Bell, C. (2017) 'Is disability studies actually white disability studies?', in Davis, L. (ed) *The Disability Studies Reader*, 5th edn, Abingdon, Oxon, Routledge, pp. 406–415.

Benn, M. (2006) 'The politics of parenting', *Guardian*, 3 June [Online]. Available at www.theguardian.com/lifeandstyle/2006/jun/03/family.family7 (Accessed 27 August 2019).

Berlant, L. (2011) *Cruel Optimism*, Durham, NC, Duke University Press.

Bick, E. (1968) 'The experience of skin in early object-relations', *International Journal of Psychoanalysis*, vol. 49, pp. 484–486.

Bion, W. (1962) 'The psycho-analytic study of thinking', *International Journal of Psychoanalysis*, vol. 43, pp. 306–310.

Bion, W. (1963) *Elements of Psychoanalysis*, London, Heinemann.

Blackman, L. and Walkerdine, V. (2001) *Mass Hysteria: Critical Psychology and Media Studies*, Basingstoke, Palgrave Macmillan.

Boyd, R., Ziviani, J., Sakzewski, L., Novak, I., Badawi, N., Pannek, K., Elliott, C., Greaves, S., Guzzetta, A., Whittingham, K., Valentine, J., Morgan, C., Wallen, M., Eliasson, A., Findlay, L., Ware, R., Fiori, S. and Rose, S. (2017) 'REACH: Study protocol of a randomised trial of rehabilitation very early in congenital hemiplegia', *BMJ Open*, vol. 7, pp. 1–18 [Online]. Available at https://bmjopen.bmj.com/content/7/9/e017204.info [doi: 10.1136/bmjopen-2017-017204] (Accessed 25 August 2019).

Brennan, T. (2004) *The Transmission of Affect*, Ithaca, NY and London, Cornell University Press.

Brock, R. (2009) '"No such thing as society": Thatcherism and Derridean hospitality in *The Fifth Child*', *Doris Lessing Studies*, vol. 28, no. 1, pp. 7–13.

Brown, P. (1995) 'Naming and framing: The social construction of diagnosis and illness', *Journal of Health and Social Behaviour* (Extra Issue: *Forty Years of Medical Sociology: The*

State of the Art and Directions for the Future), pp. 34–52 [Online]. Available at www. jstor.org/stable/2626956 [doi: 10.2307/2626956] (Accessed 21 September 2019).

Burman, E. (2008a) *Developments: Child, Image, Nation* [ebook online], Hove, East Sussex, Routledge.

Burman, E. (2008b) *Deconstructing Developmental Psychology* [ebook online], 2nd edn, Hove, East Sussex, Routledge.

Bury, M. (1982) 'Chronic illness as biographical disruption', *Sociology of Health and Illness*, vol. 4, no. 2, pp. 167–182 [Online]. Available at https://doi.org/10.1111/1467-9566.ep11339939 (Accessed 27 August 2019).

Butler, J. (1997a) *Excitable Speech: A Politics of the Performative*, Abingdon, Oxon, Routledge.

Butler, J. (1997b) *The Psychic Life of Power: Theories in Subjection*, Stanford, CA, Stanford University Press.

Callard, F. and Fitzgerald, D. (2015) *Rethinking Interdisciplinarity across the Social Sciences and Neurosciences*, Basingstoke, Palgrave Macmillan.

Caruth, C. (1995) 'Traumatic awakenings', in Parker, A. and Sedgwick, E. (eds) *Performativity and Performance*, London, Routledge, pp. 89–108.

Caselli, D. (2010) 'Kindergarten theory: Childhood, affect, critical thought', *Feminist Theory*, vol. 11, no. 3, pp. 241–254 [Online]. Available at https://doi.org/10.1177/1464700110376276 (Accessed 21 September 2019).

Chappell, A. (1998) 'Still out in the cold: People with learning disabilities and the social model of disability', in Shakespeare, T. (ed) *The Disability Reader: Social Science Perspectives*, London, Cassell, pp. 211–220.

Charmaz, K. (1983) 'Loss of self: A fundamental form of suffering in the chronically ill', *Sociology of Health and Illness*, vol. 5, no. 2, pp. 168–195 [Online]. Available at https://doi.org/10.1111/1467-9566.ep10491512 (Accessed 27 August 2019).

Chen, M. (2012) *Animacies: Biopolitics, Racial Mattering and Queer Affect*, Durham, NC, Duke University Press.

Cohen, J. (2013) *The Private Life: Why We Remain in the Dark*, London, Granta.

Cook, J. (2013) 'Creative writing as a research method', in Griffin, G. (ed) *Research Methods for English Studies*, 2nd edn, Edinburgh, Edinburgh University Press, pp. 200–217.

Coolidge, S. (2012 [1872]) *What Katy Did*, London, Vintage.

Cooper, H. (2010) 'The ideal of self-sufficiency and the physically disabled subject in contemporary Anglo-American culture', unpublished Master's dissertation, London, Birkbeck, University of London.

Cooper, H. (2013a) 'The oppressive power of normalcy in the lives of disabled children: Deploying history to denaturalize the notion of the "normal child"', in Curran, T. and Runswick-Cole, K. (eds) *Disabled Children's Childhood Studies: Critical Approaches in a Global Context*, Basingstoke, Palgrave Macmillan, pp. 136–151.

Cooper, H. (2013b) 'Defamiliarising passivity with the disabled subject: Activism, academia and the lived experience of impairment', *Graduate Journal of Social Science*, vol. 10, no. 3, pp. 125–137 [Online]. Available at http://gjss.org/sites/default/files/issues/chapters/papers/Journal-10-03-06-Cooper_0.pdf (Accessed 9 September 2019).

Cooper, H. (2015) *Making the Disabled Child: Critical Disability Studies at the Intersection of Cultural Representation and Lived Experience*, unpublished PhD thesis, London, Birkbeck, University of London.

Cooper, H. (2016) 'Passing or trespassing? Unseen disability, containment and the politics of "feeling like a fraud" in a neoliberal bureaucracy', in Mallett, R., Ogden, C. and

Slater, J. (eds) *Theorising Normalcy and the Mundane: Precarious Positions*, Chester, University of Chester Press, pp. 120–143.

Couser, G. T. (2012) *Memoir: An Introduction*, Oxford, Oxford University Press.

Critical Physiotherapy Network. (2019) *Critical Physiotherapy Network* [Online]. Available at https://criticalphysio.net (Accessed 19 August 2019).

Culler, J. (2011) *Literary Theory: A Very Short Introduction*, 2nd edn, Oxford, Oxford University Press.

Cunningham, H. (1991) *The Children of the Poor: Representations of Childhood since the Seventeenth Century*, Oxford, Blackwell Publishing.

Cunningham, H. (2005) *Children and Childhood in Western Society since 1500*, 2nd edn, Harlow, Pearson Education.

Curran, T. and Runswick-Cole, K. (2013) 'Preface', in Curran, T. and Runswick-Cole, K. (eds) *Disabled Children's Childhood Studies: Critical Approaches in a Global Context*, Basingstoke, Palgrave Macmillan, pp. ix–xi.

Cusk, R. (2008) *A Life's Work: On Becoming A Mother*, paperback edn with new introduction, London, Faber and Faber.

Cvetkovich, A. (2012) *Depression: A Public Feeling*, Durham, NC, Duke University Press.

Damasio, A. (2000) *The Feeling of What Happens: Body, Emotion and the Making of Consciousness*, London, Vintage.

Darke, P. (1999) *The Cinematic Construction of Physical Disability as Identified through the Application of the Social Model of Disability to Six Indicative Films Made since 1970: A Day in the Death of Joe Egg (1970), The Raging Moon (1970), The Elephant Man (1980), Whose Life Is It Anyway? (1981), Duet for One (1987), and My Left Foot (1989)*, unpublished PhD thesis, Coventry, University of Warwick.

David, E. and Derthick, A. (2014) 'What is internalized oppression, and so what?', in David, E. (ed) *Internalized Oppression: The Psychology of Marginalized Groups* [ebook online], New York, Springer Publishing Company, pp. 1–30.

Davis, L. (1995) *Enforcing Normalcy: Disability, Deafness, and the Body*, London and New York, Verso.

Debord, G. (1994) *The Society of the Spectacle* (trans. D. Nicholson-Smith), New York, Zone Books.

Derrida, J. (1992) *Given Time: Counterfeit Money* (trans. P. Kamuf), Chicago, IL, The University of Chicago Press.

Derrida, J. (1997) *Of Grammatology* (trans. G. Spivak), Baltimore, MD, The Johns Hopkins University Press.

Dickens, C. (1843) *A Christmas Carol. In Prose. Being a Ghost Story of Christmas. With Illustrations by John Leech*, London, Chapman and Hall [Online]. Accessed via *Literature Online* and Available at https://search-proquest-com.uea.idm.oclc.org/docview/2138576883?accountid=10637 (Accessed 8 September 2019).

Diprose, R. (1994) *The Bodies of Women: Ethics, Embodiment and Sexual Difference*, London, Routledge.

Diprose, R. (2002) *Corporeal Generosity: On Giving with Nietzsche, Merleau-Ponty and Levinas*, Albany, NY, State University of New York Press.

Edelman, L. (2004) *No Future: Queer Theory and the Death Drive*, Durham, NC, Duke University Press.

Edwards, R., Gillies, V. and Horsley, N. (2015) 'Brain science and early years policy: Hopeful ethos or "cruel optimism"?', *Critical Social Policy*, vol. 35, no. 2, pp. 167–187 [Online]. Available at https://doi.org/10.1177/0261018315574020 (Accessed 25 August 2019).

Engels, F. (1893) 'Letter to Franz Mehring' [Online]. Available at www.marxists.org/arch ive/marx/works/1893/letters/93_07_14.htm (Accessed 10 September 2019).

EQuality Training. (n.d.) 'The art of respectful language' [Online]. Available at www.equal itytraining.co.uk/images/news/language_of_respect.pdf (Accessed 22 September 2019).

Faircloth, C. (2014) 'Intensive parenting and the expansion of parenting', in Lee, E., Bristow, J., Faircloth, C. and Macvarish, J. (eds) *Parenting Culture Studies*, Basingstoke, Palgrave Macmillan, pp. 25–50.

Fanon, F. (1986) *Black Skin, White Masks* (trans. C. Markmann), London, Pluto Press.

Federici, S. (2012) 'Wages against housework', in Federici, S. (ed) *Revolution at Point Zero: Housework, Reproduction and Feminist Struggle*, Oakland, CA, PM Press, pp. 15–22.

Federici, S. and Cox, N. (2012) 'Counterplanning from the kitchen', in Federici, S. (ed) *Revolution at Point Zero: Housework, Reproduction and Feminist Struggle*, Oakland, CA, PM Press, pp. 28–40.

Felman, S. (ed) (1982) *Literature and Psychoanalysis – The Question of Reading: Otherwise*, Baltimore, MD, Johns Hopkins University Press.

Ferenczi, S. (1999) 'Confusion of tongues between adults and the child (the language of tenderness and passion)', in Borossa, J. (ed) *Selected Writings*, London, Penguin, pp. 293–303.

Fisher, P. and Goodley, D. (2007) 'The linear medical model of disability: Mothers of disabled babies resist with counter-narratives', *Sociology of Health and Illness*, vol. 29, no. 1, pp. 66–81 [Online]. Available at https://doi.org/10.1111/j.1467-9566.2007.00518.x (Accessed 22 September 2019).

Ford, G. (1999) *The Contented Little Baby Book*, London, Vermilion.

Fost, N. (2007) Contribution on the Ashley X case in Mims, C., 'The pillow angel case – Three bioethicists weigh in', *Scientific American*, 5 January [Online]. Available at www.scientificamerican.com/article/the-pillow-angel-case-th/ (Accessed 26 August 2019).

Foucault, M. (1991) *Discipline and Punish: The Birth of the Prison* (trans. A. Sheridan), London, Penguin.

Foucault, M. (2002) *The Archaeology of Knowledge* (trans. A. Sheridan Smith), London, Routledge.

Foucault, M. (2003) *Abnormal: Lectures at the College de France 1974–1975* (trans. G. Burchell), London, Verso.

Frankenberg, R. (1993) *White Women, Race Matters: The Social Construction of Whiteness*, Minneapolis, MN, University of Minnesota Press.

Freeman, E. (2019) 'Committed to the end: On carework and re-reading', lecture at Birkbeck, University of London, 24 May 2019.

Freeman, H. (2016) 'Attachment parenting: The best way to raise a child – or maternal masochism?', *Guardian*, 30 July [Online]. Available at www.theguardian.com/lifeand style/2016/jul/30/attachment-parenting-best-way-raise-child-or-maternal-masochism (Accessed 27 August 2019).

Freud, S. (1955a) 'The "uncanny"', in Strachey, J. (ed) *The Standard Edition of the Complete Psychological Works of Sigmund Freud, Volume XVII (1917–1919): An Infantile Neurosis and Other Works* (trans. J. Strachey), London, The Hogarth Press, pp. 217–256.

Freud, S. (1955b) 'From the history of an infantile neurosis', in Strachey, J. (ed) *The Standard Edition of the Complete Psychological Works of Sigmund Freud, Volume XVII (1917–1919): An Infantile Neurosis and Other Works* (trans. J. Strachey), London, The Hogarth Press, pp. 7–122.

Freud, S. (1958a) 'Remembering, repeating and working-through (further recommendations on the technique of psycho-analysis II)', in Strachey, J. (ed) *The Standard Edition of the Complete Psychological Works of Sigmund Freud, Volume XII (1911–1913): The Case of Schreber, Papers on Technique and Other Works* (trans. J. Strachey), London, The Hogarth Press, pp. 145–156.

Freud, S. (1958b) 'Formulations on the two principles of mental functioning', in Strachey, J. (ed) *The Standard Edition of the Complete Psychological Works of Sigmund Freud, Volume XII (1911–1913): The Case of Schreber, Papers on Technique and Other Works* (trans. J. Strachey), London, The Hogarth Press, pp. 213–226.

Friesen, N., Feenberg, A. and Smith, G. (2009) 'Phenomenology and surveillance studies: Returning to the things themselves', *The Information Society: An International Journal*, vol. 25, no. 2, pp. 84–90 [Online]. Available at https://doi.org/10.1080/01972240802701585 (Accessed 16 September 2019).

Frosh, S. and Baraitser, L. (2008) 'Psychoanalysis and psychosocial studies', *Psychoanalysis, Culture and Society*, vol. 13, no. 4, pp. 346–365 [Online]. Available at https://doi.org/10.1057/pcs.2008.8 (Accessed 22 September 2019).

Fuchs, T. (2005) 'Corporealized and disembodied minds: A phenomenological view of the body in melancholia and schizophrenia', *Philosophy, Psychiatry, and Psychology*, vol. 12, no. 2, pp. 95–107 [Online]. Available at https://muse.jhu.edu/article/190379 (Accessed 22 September 2019).

Gallop, J. (2002) *Anecdotal Theory*, Durham, NC, Duke University Press.

Garland-Thomson, R. (2005) 'Staring at the other', *Disability Studies Quarterly*, vol. 25, no. 4 [Online]. Available at http://dsq-sds.org/article/view/610/787 (Accessed 10 September 2019).

Garland-Thomson, R. (2009) *Staring: How We Look*, Oxford, Oxford University Press.

Garland-Thomson, R. (2011) 'Misfits: A feminist materialist disability concept', *Hypatia*, vol. 26, no. 3, pp. 591–609 [Online]. Available at https://doi.org/10.1111/j.1527-2001.2011.01206.x (Accessed 22 September 2019).

Gawande, A. (2002) *Complications: A Surgeon's Notes on an Imperfect Science*, New York, Metropolitan Books.

Gerhardt, S. (2004) *Why Love Matters: How Affection Shapes a Baby's Brain*, Hove, East Sussex, Brunner-Routledge.

Gherovici, P. (2011) 'Psychoanalysis needs a sex change', *Gay & Lesbian Issues and Psychology Review*, vol. 7, no. 1, pp. 3–18 [Online]. Available at https://groups.psychology.org.au/Assets/Files/GLIP%20Review%20Vol%207%20No%201.pdf (Accessed 23 September, 2019).

Gibson, B. (2015) *Rehabilitation: A Post-Critical Approach*, Boca Raton, FL, CRC Press, Taylor and Francis Group.

Gill, J. (ed) (2006) *Modern Confessional Writing: New Critical Essays*, Abingdon, Oxon, Routledge.

Gleitzman, M. (1989) *Two Weeks with the Queen*, London, Blackie and Son.

Goffman, E. (1990) *Stigma: Notes on the Management of Spoiled Identity*, London, Penguin.

Goldstein, R. (1991) 'The implicated and the immune: Responses to AIDS in the arts and popular culture', in Nelkin, D., Willis, D. and Parris, S. (eds) *A Disease of Society: Cultural and Institutional Responses to AIDS*, Cambridge, Cambridge University Press, pp. 17–42.

Goodley, D. (2000) *Self-Advocacy in the Lives of People with Learning Difficulties*, Buckingham, Open University Press.

Goodley, D. (2001) '"Learning difficulties", the social model of disability and impairment: Challenging epistemologies', *Disability and Society*, vol. 16, no. 2, pp. 207–231 [Online]. Available at https://doi.org/10.1080/09687590120035816 (Accessed 21 September 2019).

Goodley, D. (2011) *Disability Studies: An Interdisciplinary Introduction*, London, Sage.

Goodley, D. and Lawthom, R. (2013) 'The disavowal of uncanny disabled children: Why non-disabled people are so messed up around childhood disability', in Curran, T. and Runswick-Cole, K. (eds) *Disabled Children's Childhood Studies: Critical Approaches in a Global Context*, Basingstoke, Palgrave Macmillan, pp. 164–179.

Gramsci, A. (1971) *Selections from the Prison Notebooks of Antonio Gramsci* (eds. and trans. Q. Hoare and G. Nowell Smith), London, Lawrence and Wishart.

Grech, S. and Soldatic, K. (2015) 'Introduction: Disability and colonialism: (Dis)encounters and anxious intersectionalities', *Social Identities*, vol. 21, no. 1, pp. 1–5.

Griffin, G. (2013) 'Research methods for English studies: An introduction', in Griffin, G. (ed) *Research Methods for English Studies*, 2nd edn, Edinburgh, Edinburgh University Press, pp. 1–17.

Gunther, D. and Diekema, D. (2006) 'Attenuating growth in children with profound developmental disability: A new approach to an old dilemma', *Archives of Pediatrics and Adolescent Medicine*, vol. 160, no. 10, pp. 1013–1017 [Online]. Available at http://arch pedi.jamanetwork.com/article.aspx?articleid=205567 (Accessed 21 September 2019).

Habermas, J. (1994) 'Some questions concerning the theory of power: Foucault again', in Kelly, M. (ed) *Critique and Power: Recasting the Foucault/Habermas Debate*, Cambridge, MA, MIT Press, pp. 79–107.

Hall, K. (2014) 'Towards a queer crip feminist politics of food', *PhiloSOPHIA*, vol. 4, no. 2, pp. 177–196 [Online]. Available at https://muse.jhu.edu/article/565882 (Accessed 23 September 2019).

Han, B.-C. (2017) *Psychopolitics: Neoliberalism and the New Technologies of Power*, London, Verso.

Hand, S. (2009) *Emmanuel Levinas*, Abingdon, Oxon, Routledge.

Hanisch, C. (1969) 'The personal is political' [Online]. Available at www.carolhanisch.org/CHwritings/PIP.html (Accessed 21 September 2019).

Harrang, C. (2012) 'Psychic skin and narcissistic rage: Reflections on Almodóvar's *The Skin I Live In*', *International Journal of Psychoanalysis*, vol. 93, pp. 1301–1308 [Online]. Available at https://doi.org/10.1111/j.1745-8315.2012.00633.x (Accessed 22 September 2019).

Harris, A. (1987) 'The rationalization of infancy', in Broughton, J. (ed) *Critical Theories of Psychological Development*, New York, Plenum Press, Yes, pp. 31–59.

Hass, A. (2011) 'Discipline beyond disciplines', in Walton, H. (ed) *Literature and Theology: New Interdisciplinary Spaces*, Abingdon, Oxon, Routledge, pp. 19–36.

Heti, S. (2018) *Motherhood*, London, Harvill Secker.

Hickman, M. (2005) 'The battle of the baby gurus', *Independent*, 13 December [Online]. Available at www.independent.co.uk/life-style/health-and-families/health-news/battle-of-the-baby-gurus-519272.html (Accessed 27 August 2019).

Hockey, J. and James, A. (1993) *Growing Up and Growing Old: Ageing and Dependency in the Life Course*, London, Sage.

Hocking, N. (2014) 'Letting the *Skyfall* or: How I learned to stop worrying and love James Bond', in Jones, S., Cooper, H. and Bigman, F., *Non-Reproduction: Politics, Ethics, Aesthetics*, a special issue of *Studies in the Maternal*, vol. 6, no. 1, pp. 1–23 [Online]. Available at http://doi.org/10.16995/sim.7 (Accessed 22 September 2019).

Hodgson Burnett, F. (1987 [1911]) *The Secret Garden*, Oxford, Oxford University Press.

Hollway, W. and Jefferson, T. (2013) *Doing Qualitative Research Differently: A Psychosocial Approach*, 2nd edn, London, Sage.

Hughes, B. (1999) 'The constitution of impairment: Modernity and the aesthetic of oppression', *Disability and Society*, vol. 14, no. 2, pp. 155–172 [Online]. Available at https://doi.org/10.1080/09687599926244 (Accessed 23 September 2019).

Jacques, J. (2015) *Trans: A Memoir*, London, Verso.

James, A., Jenks, C. and Prout, A. (1998) *Theorizing Childhood*, Cambridge, Polity Press.

Jardine, C. (2010) 'Britain's baby gurus go to war', *Telegraph*, 23 April [Online]. Available at www.telegraph.co.uk/women/mother-tongue/7620961/Britains-baby-gurus-go-to-war.html (Accessed 27 August 2019).

Jay, M. (1993) *Downcast Eyes: The Denigration of Vision in Twentieth-Century French Thought*, Berkeley, CA, University of California Press.

Johnson, B. (1986) 'Apostrophe, animation, and abortion', *Diacritics*, vol. 16, no. 1, pp. 28–47 [Online]. Available at www.jstor.org/stable/464649 [doi: 10.2307/464649] (Accessed 24 August 2019).

Jones, S., Cooper, H. and Bigman, F. (2014) 'Editorial – Non-reproduction: A conversation', *Non-Reproduction: Politics, Ethics, Aesthetics* a special issue of *Studies in the Maternal*, vol. 6, no. 1, n. p. [Online]. Available at http://doi.org/10.16995/sim.1 (Accessed 22 September 2019).

Jutel, A. (2015) 'Beyond the sociology of diagnosis', *Sociology Compass*, vol. 9, no. 9, pp. 841–852 [Online]. Available at https://doi.org/10.1111/soc4.12296 (Accessed 22 September 2019).

Jutel, A. and Nettleton, S. (2011) 'Towards a sociology of diagnosis: Reflections and opportunities', *Social Science and Medicine* (Special issue on sociology of diagnosis), vol. 73, no. 6, pp. 793–800 [Online]. Available at http://doi.org/10.1353/chq.0.1168 (Accessed 22 September 2019).

Kafer, A. (2013) *Feminist, Queer, Crip*, Bloomington, IN and Indianapolis, IN, Indiana University Press.

Katz Rothman, B. (2004) 'Motherhood under capitalism', in Taylor, J., Layne, L. and Wozniak, D. (eds) *Consuming Motherhood*, New Brunswick, Rutgers University Press, pp. 19–30.

Keith, L. (2001) *Take Up Thy Bed and Walk: Death, Disability and Cure in Classic Fiction for Girls*, London, The Women's Press.

Kleege, G. (1999) *Sight Unseen*, New Haven, CT and London, Yale University Press.

Klein, M. (1997a) 'Notes on some schizoid mechanisms', in Segal, H. (ed) *Envy and Gratitude and Other Works 1946–1963*, London, Vintage, pp. 1–24.

Klein, M. (1997b) 'Some theoretical conclusions regarding the emotional life of the infant', in Segal, H. (ed) *Envy and Gratitude and Other Works 1946–1963*, London, Vintage, pp. 61–93.

Kristeva, J. (1984) *Revolution in Poetic Language* (trans. M. Waller), New York, Columbia University Press.

Kumari Campbell, F. (2008) 'Exploring internalized ableism using critical race theory', *Disability and Society*, vol. 23, no. 2, pp. 151–162 [Online]. Available at https://doi.org/10.1080/09687590701841190 (Accessed 22 August 2019).

Lacey, E. (2016) 'Child's play: Illustrated bodies and traces of disability', *Textual Practice*, vol. 30, no. 5, pp. 795–813.

Landsman, G. (1999) 'Does god give special kids to special parents? Personhood and the child with disabilities as gift and giver', in Layne, L. (ed) *Transformative Motherhood: On Giving and Getting in a Consumer Culture*, New York, New York University Press, pp. 133–165.

Landsman, G. (2004) '"Too bad you got a lemon": Peter Singer, mothers of children with disabilities, and the critique of consumer culture', in Taylor, J., Layne, L. and Wozniak, D. (eds) *Consuming Motherhood*, New Brunswick, Rutgers University Press, pp. 100–121.

Lapper, A. (2006) *My Life in My Hands*, London, Pocket Books.

Latour, B. and Woolgar, S. (1986) *Laboratory Life: The Construction of Scientific Facts*, 2nd edn, Princeton, NJ and Chichester, Princeton University Press.

Law, J. (2004) *After Method: Mess in Social Science Research*, Abingdon, Oxon, Routledge.

Layne, L. (1999) 'The child as gift: New directions in the study of Euro-American gift exchange', in Layne, L. (ed) *Transformative Motherhood: On Giving and Getting in a Consumer Culture*, New York, New York University Press, pp. 1–27.

Leader, D. and Corfield, D. (2008) *Why Do People Get Ill?* London, Penguin.

Leary, K. (1999) 'Passing, posing and "keeping it real"', *Constellations*, vol. 6, no. 1, pp. 85–96 [Online]. Available at https://doi.org/10.1111/1467-8675.00122 (Accessed 21 September 2019).

Lemma, A. (2012) 'A perfectly modern Frankenstein: Almodóvar's *The Skin I Live In* (2011, Sony Pictures Classics)', *International Journal of Psychoanalysis*, vol. 93, pp. 1291–1300 [Online]. Available at https://doi.org/10.1111/j.1745-8315.2012.00634.x (Accessed 21 September 2019).

Lemma, A. (2013) 'The body one has and the body one is: Understanding the transsexual's need to be seen', *International Journal of Psychoanalysis*, vol. 94, pp. 277–292 [Online]. Available at https://doi.org/10.1111/j.1745-8315.2012.00663.x (Accessed 19 September 2019).

Lesnik-Oberstein, K. (2008) *On Having an Own Child: Reproductive Technologies and the Cultural Construction of Childhood* [ebook reader], London, Karnac.

Lesnik-Oberstein, K. (2011) 'Introduction: Voice, agency and the child', in Lesnik-Oberstein, K. (ed) *Children in Culture, Revisited: Further Approaches to Childhood*, Basingstoke, Palgrave Macmillan, pp. 1–17.

Lessing, D. (2007 [1988]) *The Fifth Child*, London, Harper Perennial.

Letherby, G., Scott, J. and Williams, M. (2013) *Objectivity and Subjectivity in Social Research*, London, Sage.

Levinas, E. (1985) 'The face', in Levinas, E. (ed) *Ethics and Infinity: Conversations with Philippe Nemo* (trans. R. Cohen), Pittsburgh, PA, Duquesne University Press, pp. 83–92.

Lingsom, S. (2008) 'Invisible impairments: Dilemmas of concealment and disclosure', *Scandinavian Journal of Disability Research*, vol. 10, no. 1, pp. 2–16 [Online]. Available at https://doi.org/10.1080/15017410701391567 (Accessed 21 September 2019).

Lukács, G. (1971) 'Reification and the consciousness of the proletariat', in Lukács, G. (ed) *History and Class Consciousness: Studies in Marxist Dialectics* (trans. R. Livingstone), London, The Merlin Press, pp. 83–222.

Machan, T. (1990) 'Politics and generosity', *Journal of Applied Philosophy*, vol. 7, no. 1, pp. 61–73 [Online]. Available at https://doi.org/10.1111/j.1468-5930.1990.tb00254.x (Accessed 23 September 2019).

Mairs, N. (1996) *Waist-High in the World: A Life among the Non-Disabled*, Boston, MA, Beacon Press.

Mallett, R. and Runswick-Cole, K. (2016) 'The "urge to know" normal: Theorising how impairment labels function', in Mallett, R., Ogden, C. and Slater, J. (eds) *Theorising Normalcy and the Mundane: Precarious Positions*, Chester, University of Chester Press, pp. 95–119.

Marks, D. (1999) *Disability: Controversial Debates and Psychosocial Perspectives*, Abingdon, Oxon, Routledge.

Martinez, F. (2014) *What the **** Is Normal?!* London, Penguin Random House.

Marx, K. (1976) *Capital: Volume 1* (trans. B. Fowkes), Harmondsworth, Penguin.

Mason, M. (1992) 'Internalised oppression', in Rieser, R. and Mason, M. (eds) *Disability Equality in the Classroom: A Human Rights Issue*, revised edn, London, Disability Equality in Education, pp. 27–28.

McDougall, J. (1989) *Theatres of the Body: A Psychoanalytic Approach to Psychosomatic Illness*, London, Free Association Books.

McLeod, C. (2001) 'Does gift language elevate devalued forms of motherhood?', Review of *Transformative Motherhood: On Giving and Getting in a Consumer Culture*, *Medical Humanities Review*, vol. 15, no. 1, pp. 67–70.

McRobbie, A. (2013) 'Feminism, the family and the new 'mediated' maternalism', *New Formations: A Journal of Theory/Culture/Politics*, vol. 80–81, pp. 119–137 [Online]. Available at www.lwbooks.co.uk/new-formations/80-81/feminism-the-family-and-the-new-'mediated'-maternalism (Accessed 22 September 2019).

McRuer, R. (1998) 'Reading and writing "immunity": Children and the anti-body', *Children's Literature Association Quarterly*, vol. 23, no. 3, pp. 134–142 [Online]. Available at http://doi.org/10.1353/chq.0.1168 (Accessed 22 September 2019).

McRuer, R. (2010) 'Disability nationalism in crip times', *Journal of Literary and Cultural Disability Studies*, vol. 4, no. 2, pp. 163–178 [Online]. Available at https://doi.org/10.3828/jlcds.2010.13 (Accessed 23 August 2019).

Merleau-Ponty, M. (2002) *Phenomenology of Perception* (trans. C. Smith), London, Routledge.

Messer, J. (2013) 'Reconceptualizing maternal work: Dejours, Ruddick and Lionel Shriver's *We Need to Talk about Kevin*', *Women's Studies International Forum*, vol. 38, pp. 11–20 [Online]. Available at https://doi.org/10.1016/j.wsif.2013.01.015 (Accessed 22 September 2019).

Michalko, R. (2003) '"I've got a blind prof": The place of blindness in the academy', in Freedman, D. and Stoddard Holmes, M. (eds) *The Teacher's Body: Embodiment, Authority and Identity in the Academy*, New York, SUNY Press, pp. 69–81.

Miller, N. (2002) *But Enough about Me: Why We Read Other People's Lives*, New York, Columbia University Press.

Mitchell, D. and Snyder, S. (2000) *Narrative Prosthesis: Disability and the Dependencies of Discourse*, Ann Arbor, MI, University of Michigan Press.

Mitchell, S. (1988) *Relational Concepts in Psychoanalysis: An Integration*, Cambridge, MA and London, Harvard University Press.

Mollow, A. (2012) 'Is sex disability? Queer theory and the disability drive', in McRuer, R. and Mollow, A. (eds) *Sex and Disability*, Durham, NC, Duke University Press, pp. 285–312.

Morrison, T. (1993) *Nobel Lecture*, 7 December [Online]. Available at www.nobelprize.org/nobel_prizes/literature/laureates/1993/morrison-lecture.html (Accessed 23 September 2019).

Moto, M. (2012) *The Uncanny Valley*, English edn (trans. K. MacDorman and N. Kageki) [Online]. Available at http://spectrum.ieee.org/automaton/robotics/humanoids/the-uncanny-valley (Accessed 23 September 2019).

Mulvey, L. (1975) 'Visual pleasure and narrative cinema', *Screen*, vol. 16, no. 3, pp. 6–18 [Online]. Available at https://doi.org/10.1093/screen/16.3.6 (Accessed 23 September 2019).

Muncey, T. (2010) *Creating Autoethnographies*, London, Sage.

Murphy, R. (2001) *The Body Silent*, reissued edn, New York, Norton.

Nelson, M. (2016) *The Argonauts*, UK edn, London, Melville House.

Nicholls, S. (2008) *Ways to Live Forever*, London, Marion Lloyd Books.

Nichols, P. (1967) *A Day in the Death of Joe Egg*, London, Faber and Faber.

Nichols, P. (2013) 'An Introduction by Peter Nichols', programme for a production of *A Day in the Death of Joe Egg*, Rose Theatre, Kingston, UK, 30 April–18 May 2013, pp. 5–6.

Oakley, A. (2018) *The Sociology of Housework*, reissued edn, Bristol, Policy Press.

Oliver, M. (1983) *Social Work with Disabled People*, London, Macmillan.

Oliver, M. (1993) 'What's so wonderful about walking?' *Inaugural Professorial Lecture*, University of Greenwich, London, 9 February. Published in The Disability Archive, University of Leeds [Online]. Available at https://disability-studies.leeds.ac.uk/wp-content/uploads/sites/40/library/Oliver-PROFLEC.pdf (Accessed 16 August 2019).

Oxford English Dictionary. (2019) *Oxford English Dictionary* [Online]. Available at www.oed.com/ (Accessed 29 August 2019).

Parker, R. (1997) 'The production and purposes of maternal ambivalence', in Wendy Hollway, W. and Featherstone, B. (eds) *Mothering and Ambivalence*, London, Routledge, pp. 17–35.

Pilkington, E. (2007) 'Frozen in time: The disabled nine-year-old girl who will remain a child all her life', *Guardian*, 4 January [Online]. Available at www.theguardian.com/world/2007/jan/04/health.topstories3 (Accessed 26 August 2019).

Pilkington, E. (2012) 'The Ashley Treatment: "Her life is as good as we can possibly make it"' [email interview with Ashley's father], *Guardian*, 15 March [Online]. Available at www.guardian.co.uk/society/2012/mar/15/ashley-treatment-email-exchange (Accessed 26 August 2019).

Preciado, P. (2013) *Testo Junkie: Sex, Drugs and Biopolitics in the Pharmacopornographic Era* (trans. B. Benderson), New York, The Feminist Press at the City University of New York.

Prosser, J. (1998) *Second Skins: The Body Narratives of Transsexuality*, New York, Columbia University Press.

Prout, A. (2005) *The Future of Childhood: Towards the Interdisciplinary Study of Children*, Abingdon, Oxon, RoutledgeFalmer.

Puar, J. (2009) 'Prognosis time: Towards a geopolitics of affect, debility and capacity', *Women and Performance: A Journal of Feminist Theory*, vol. 19, no. 2, pp. 161–172 [Online]. Available at https://doi.org/10.1080/07407700903034147 (Accessed 29 August 2019).

Puar, J. (2015) 'The "right" to maim: Disablement and inhumanist biopolitics in palestine', *Borderlands E-journal*, vol. 14, no. 1, pp. 1–27 [Online]. Available at www.borderlands.net.au/vol14no1_2015/puar_maim.pdf (Accessed 23 August 2019).

Puar, J. (2017a) *The Right to Maim: Debility, Capacity, Disability*, Durham, NC, Duke University Press.

Puar, J. (2017b) *Terrorist Assemblages: Homonationalism in Queer Times*, 2nd edn, Durham, NC, Duke University Press.

Pyne, J. (2017) 'Arresting Ashley X: Trans youth, puberty blockers and the question of whether time is on your side', *Somatechnics*, vol. 7, no. 1, pp. 95–123 [Online]. Available at https://doi.org/10.3366/soma.2017.0208 (Accessed 26 August 2019).

Quiney, R. (2007) 'Confessions of the new capitalist mother: Twenty-first-century writing on motherhood as trauma', *Women: A Cultural Review*, vol. 18, no. 1, pp. 19–40 [Online].

Available at https://doi.org/10.1080/09574040701276704 (Accessed 22 September 2019).

Rapp, R. (1999) 'Foreword', in Layne, L. (ed) *Transformative Motherhood: On Giving and Getting in a Consumer Culture*, New York, New York University Press, pp. xi–xix.

Reeve, D. (2001) 'Review of *What Psychotherapists Should Know about Disability*, by Rhoda Olkin', *Disability and Society*, vol. 16, no. 4, pp. 626–629 [Online]. Available at https://doi.org/10.1080/09687590120059577 (Accessed 23 September 2019).

Reeve, D. (2008) *Negotiating Disability in Everyday Life: The Experience of Psycho-Emotional Disablism*, unpublished PhD thesis, Lancaster, Lancaster University.

Rivkin, J. and Ryan, M. (2004) *Literary Theory: An Anthology*, 2nd edn, Oxford, Blackwell Publishing.

Rose, J. (1984) *The Case of Peter Pan, or the Impossibility of Children's Fiction*, London and Basingstoke, Macmillan.

Rose, N. (1999) *Governing the Soul: The Shaping of the Private Self*, 2nd edn, London, Free Association Books.

Roustang, F. (1984) 'On the epistemology of psychoanalysis', *MLN*, vol. 99, no. 4 (French Issue), pp. 928–940 [Online]. Available at www.jstor.org/stable/2905509 [doi: 10.2307/2905509] (Accessed 29 October 2019).

Salecl, R. (2010) *The Tyranny of Choice*, London, Profile Books.

Samuels, A. (2009) 'Possibilities and limitations of the therapeutic approach to conflict resolution', paper presented at *Psycho-Political Resistance in Israel-Palestine*, Birkbeck Institute for Social Research, 15–16 October 2009 [Online]. Available at http://backdoor broadcasting.net/2009/10/andrew-samuels-possibilities-and-limitationsof-the-thera peutic-approaches-to-conflict-resolution/ (Accessed 22 September 2019).

Samuels, E. (2003) 'My body, my closet: Invisible disability and the limits of the coming-out discourse', *GLQ: A Journal of Lesbian and Gay Studies*, vol. 9, pp. 233–255 [Online]. Available at https://muse.jhu.edu/article/40803 (Accessed 22 September 2019).

Sartre, J.-P. (2003) 'The look', in Sartre, J.-P. (ed) *Being and Nothingness* (trans. H. Barnes), Abingdon, Oxon, Routledge, pp. 276–326.

Scarry, E. (1985) *The Body in Pain: The Making and Unmaking of the World*, Oxford, Oxford University Press.

Scully, J. L., Shakespeare, T. and Banks, S. (2006) 'Gift not commodity? Lay people deliberating social sex selection', *Sociology of Health and Illness*, vol. 28, no. 6, pp. 749–767.

Sears, B. and Sears, M. (2001) *The Attachment Parenting Book: A Commonsense Guide to Understanding and Nurturing Your Baby*, New York, Boston, MA and London, Little, Brown and Company.

Sedgwick, E. (2003) 'Paranoid reading and reparative reading, or, you're so paranoid, you probably think this essay is about you', in Sedgwick, E. (ed) *Touching Feeling: Affect, Pedagogy, Performativity*, Durham, NC, Duke University Press, pp. 123–151.

Segal, L. (2009) 'Who do you think you are? Feminist memoir writing', *New Formations, Special Issue: Reading Life Writing*, vol. 67, pp. 120–136 [Online]. Available at www. lwbooks.co.uk/new-formations/67/who-do-you-think-you-are-feminist-memoir-writing (Accessed 22 September 2019).

Siebers, T. (2004) 'Disability as masquerade', *Literature and Medicine*, vol. 23, no. 1, pp. 1–22 [Online]. Available at https://muse.jhu.edu/article/170316 [doi: 10.1353/lm.2004.0010] (Accessed 23 September 2019).

Slater, J. (2016) *Youth and Disability: A Challenge to Mr Reasonable*, Abingdon, Oxon, Routledge.

Slater, J. and Liddiard, K. (2018) 'Why disability studies scholars must challenge transmisogyny and transphobia', *Canadian Journal of Disability Studies*, vol. 7, no. 2, pp. 83–93 [Online]. Available at https://doi.org/10.15353/cjds.v7i2.424 (Accessed 23 September 2019).

Soth, M. (2010/11) 'The return of the repressed body – Not a smooth affair', *The Psychotherapist*, no. 47 (Winter), pp. 19–21.

Spivak, G. (1987) 'Subaltern studies: Deconstructing historiography', in Spivak, G. (ed) *In Other Worlds: Essays in Cultural Politics*, New York, Methuen, pp. 197–221.

Spyri, J. (2009 [1880]) *Heidi* (trans E. Hall), London, Penguin.

Stacey, J. (1997) *Teratologies: A Cultural Study of Cancer*, Abingdon, Oxon, Routledge.

Steedman, C. (1995) *Strange Dislocations: Childhood and the Idea of Human Interiority, 1780–1930*, London, Virago Press.

Stern, D. (1991) *Diary of a Baby*, London, Fontana.

Sullivan, N. (2003) *A Critical Introduction to Queer Theory*, Edinburgh, Edinburgh University Press.

Taylor, B. (2014) *The Last Asylum: A Memoir of Madness in Our Times*, London, Hamish Hamilton.

Thatcher, M. (1987) 'Interview for *Woman's Own* ("no such thing as society")', 23 September 1987, published by the Margaret Thatcher Foundation [Online]. Available at www.margaretthatcher.org/document/106689 (Accessed 16 September 2019).

The Secret Garden (1993) Directed by Agnieszka Holland [Film]. United States, Warner Bros. Pictures.

The Secret Garden (2020) Directed by Marc Munden [Film]. United Kingdom, Studiocanal/ Heyday Films.

The Skin I Live In (2011) Directed by Pedro Almodóvar [Film]. Spain, Warner Bros. Pictures.

The Union of the Physically Impaired Against Segregation (UPIAS) and The Disability Alliance. (1976) 'The union comments on the discussion', in *Fundamental Principles of Disability*, London, UPIAS and The Disability Alliance, pp. 11–20.

Thomas, C. (1999) *Female Forms: Experiencing and Understanding Disability*, Buckingham, Open University Press.

Titchkosky, T. (2003) *Disability, Self and Society*, Toronto, University of Toronto Press.

Tremain, S. (2006) 'Reproductive freedom, self-regulation and the government of impairment in utero', *Hypatia*, vol. 21, no. 2, pp. 35–53 [Online]. Available at https://doi.org/ 10.1111/j.1527-2001.2006.tb00963.x (Accessed 20 September 2019).

Tustin, F. (1990) *The Protective Shell in Children and Adults*, London, Karnac.

United Nations. (1990) *UN Convention on the Rights of the Child*, London, UNICEF [Online]. Available at https://downloads.unicef.org.uk/wp-content/uploads/2010/05/ UNCRC_united_nations_convention_on_the_rights_of_the_child.pdf?_ga= 2.252403977.1443165817.1568474095-699488456.1568474095 (Accessed 14 September 2019).

Unwin, S. (2013a) 'Welcome', programme for a production of *A Day in the Death of Joe Egg*, Rose Theatre, Kingston, 30 April–18 May 2013, p. 2.

Unwin, S. (2013b) 'How my son's disability is helping me to direct Joe Egg', *Independent*, 3rd April [Online]. Available at www.independent.co.uk/arts-entertainment/theatre-dance/features/how-my-sons-disability-is-helping-me-to-direct-joe-egg-8557342.html (Accessed 23 September 2019).

Vidali, A. (2010) 'Seeing what we know: Disability and theories of metaphor', *Journal of Literary and Cultural Disability Studies*, vol. 4, no. 1, pp. 33–54 [Online]. Available at https://doi.org/10.1353/jlc.0.0032 (Accessed 24 August 2019).

Watermeyer, B. (2013) *Towards a Contextual Psychology of Disablism*, Abingdon, Oxon, Routledge.

Watermeyer, B., McKenzie, J. and Swartz, L. (2019) 'Introduction', in Watermeyer, B., McKenzie, J. and Swartz, L. (eds) *The Palgrave Handbook of Disability and Citizenship in the Global South* [ebook online], Cham, Switzerland, Palgrave Macmillan, pp. 1–9.

Wells, K. (2009) *Childhood in a Global Perspective*, Cambridge, Polity Press.

Wiegman, R. (2012) *Object Lessons*, Durham, NC, Duke University Press.

Wiegman, R. (2014) 'The times we're in: Queer feminist criticism and the reparative "turn"', *Feminist Theory*, vol. 15, no. 1, pp. 4–25 [Online]. Available at https://doi.org/10.1177/1464700113513081a (Accessed 23 August 2019).

Williams, G. (1984) 'The genesis of chronic illness: Narrative re-construction', *Sociology of Health and Illness*, vol. 6, no. 2, pp. 175–200 [Online]. Available at https://doi.org/10.1111/1467-9566.ep10778250 (Accessed 27 August 2019).

Williams, R. (1977) 'Dominant, residual, and emergent', in Williams, R. (ed) *Marxism and Literature*, Oxford, Oxford University Press, pp. 121–127.

Wilson, J. and Chivers Yochim, E. (2015) 'Pinning happiness: Affect, social media and the work of mothers', in Levine, E. (ed) *Cupcakes, Pinterest and Ladyporn: Feminized Popular Culture in the Early Twenty-First Century* [ebook online], Urbana, IL, Chicago, IL and Springfield, IL, University of Illinois Press, pp. 232–248.

Winnicott, D. (1957) *The Child and the Family: First Relationships*, London, Tavistock.

Winnicott, D. (1971a) 'Mirror-role of mother and family in child development', in Winnicott, D. (ed) *Playing and Reality*, London, Tavistock, pp. 111–118.

Winnicott, D. (1971b) 'Transitional objects and transitional phenomena', in Winnicott, D. (ed) *Playing and Reality*, London, Tavistock, pp. 1–25.

Winnicott, D. (1990a) 'The theory of the parent-infant relationship', in Khan, M. (ed) *The Maturational Processes and the Facilitating Environment*, London, Karnac, pp. 37–55.

Winnicott, D. (1990b) 'Ego distortion in terms of true and false self', in Khan, M. (ed) *The Maturational Processes and the Facilitating Environment*, London, Karnac, pp. 140–152.

Winning, J. (2012) 'The meaning of skin and surgical subjectivity', keynote presentation at *Precarious Bodies: Doctoral Symposium*, author's unpublished manuscript, Zurich, University of Zurich, 23 November 2012.

Wright, K. (1991) *Vision and Separation: Between Mother and Baby*, London, Free Association Books.

Young, I. (1980) 'Throwing like a girl: A phenomenology of feminine body comportment, motility and spatiality', *Human Studies*, vol. 3, no. 2, pp. 137–156 [Online]. Available at https://doi.org/10.1007/BF02331805 (Accessed 22 September 2019).

Zelizer, V. (1994) *Pricing the Priceless Child: The Changing Social Value of Children*, Princeton, NJ, Princeton University Press.

Index

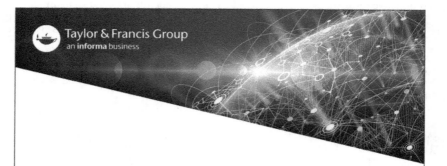